MW00445448

The International Instant Business Plan Book

12 Quick-and-Easy Steps to a Profitable Business

by Gustav Berle, Ph.D. and Paul Kirschner

PUMA PUBLISHING COMPANY
Santa Maria, California, U.S.A.
1996

Copyright ©1996
Puma Publishing Company
Santa Maria, California
All Rights Reserved
1st Printing April 1996
2nd Printing September 1996

Library of Congress Cataloging-in-Publication Data

Berle, Gustav, 1920–
    The international instant business plan book: 12 quick-and-easy steps to a profitable business /
by Gustav Berle and Paul Kirschner.
      p. cm.
    Includes index.
    ISBN 0-940673-81-9
    1. International business enterprises - - Planning - - handbooks, manuals, *etc.*
    2. Business planning - - handbooks, manuals, *etc.*
    I. Kirschner, Paul, 1917– . II. Title.
    HD62.4.B477 1996
    658.4'012—dc20

95-52146 CIP

ABOUT THE AUTHORS

Paul Kirschner has traveled throughout the world, giving seminars on business plan preparations. He was former marketing director of SCORE/SBA, commandant of a 1,500-student Army Reserve School and taught college-level army courses. He has been an analyst of more than 100 diverse small business operations and counseled over 1,000 clients. His career includes managing and controlling manufacturing firms grossing from $500,000 to $25,000,000 and working with manufacturers in the Far East, Latin America, Russia, Hungary, Kenya, Egypt and the Caribbean.

Gustav Berle is the author of *Free Help from Uncle Sam to Start Your Business* (3rd ed.), published by Puma Publishing, Inc., as well as ten other books for Wiley, McGraw-Hill and Prentice-Hall. Berle teaches at Florida International University and has a Ph.D. in business administration. He was formerly National Communications Director of SCORE/SBA, as well as a publisher, editor and public relations consultant.

ACKNOWLEDGEMENTS

Special thanks are due to the directors and officials of the U.S Department of Commerce and the U.S. Small Business Administration; to Bill Valenta for his suggested changes which greatly improved this book; to Wade Simola for his fine cover design, and to Elaine at *Graphics Limited*. As usual, Curt Scott of *Crown Publishing* went beyond the call of duty to design and edit these pages. His devotion to excellence is rare these days.

TABLE OF CONTENTS

Coupon for your own up-to-the-minute copy of Puma Publishing's (Free!) *Internet Resources Roster* 249

The International Instant Business Plan

What is a Business Plan Anyway?

During the past few years the use of a business plan in starting a small business or making application for a business loan has become requisite. This trend has been accepted virtually all over the commercial world.

Having a business plan is good for the entrepreneur as well. Without it the business person might be traveling in a strange land without a road map. The problem is not with the acceptance and the logic of the business plan, but with the assumed complexity of it. It need not be complicated, however.

In Germany, France, England, Russia, Italy, Latin America or Scandinavia the need of a business plan is the same. Business is conducted in almost every country very similarly. Money is needed and money is borrowed in every country under similar circumstances—you ask for a certain amount, you offer proof of your need, you present the lender with security or collateral, you make arrangements to pay back the loan and you pay interest.

The preparation and presentation of a business plan only details the need and offers proof of the borrower's viability and ability to repay the loan. It also shows that the entrepreneur is a professional, is serious about running the business, and has prepared well. This book will show you the way—with a minimum of confusion, double talk and unnecessary detail.

In this book the authors are making two assumptions:
…that you are a small-business person who wants to go into an enterprise of your own, expand a business you already own, or want to borrow money from either a personal or commercial source; and

With your business plan, you become a professional.

…that you have a general idea that a business plan is desirable, even necessary (if you are going for a loan), but that you need more guidance and specific help.

There is rarely one single way of preparing a business plan. However, there are some specific ground rules that the authors have developed. In this book they have narrowed down the why and how of preparing a business plan into 12 easy steps.

What is a business plan anyway?

Your blueprint. Your map. Your statement of plans and hopes. Your compass. Your guidepost or guidelines to planned action. Your business philosophy backed by realism. Your current and futuristic X-ray of your business. Your reminder system. It is all of these and more. In a previous book, *The Small Business Information Handbook,* author Gustav Berle offers the following detailed explanation:

> "To plan and operate a successful business, it has always been
> necessary to have a business plan. In recent years it has re-
> emerged as a major topic of business talk, as if it were a unique
> discovery. What is a business plan? It is your guidepost for
> your business's existence, your roadmap that shows you how to
> go forward on your road to success, your blueprint for building
> your enterprise, and the key that can open the door to your
> bank loan. Without a viable, complete, credible business plan,
> as an owner you are groping in the maze of entrepreneurship.
> With your business plan, you become a professional. It can
> lead to riches, or it can reveal to you pitfalls that you have
> ignored. Revealed pitfalls are not unconquerable stumbling
> blocks—they are incentives for you to do more research, learn
> more, do more checking, rein-in enthusiasm until your
> knowledge catches up with it. Your business plan is the heart
> of your business's start."

You can aid the survival rate by developing a business plan.

You need a business plan:
- • when you want to start a new business;
- • when you want to correct a losing trend;
- • when you want to expand a business;
- • when you want to sell or pass on a business;
- • when you want to get a loan.

The latter reason is generally thought to be the most important one, even though in practice it is not. The most important consideration especially when you are asking for somebody else's money, is management… in short: YOU.

We will cover the "You Factor" later in the book. Here we will consider the first reason as the one that most entrepreneurs need a business plan. Again, a couple of reasons mandate this emphasis. For one, many new companies are incorporated each year, and perhaps twice as many just start up a business as a sole proprietorship or partnership, without the legal umbrella known as a "corporation"; abbreviations that signify corporate limited-liability status include *"Inc.," "Corp.,"* and *"Ltd.,"* as well as *"GmbH"* (German for *Gesellschaft mit beschränkter Haftung*, which means, quite literally, "company with limited liability"), *N.V.* (Dutch for *Naamloze Vennootschap*), *Lte.* (French) and *"SpA"* (Italian). It is at startup that a business plan is most vital, and here is where we'll cast our spotlight. At the genesis of a new business, we sometimes need to pull on the balloon string to bring the airborne, free-spirited sphere back to earth a bit.

Business ideas are often generated over the breakfast table, while lolling on a beach during a vacation break, or at a moment of frustration with the status quo. This idea is then developed into an embryo with further discussion and research, soul-searching and questioning. The formation of the fetus, the final stage before birth, becomes then a matter of intense activity. Unfortunately, business starts, unlike the majority of births, do not have a definite gestation period. Some businesses are stillborn or do not survive through adolescence. Those that mature into adulthood after five years, amount to a bare 20 percent. We can aid the survival rate by developing a business plan. But instead of thinking of the business plan as a lifesaver to be tossed to us by a banker or business consultant, why not use it to construct the business from the start, along sound and firm lines?

A Checklist of Information Needed for a Complete Business Plan

Type of business or service: You must have training or experience in the type of business under consideration. You cannot hire a person who has the experience you lack, in hopes that his or her knowledge will make the business go.

Capital: It takes money to start your business. Borrowing money is possible, but only if you have sufficient funds of your own in cash, inventory and/or equipment to provide a reasonable equity for loan consideration. Sufficient funds should be available to meet overhead and take advantage of discounts. You'll also need the ability to arrange credit to handle unexpected financial challenges.

Location: Space leased or owned must be sufficient to meet the needs of the business considered. Location should consistent with your purposes.

Product or Service: Is there a need for your product or service? If not apparent, can a demand for it be developed through advertising and provide a profitable return on the time and money you will be investing?

Bookkeeping: All transactions of your business must be accounted for to provide records for your own knowledge, as well as for reports required to meet reporting required by the government.

Records: Reports should be prepared for your own use. These should cover receivables, payables, inventory, payrolls, insurance, financial statements and periodic operating statements.

Management: This is the crucial element that either creates your success or expedites your failure. A study of and understanding of financial records and pertinent management experience will contribute to a successful operation.

Personnel: If your business goes beyond a one-man enterprise, sufficient, experienced staff must be available and trained properly to accommodate customers.

Inventory: Sufficient in quantity and quality to meet customer demand through all seasons.

Advertising: A necessary tool to help business grow, using experienced personnel or an ad agency to select the most effective media with professionally-developed messages.

Free Publicity: It's easier than you might think. Issue professionally-written news releases as appropriate, to national or regional media. Call up your local newspaper(s) radio and TV station(s) and suggest an interview.

Tax payments: Your government is a partner and an alert one. Make all payments accurately and on time, especially payments withheld from employees and held in trust by you.

Attorney: A reliable, business-experienced lawyer is needed to oversee the formation of proprietorship, partnership or corporation, to check leases and buy-and-sell agreements.

License and registration: You must be sure that the business you are considering is properly registered or licensed. Get a checklist from the local licensing bureau, chamber of commerce, or consult an attorney or accountant.

Outside assistance: Much outside help is available to you, most of it free, from government sources ; from business organizations such as the local chamber of commerce; or from business development offices that might be located in capitols and major cities. Also check your library for books and journals that will help to guide and inform you.

Accounting: Necessary but not Necessarily Mysterious

Your business plan will of necessity be heavily laced with accounting figures. It is perhaps regrettable that so many entrepreneurs have a weakness for this extremely important ingredient and a business plan is, after all, the first step in organizing and funding a new business. Many accountants are quite competent to help you prepare a practical and

The Executive Summary is a condensed outline of your entire business plan. Put it up front.

acceptable business plan. This book, however, will take you a long way down the path of accounting proficiency. It might not teach you accounting, but it could provide you with sufficient inside knowledge to produce the kind of business plan that will serve as your guide, and as a creditable adjunct to a loan application. What is it then, that accounting pros could provide for you? What are bank loan officers and potential investors looking for in the plan you are about to produce for your business? Here are the critical elements.

Executive Summary

Put yourself into the place of a loan officer or investor who does not know you or your business idea. He gets dozens and even hundreds of proposals and applications each year. His time must be concentrated on those that are professionally prepared, complete and appear realistic. He wants to know, quickly, what it is all about. The "Executive Summary" is a condensed outline—a "wrap-up"—of your entire business plan. Put it up front in one to two pages and answer the salient question the reviewer will have: *"What's in it for me and how secure will my investment be?"* Having answered all of that in brief fashion, append the table of contents and go to Step Two.

Your new business (most business plans are prepared for fledgling enterprises) probably does not have much of a creditable track record. As a substitute, offer an analysis of the market. Make thorough estimates, be critical, logical and probable. Don't just talk about your dreams, but about your expectations of realistic goals. Define your business in crystal-clear terms and state your goals and projections as honestly as you can at this point in time. What plan do you have to produce that better mousetrap, to have customers beat a path to your door, who will do each job and what his or her qualifications are, and how you expect to pay back the capital you expect to borrow.

Your financial projections should be tied to reality, to demonstrable industry figures. Lenders are usually pros in the money business, and they will spot unrealistic figures quickly.

Stick to your facts and do not malign the competition, but show your favored position in any competitive situation. Negativism has a way of coming back to haunt you, as many a politician has discovered.

There is much talk these days about 'innovative financing'—and indeed, there is no harm in being creative. Many lenders appreciate a pragmatic display of creativity, as long as it remains objective. Potential financial backers' first interest is their own interest.

Even if you prepare most of the business plan yourself, it will be well to include the actual services, or at least the names and references, of a professional accountant and attorney. The addition of professionals will assure that your plan is regarded as being soundly structured and will minimize unforeseen future liabilities.

While a business plan should be thorough, it should also be concise. A ponderous presentation could turn an outsider off. If you feel that corroborating evidence and appendices are necessary, put them in a separate addendum. The financier then will have the option to peruse the additional material.

If but one of the pieces of information in this book applies to you and your enterprise, then this book will have paid for itself. Even if a professional prepares a business plan for you and charges you thousands, you will have to supply the inside information. Be patient and study this book. It can not only save you money, but provide an invaluable learning process that can lead to one of the important and valuable tools of your new or expanding business.

Chapter 1

Are You Ready for the Demands of Entrepreneurship?

- Your Entrepreneurial Test

- Your General Outline for a Professional Business Plan:
  A Banker's Viewpoint

- Your Instant Business Plan

The Spirit of Entrepreneurship is an elusive characteristic. It appears to crop up more frequently among some people than others; among some ethnic groups more so than those who have rarely, if ever, been exposed to buying and selling, or the creative process, or working for oneself. It isn't all education and knowledge, though these certainly will help. Having the right upbringing such as a successful father or other family member "in the business" can be immeasurably useful, but this cannot be ordained or created.

In Figure 1 on the next page, we have showcased the POE Factor to try and explain the *Entrepreneurial Spirit*. POE stands for *Persistence, Optimism and Expertise*. Some people may learn the first two, but most cannot. You will develop expertise through diligent work and study. There are a few other, less-concrete ingredients, such as luck, opportunity, and a rich relative leaving you a large amount of money.

Luck borders on superstition. Opportunity, which often creeps silently into view, must be heard and seen to be realized. And depending on a financial windfall is worse than betting the slowest horse in a race to come in first. So where do we go from here?

> **No entrepreneur need feel lonely or in need of encouragement.**

What Puts the $ into a $uccessful Entrepreneur?

Figure 1

The POE Factor. It stands for *Persistence, Optimism, Expertise*. Put the three together and it sounds like the tintinnabulations of $uccess. The steps to POE can include motivation to achieve and succeed, no matter how steep the road. Perpetual striving for quality in product and service not necessarily perfection, but constant improvement. Veneration for the customer who is, after all, the the objective of all business planning. Long-term goals rather than quick-fix short-term gains. Dependence, despite a king-sized sense of individualism, on peers and peer groups who can boost the entrepreneur's well-being. Encouragement of entrepreneurial dreams that can lead to innovation and often, but not always, to profit-achievement. The true entrepreneur rarely recognizes setbacks, but takes them as challenges to betterment, or simply to another road less traveled. Add to this potpourri a dollop of enthusiasm, plus an endless quest for knowledge, and the entrepreneur YOU will be an unbeatable economic force. Your Business Plan should express all of these ingredients. Like a cake in the oven, half-baked it will fall flat. Well prepared and executed, it is ambrosia that tinkles pleasantly in the till.

Remember: entrepreneurs average 3.8 failures before final success. A sound Business Plan, aided by persistence and knowledge, will enhance your chances for success. Like Armand Hammer, the oil tycoon, said "*When I work 14 hours a day, seven days a week, I get lucky.*" It was his key to $uccess.

To find out whether *you* are ready to be an entrepreneur will take all of the above, and a little more. It takes good management and it takes money in that order.

Notice that when we named the two main ingredients of entrepreneurial success, we mentioned management first, and money second. Think about that for a moment.

There have been hundreds of good companies during the past years that were well financed, but eventually went bankrupt. Unlike federal governments which can borrow freely and print more money when needed, business people cannot practice deficit financing and survive. While money is always helpful and sometimes can even be a lifesaver, it is less important than a smart business leader who can plan and foresee problems before they occur, manage money astutely, and never accumulate more debts than assets.

Yes, money is important, but it takes backseat to management. That's where you may be armed with a few competitive advantages that another business operator may not have—Persistence, Optimism, Expertise. The POE Factor.

Persistence to keep on going when the going gets rough, and it invariably will, especially during the troublesome startup years. *Optimism* to know instinctively that there is always an alternative, that pitfalls are only holes in the road to be filled with opportunity. *Expertise* to be creative, innovative, reliable, quality-conscious, and forever seeking more knowledge to forge ahead.

And now we are ready if you are to see what makes you tick. Here is an Entrepreneurial Test that may give you a hint:

Your Entrepreneurial Test

This is an examination of the most important ingredient in your business: *you.* It does not provide all your answers nor any magic solution, but it provides some guidelines, some parameters, that establish that *you* have a better-than-even chance for success in a business of your own. Nobody will judge the results of this test except *you,* for you are judge and jury of

> **When we named the two main ingredients of entrepreneurial success, we mentioned management first, and money second. Think about that.**

your own fate. (Who said, "If it's to be, it's up to me"?) Your Entrepreneurial Test is a good exercise for you before you spend any money.

1. Being optimistic is one positive, even necessary trait, of the entrepreneur. Do you think you are? ___YES ___NO

2. The repetitiveness of industrial jobs can be boring. You, too, are easily bored by ordinary, rote tasks. In fact, you might even judge yourself to be a restless type of personality? ___YES ___NO

3. The children of immigrants are among the most successful entrepreneurs. Are you the progeny of an immigrant? ___YES ___NO

4. You'd think that brilliant students would make the best entrepreneurs, but that hasn't been borne out by fact. Most entrepreneurs were only average students, and developed later. Were you? ___YES ___NO

5. Entrepreneurial personalities were usually self-contained youngsters—rarely members of athletic teams or tight groups. Were you always pretty self-sufficient? ___YES ___NO

6. Along similar lines, were you content as a youngster when you were alone? ___YES ___NO

7. When you were still in school, did you engage in any paid, entrepreneurial activities, such as babysitting, newspaper delivery, part-timing in an office or store, or helping run things at school? ___YES ___NO

8. Stubbornness as a child, or better said, determination, is a measurable trait. Do you think you were stubborn? ___YES ___NO

9. Did you handle any money as a youngster? Were you quite good at managing it? ___YES ___NO

10. Do you usually write down things? Make memos to yourself of tasks you have to do? Take good notes? ___YES ___NO

11. Entrepreneurs are calculated risk-takers and often venture into previously-uncharted areas. Do you think that you are that type? ___YES ___NO

12. Some take well-trod paths; others make paths for followers. Do you feel you are adventurous enough to venture into different directions? ___YES ___NO

13. Does getting stuck in a rut make you anxious, propel you into new areas and motivate you to think about going into new businesses or associations? ___YES ___NO

14. Put yourself into the seat of a loan officer at a financial institution. Would you regard an entrepreneur such as you as an acceptable risk? ___YES ___NO

15. Entrepreneurship takes determination and perseverance. Supposing your business went broke; would you start up again in a different direction? ___YES ___NO

16. Being in business is forgetting about the clock. Could you, or would you, devote the hours to being a successful entrepreneur that business independence often demands? ___YES ___NO

17. Are you the type who usually tackles two or more projects at the same time or overlapping? Finishes one task and begins another one right away? ___YES ___NO

18. While it is usually good to use the OPM (other people's money) method in business startups, would you risk your own savings to start up or expand a business of your own? ___YES ___NO

19. If you are willing to risk your own money, are you so convinced about the soundness of your business that you would ask others to risk their investment also? ___YES ___NO

20. Despite your entrepreneurial penchant and willingness to take calculated risks, would you rather research and market-test an idea first, or surge ahead and depend entirely on your gut feeling? You admit that you would act on the side of caution in this case, or would you? ___YES ___NO

OK, there it is. How did you make out? Frankly now how many times could you unequivocally and honestly say 'Yes'? If the overwhelming majority of answers were 'Yes,' go ahead. You will make a great entrepreneur. If not, better recheck your plans…

A Banker's Viewpoint of Your Business Plan

By this time you have hopefully been convinced that a business plan is a necessity if you want to start, operate and profit in a business of your own. It is doubly necessary if you have to rely on others to furnish you with capital.

There is no single way to prepare a business plan. Different business counselors, bankers, financial officers, accountants, lawyers and writers have various ideas as to the most effective method to make a presentation. So, with some humility, we present here a cross-section of what we feel is the most logical, acceptable and feasible way to create your business plan.

Look at your Business Plan as the Constitution of your enterprise. Once it is completed, it will form the foundation, the platform, the basis of your business. Over the years, you may want to make additions and alterations to fit circumstances just like a Constitution would receive..

Now look at the other side of the table. If you need startup and operating capital for your business, you will first of all search your own resources; then approach others, at banks or lending institutions, who are usually strangers to you. Here, then, sits that stranger. All he usually knows about you is what you have written down on those sheets of paper, called your business plan. To him, you are a commodity from which he and his bank or institution intend to make a profit, and which will pay his salary. Got the picture? Now try to fill the frame.

Like a precious perfume, your business plan requires attractive packaging. The aromatic elixir is encased in a costly bottle, ensconced in a box and then wrapped in costly foil. Your business plan too, must be wrapped for attraction.

Many years ago when we first ventured out into the business world, an older friend gave us this bit of sage advice, which we have never forgotten. We'll pass it on to you, for what it's worth: *"When applying for a job, always present yourself in good clothes."*

What all this preamble comes down to is this: If you think that your business plan is worth the paper it is written on, use the finest paper you can afford. Type, or have your business plan typed, on the best stationery possible, neatly, professionally and flawlessly. Then encase it in a folder or spiral-bound clear plastic.

Complete your business plan. Use professional help, if you believe you need it especially in perfecting the financials. Be as thorough, as candid, as realistic as you can. You cannot fool yourself, and you certainly won't fool the professionals who examine your presentation and make the decision to lend many thousands of dollars to you, based on the premise and promise of your business plan.

Once your complete business plan is done, turn yourself into a critic. Make believe that you are going to consider that business plan, but you certainly want to know what it contains. You have little time and perhaps less patience. There are 49,999 other business plans out there from which you could choose. So why should you risk your firm's funds on this one?

After your final polishing is done, have the plan checked by several others—including a qualified proofreader (or two). One additional word to the wise: Your business plan will project a much more polished and professional appearance if you prepare your plan with a good word processor. Additionally, using a computer word processor or page-layout program makes it much easier and faster to make changes to both the content and the appearance of your plan. If you aren't skilled in using word processing software, a phone call to a computer users' group or a secretarial service should provide you with someone qualified to do it for you for a reasonable fee.

By this time, we believe you can empathize with the financial officer who is going to peruse your business plan. So to make it more enticing, interesting and plausible your next step is to write a Summary. It will be concise, exact, unadorned. It will be short and it is the key that will open the locked door to a loan.

Even though the Summary is the first thing the prospective lender will read in your business plan, you are most likely to write it last. But remember that it is first impressions that last.

There are a dozen parts in this business plan. They are The 12 Steps and consist of:

1. Cover letter

2. Business identification

3. Business Purpose and Goals

4. Description of business

5. Your market research

6. Competition

7. Management
   - Business Asset Management
   - Personnel Management

8. Location

9. Your Market Strategy

10. Financial information

11. Keeping records

12. Executive Summary

Buying a Business

The following section of the business plan is necessary only if you are acquiring somebody else's business, rather than starting your own. We need not be too concerned here with the philosophies behind such a move, but only with its impact on your business plan and your ability to borrow additional capital.

Buying somebody else's business is often a shortcut to profitable operations, since the business is already up and running. It's like refueling an airplane in midair or having it land to begin the takeoff procedure anew. With this advantage, however, come a few cautions:

• You might need more capital up front to take over somebody else's operating business;

• You need to know a great deal about the business you are acquiring; just because it is (hopefully) a well-run enterprise does not guarantee it will continue to be so, unless you truly understand it;

• You need to make sure that any inventory is clean, current, market valued and that employees and customers will remain loyal to you, and

• Have you determined why the seller wants to sell his business if it is running so well?

An experienced accountant, lawyer, and banker on your side can be of immeasurable assistance, rather than relying on your gut feeling or even on the "advice" of the seller's broker.

Summation of the SUMMARY

When preparing your business plan for a loan application, it is customary to start out with an *Executive Summary* up front. The reason is that the loan officer is extremely busy. He or she wants to know immediately what your business is all about, how much money you want, how you plan to pay it back and what security you have to back the loan. Knowing this, you will prepare the entire business plan first; then extract the above four points from the body of the plan and put a synopsis of them up front in the "Summary." It will be useful to make this summary as complete, concise and dramatic as possible. If your business revolves around a product, enclose a picture of the product. If it is a building or a business location, include a picture of that structure or plan of the location. If you have illustrative or explanatory literature, such as catalog sheets or brochures, attach them also. It's the old story: make your first impression a lasting one.

Here are the key elements of the summary

- Description of Business—what does it do; how long has it been in business; what is your management team like; why did you pick your particular location; what is your business's growth potential?

- Amount of Loan Request—what do you need the money for; for how long do you need it; how would you prefer the loan to be paid?

- The Payback Plan—amount, number and timing of the payback; where will you get the money to repay the lender; what backup plan do you have in case your money for the payback does not come in as readily as you envision.

- Security for Loan—what is the true, current value of your collateral; how was this value appraised; how readily is it available in an emergency?

Buying somebody else's business is often a shortcut to profitable operations.

Chapter II

12 *Quick-and-Easy* Steps to Your Business Plan

Step 1: Introduction to the Business Plan

As you develop your thoughts, notes and figures for your Business Plan, determine first of all:

- How much you really need to borrow;

- How long will you need borrowed money;

- For how long a period you need it;

- Where you will get the money;

- A backup plan in case your present projection doesn't work out;

- What security will be offered as collateral;

- The current appraisal of your security and its availability.

There are three preliminary steps you need to take to start your actual Business Plan:

1.1 The Cover Letter

You need some good stationery on which to write this cover letter. The quality and design of your stationery is the first impression. Let it reflect your best effort, your quality, your image. The cost is minor when compared with the intended results.

It is said that *"You don't need to be a millionaire to dress like one."* Still, people judge you first by what they see on the outside. This is the way products are packaged. This is the way applicants, whether for loans or jobs, are regarded. This is one of the ways your business plan will be judged.

If your business plan is to be used as a presentation to a potential lender or financial institution, a cover letter, printed on good stationery, should introduce you and the purpose of your presentation. Here is an example:

****

Dear (name):

We are requesting your granting us a loan of $_____ for the purpose of _____. Repayment is anticipated over a period of _____. The source of repayment will be _____. We are offering you as collateral the items listed on the accompanying exhibit, complete with appraised valuation, having an approximate current value of $_____, conservatively stated.

We will greatly appreciate your serious consideration of this loan request, since this loan will be vital to the successful and profitable execution of our business plan, as enclosed. Should you require further information, please contact us at (phone number) _____.

Cordially,

(Signature[s])

Name(s)

Title(s)

Encl: Business Plan for _____
                                            (your company name)

****

Business Plan

for

(Your Company Name)

Prepared especially for

(Financial Officer's Name &

Lending Institution's Company Name)

1.3 Table of Contents

Step 2. Business Identification

This is the name you give your business, which then will appear on all of your stationery and anything that is imprinted with your business name—the outside sign(s), wrappings and cartons, vehicles and advertising. It is like the baptism of your business and very likely you will live with this name for the rest of your business life.

The real importance, in addition to identification, is to let your name tell your customers and clients who you are and what you do. It is important to give considerable attention to this vital function.

The business identification should not be the creation of a whim or something dashed off on the kitchen table between the cereal and the coffee. A good name will be appropriate to your business or profession, identify either you or your business function or location, and make a positive impact in the telephone directory, in your signage, your business card, and wherever it may come to the attention of someone who can influence your enterprise.

Business Identification Worksheet

1. The name of the business is

2. Business address

3. Actual location

4. Telephone

5. Tax or business registration number

6. Principals involved in business and contact addresse

7. Accountant of record and address and phone

8. Attorney of record and address and phone

9. Banker, location and phone

10. Insurance agent and address and phone

11. Other business consultant or advisor, address and phone

Step 3. Purpose

The purpose of your business might appear obvious to you when that bright idea first hits your mind. But will it still be pertinent a year down the road? Will the financial officer who examines your business plan be convinced that your purpose is realistic and destined for success?

This section of your business plan might require deeper thought than you first gave it. The old adage *"Sleep on it!"* might apply here. Of course, you have personal needs: making money and improving your lifestyle. These, the wealth-creating functions, are the obvious, external reasons.

More reasons of your purpose are the sometimes subtle needs of our society: making a contribution to the endangered environment, improving the ethical conduct of your type of business, providing employment to your fellowman. If you spell out all these additional purposes of entrepreneurial creation, you will be more satisfied with yourself and with your business plan and so will your investors or lenders.

Will the financial officer be convinced your purpose is realistic?

Purpose (worksheet)

1. The goals of my proposed business are

   _____

   _____

   _____

2. If an existing business, state purpose(s) of acquisition or expansion

   _____

3. Your experience to enable you to successfully manage the above-described enterprise consists of

   _____

   _____

4. How much money will be needed from:

   • Your own investment? . . . . . .$ _____

   • Other personal lenders? . . . . .$ _____

   • Loan from this institution? . .$ _____

5. How long will you make use of these funds? _____

6. How will these funds benefit the proposed business, in terms of:

   • Machinery or equipment _____

   • Inventory _____

   • Working Capital _____

   • Other _____

7. Over what period of time do you intend to repay this loan? _____

8. Where will the funds for the repayment come from?

   _____

   _____

9. Your collateral and market value _____ [$_____]

10. Who owns the collateral (described in #9)? _____

Step 4. Description of Business

It seems simple to say that your business does this and that, and that you are either a proprietorship, a partnership or a Corporation. But there's more to it; in fact, there are a number of points that must be accounted for.

In 1624 (in his *Meditation 17*) English poet John Donne wrote *"No man is an island,"* an admonition that each of us and each of our endeavours is dependent upon and interdependent with other individuals and other institutions. Your enterprise itself will be functioning within the context of a larger society. Your choice of individuals and institutions with whom you will be associating can speak volumes about the viability of your enterprise, and can serve to determine the level of its success.

Many professionals and peers with whom you surround yourself and with whom you will do business will be helpmates, suppliers, and underwriters of your future success.

Your choices of banker, lawyer, accountant and insurance carrier, for example, indicate that you have planned carefully and thoroughly, and are planning to stay on this course for the long haul. If these advisors are recognized to be of sterling caliber, their implied association with you will enhance your status.

Equal advantages can come from your association with professional and trade societies, chambers of commerce, and leadership in professional, civic and academic organizations.

Description of Business (worksheet)

1. The legal description of the proposed business

   _____

2. If corporation, where is it *or will it be* incorporated? _____

3. Other pertinent information _____

4. Classification or government code of corporate business _____

5. Is this a new business, expansion of your existing business, or purchase of an existing business? _____

6. When are you projecting to begin operation? _____

7. If this is an existing business, outline its history

   _____

   _____

   _____

   _____

8. Your projected operating schedule of business

   _____

9. Is this a: Seasonal business? ____ Year-around business? ____

10. Describe your plans for managing the business, including personnel, stock and inventory:

    _____

    _____

    _____

    _____

11. Who are your outside vendors and what will they be providing?
    - vendor: _____ supplying: _____
    - vendor: _____ supplying: _____
    - vendor: _____ supplying: _____
    - vendor: _____ supplying: _____
    - vendor: _____ supplying: _____

12. Terms of supply acquisition or credit available:

_____

13. What specific prices and discounts have been quoted by the suppliers for the above-mentioned products?

_____

_____

_____

14. What (if any) technical or management assistance will suppliers render? _____

_____

15. Who are your outside contractors and what will they be providing?
    • contractor: _____ providing: _____
    • contractor: _____ providing: _____
    • contractor: _____ providing: _____
    • contractor: _____ providing: _____
    • contractor: _____ providing: _____

    Their terms? _____

16. If you are planning to construct a building, supply all specifics, costs, titles: _____

_____

17. Why will this business be successful and profitable? _____

_____

18. Who started the business you are buying and when? _____

19. What do you think are the real reasons that this business is for sale?

_____

Step 5. Market Research

YOUR MARKET RESEARCH—
Pre-Business Plan Planning

If you are planning to build a better mousetrap, make sure that there are mice out there. While this might sound like a simplistic statement, it will surely come as no surprise that many businesses lose or even go bankrupt because, there were no mice to catch in their "better mousetrap."

The answer, of course, is to do your planning before you make a marketing decision, and especially before you spend any money. All too often, one major factor, typical among entrepreneurs, gets in the way of this simple logic: *enthusiasm for the new idea and the conviction that the world is waiting to beat a path to your door.* Sometimes it is; most often it isn't.

This pre-planning is called Market Research. It sounds like a very ponderous, costly and time consuming process—and it can be. However, there are some shortcuts that can be taken. Suffice to say—doing market research now is a lot less time and energy consuming, and certainly a great deal more cost-effective, than doing it later and possibly failing.

Market research is called for; complete, in-depth investigation that will provide you with pragmatic and rational answers. Limited and falsely directed research will only lead to wrong conclusions.

It is unlikely that an enthusiastic entrepreneur will long hesitate on the side of apathy and inertia. This, too, can be deadly. As Breen and Blankenship point out in their very useful book, "Do-It-Yourself Market Research," *"It is too easy to say 'no' to a new product or a new idea. An action that is never taken cannot fail. It might have been profitable, but no one will ever know."*

Steven Harper in his book, "Starting Your Own Business," compared the market to a horse and you, the entrepreneur, as the rider. As he put it, *"No jockey ever carried his horse across the finish line."* In other words, the market must be there to support your product or service. If there is any doubt in your mind that the need exists, or that you have the skill and means to create a market niche, better go over your plan again.

> *The best-built mousetrap will not attract customers unless there is a clearly-defined path on which potential buyers can approach.*

With all the caveats that we dredge up to make you more cautious about potential risks, intuition, imagination and ideas still play a big role. Even market research cannot always substitute for the innate tools of the entrepreneur. However, market research can fill in the gaps that intuition cannot account for.

Take one example: Saturation Statistics. These figures tell how many people it takes to enable a business to survive and prosper in urban areas in western industrialized countries. These figures, obviously, may vary considerably from country to country.

- Hardware Store—requires at least 8,000 people within the immediate market

- Barber shop—2,200

- Florist shop—8,600

- Nursery and garden supplies—26,000

- Restaurant—8,500

- Ladies' fashion store—5,000

- Furniture store—3,000

- Bookstore—26,000

- Stationery store—60,000

One caution: the above figures are conservative and depend upon your ambition. They also refer to existing population, not potential customers. In a new area or a new shopping center, your research must take into consideration potential development, future competition in reaction to population growth, and even the type of competition—franchise, highly promotional businesses, anticipated road pattern changes, proximity of customer-centers that exist or are projected, and other factors.

The more meaningful figures that you have at your disposal, the easier it will be to prepare a business plan that will work for you—and open the doors to potential loan demands.

FIVE TYPES OF MARKETING RESEARCH YOU CAN DO

1. Market Research: Finding out the real needs and wants of potential buyers, determining the specific market segment, assessing the market area, evaluating competition, spotting trends heretofore obscured.

2. Promotion Research: Determining the best strategy to reach your market, evaluating media, comparing costs and results.

3. Product Research: Ascertaining the public's receptivity, assuring pricing in the marketplace and in relation to competition, determining quality of product in actual use, checking distribution, naming, and packaging methods.

4. Sales Research: Evaluating performance, training and compensation of internal and external sales personnel, empathy with product, service follow-up, assigned territories or job station.

5. Company Research: Checking overall trends in your business, assessing company image, adequacy of location, morale, quality control, company ethics, adherence to environmental concerns and government regulations.

Methods of marketing research can include surveys (personal interviews, telephone calls or mail questionnaires), observation (observing customer behavior by eye-contact or electronic equipment), and/or experimental methods (actually establishing test situations in a store, trade show booth, display, or test-advertisements). Because products and services needs and consumers are constantly changing, marketing research should be a continuing part of your business operation.

Step 6. Competition

Competition will invariably exist. If you think you have an exclusive niche in your market, take advantage of it as much as possible. The chances are, however, that you will have plenty of competition who will compete, directly or indirectly, for the same market as you do. You can learn a great

So if you want to learn quickly, see what your competitors have done right and what they have done wrong.

deal from a larger and older competitor. Many of these have proven themselves as vulnerable to time and change as other enterprises, and many famed companies have disappeared from view—usually more because of faulty management than lack of financing—it was invariably competition that did them in. Somebody built a better company.

So if you want to learn quickly, see what your competitors have done right and what they have done wrong. Sometimes you can learn a lot from a non-competitor in the same business, who happens to be located in another market or in another city. Such a study can be more valuable than hiring a costly consultant—and it looks ever so good in your business plan.

Competition Worksheet

1. Names and locations of your nearest competitors:

   _____

2. Do you have any realistic information on their status? Proof?

   _____

3. In what ways will you be competitive (or better)? _____

   _____

4. How will you be different? Be specific about your advantages and how you can meet and beat competition, if needed.

   _____

   _____

   _____

5. What is your estimate of the competition's market share?

   _____

6. What strategies can you generate to obtain some of that market share? Over what time period? At what cost?

   _____

   _____

Step 7. Management

Management is perhaps the very first and foremost consideration in any business. The person or persons who run the business will determine, more than any of the other factors, whether the enterprise has a chance to succeed or is doomed to crash with the first ill wind. While a single proprietorship is easy to describe, providing you are completely candid with yourself, a multiple-management business is fraught with complications.

Other members of the management team need to be analyzed with a magnifying glass and complete frankness. Partners, especially, will come under scrutiny, as will specialized executives who are slated to perform functions that you cannot do. Such dependency makes you vulnerable and all possibilities must be taken into account when creating a workable and pragmatic business plan.

We cannot emphasize enough that management is the Number One reason businesses succeed or fail. Money is important, of course, and in the minds of many startup entrepreneurs, money is the first consideration. But experienced business people, and certainly financial officers, know that the "You Factor" determines whether an enterprise will likely grow or crash.

The determination of this step is difficult also for emotional reasons. As an entrepreneur you are ready, willing and able. It is indeed difficult to admit that you have shortcomings. But it's your life and your money. If you need more counsel, more training, more knowledge, get it now before you spend your hard-earned money and time.

We cannot emphasize enough that management is the Number One reason businesses succeed or fail.

Management Worksheet

1. Attach detailed resume of each principal in the business

2. Name each principal and related business experience in reference to the new business _____
_____

3. What are job descriptions of each of the above? Salaries? Costs of benefits? _____
_____
_____
_____

4. What external management assistance can you call on, if and when necessary? _____
_____
_____
_____

Personnel

Personnel is also a weighty decision that must be accounted for in the business plan. At the beginning of many small enterprises, the owner and his family do double-duty or, at best, arrangement can be made to utilize part-time personnel that work usually less than 20 hours a week, or on a basis other than a firm salary or hourly rate.

For purposes of your planning, this determination must be made as accurately as possible, since it impacts your cash needs. Personnel compensation must usually be made immediately and usually before income is derived from their contributions. The fiscal officer who might examine your business plan is especially interested in your commitments to hired personnel and its long-range implications on your cash flow. Remember, too, that it is wise to establish a clearly-understood and -written employee policy.

Personnel Worksheet

1. Will you need to hire any people? If so, what are the job titles, functions and expected salaries? _____

   _____

   _____

   _____

2. What training and additional benefits must you provide? _____

   _____

   _____

   _____

3. Can your business employ part-time employees? _____

   _____

   _____

   _____

4. Are any of the proposed employees your family members? _____

   _____

   _____

   _____

5. Briefly detail a succession policy, in the event you become incapable of managing the business yourself: _____

   _____

   _____

   _____

   _____

Step 8. Location

Location will be of primary interest to your interviewer at the bank or lending institution. Business experts have learned that there are three factors that will affect the health of your retail business: location, location, location.

In other sections of this book we have mentioned some of the criteria that need to be weighed in choosing a location for your business and the pitfalls that need to be regarded before signing any lease obligation. This section in your business plan needs to be completed carefully, both for your own protection and guidance, and for the examining lending officer. He knows, as you should, that a misstep in this section can cost you your business and obligate you for many years to come.

If your business is operating out of your home—and a growing number of small startups and "second time around" business are home-based—you need to make sure that the space is adequate to your needs, relatively free of family interference and temptations, and is zoned appropriately. There are tax advantages that may be considered, too.

If you sign a lease for external premises, do some quick arithmetic for your own information and for the business plan:

100 sq. meters office @ 600*francs* ($120 USD) per sq. meter
for 3 years =180.000*f* ($36,000 USD)

200 sq. meters retail store @ 500*francs* ($100 USD) per sq. meters.
for 5 years = 500.000*f* ($100,000 USD)

500 sq. meters warehouse @ 250*francs* ($50 USD) per sq. meter
for 2 years = 250.000*f* ($50,000 USD)

Add to these costs such "peripheral expenditures" as utilities, shared maintenance costs, refuse removal, improvements, *et al.*

Location Worksheet

1. State your reason(s) for choosing the location you've selected:

   _____

   _____

2. Is the neighborhood appropriate for your business? _____

3. What are the zoning restrictions? _____

4. Other area businesses? Any competitive? _____

5. Why is this location your first choice? _____

   _____

6. What other locations have you explored? _____

   _____

7. What is the rental or purchase cost? _____

8. Is this location permanent? If not, when will it change? _____

9. Do you own or lease the building you are in? _____

10. Describe the lease terms, taxes, future increases clause: _____

    _____

    _____

    _____

11. Enclose a floor plan of the facility.

12. If you need to make alterations or renovations, attach revised floor plans and cost estimates. Will the landlord pay all or part of these leasehold improvements?

Business experts have learned that there are three factors that will affect the success of your retail business: location, location, location.

Location Evaluations of Different Sites

The following worksheet can help you to decide which prospective locations would be best for your business planning. Use a rating of 1-to-5 in ascending order with 5 being the most favorable. All factors may not be relevant for all types of businesses, so disregard those not relevant to your business, and divide your total score by the number of applicable questions × five. For example, if 17 of the questions are applicable to your business, your maximum *possible* count is 17 × 5, or 85. If your total count is 78, then 78 ÷ 85 = 92%.

LOCATION ....Worse ⬅——————➡ Better

FACTOR	1	2	3	4	5
Busy shopping area	——	——	——	——	——
Street access to premises	——	——	——	——	——
Traffic flow	——	——	——	——	——
Pedestrian traffic	——	——	——	——	——
Parking facilities	——	——	——	——	——
Public transportation	——	——	——	——	——
Street location	——	——	——	——	——
Nearest competition	——	——	——	——	——
Display area	——	——	——	——	——
Ease of entry and exit	——	——	——	——	——
Rear access for deliveries	——	——	——	——	——
Required utilities	——	——	——	——	——
Building condition	——	——	——	——	——

Required improvements   ___ ___ ___ ___ ___

Cost of rent   ___ ___ ___ ___ ___

Length of lease   ___ ___ ___ ___ ___

Location vacancy rate   ___ ___ ___ ___ ___

History of site   ___ ___ ___ ___ ___

Property Taxes   ___ ___ ___ ___ ___

Suitable zoning   ___ ___ ___ ___ ___

Total count: _____ (divide this number by your maximum possible count to determine your score; the closer to 100%, the better your location)

Step 9. Your Market Strategy

Marketing is the strategic plan to put you in touch with the customer in order to satisfy their NEEDS, WANTS or DESIRES. This should be based on your market research and plays a vital role in successful business ventures. The key element of a successful marketing plan is to know your customers—their likes, dislikes, and expectations. By identifying these factors, you can develop a marketing strategy that will allow you to arouse and fulfill their needs.

You must understand your customer before you can develop or offer a product or service that they will want to buy.

If you are introducing an innovative or new product, you must try to create a desire for the product, but this will take a great deal of marketing effort both in advertising publicity, sales promotion, and public relations. Novelty products have a shorter life than products that will fill a need.

COMPETITION

Competition is a way of life: your business's competition exists now or will develop soon. Nations compete in the global marketplace, as do domestic entrepreneurs in their local spheres of interest.

IBM is a current example of intense competition in the personal computer field. A newspaper report recently stated *"IBM, struggling again to salvage its fortunes as the world's premier computer company, announced sharp cutbacks in jobs and production lines and said it would probably lay off workers for the first time in its 78-year history."* The past few years have seen this reduction in work forces with many large firms worldwide.

Start a file on each of your competitors' advertising and promotional materials and their pricing strategy techniques. Review these files periodically, to monitor when and how often they advertise, sponsor promotions and offer sales. Use this information to determine your marketing strategy.

PRICING AND SALES

Pricing strategy is another marketing technique you can use to improve your overall competitiveness. It is a good idea to get a feel for the pricing strategy that your competitors are using. Do not let your competitors determine your pricing, remember that price is only one part of the overall image the service you provide your customers is equally or more important. Some of the pricing strategies you may consider are:

1. Direct product or service cost + operating expenses + desired profit

2. Be in a competitive position

3. Pricing below or above competition

4. Multiple pricing for quantities or different levels

The key to success is to have a well-planned strategy, to establish your policies, constantly monitor inventory turns, prices and operating costs to ensure profits. Keep abreast of the changes in the marketplace, because these changes will affect your competitiveness and profit margins.

ADVERTISING AND PUBLIC RELATIONS

You must not forget that money you borrow must be paid back; this money must be earned out of the proceeds of your business.

The purpose of advertising and publicity functions is to help move goods and services. Virtually every successful enterprise incorporates a measured investment of their marketing budget into these functions.

For your own reference, 2 to 5 percent of sales revenue for advertising might be appropriate based on your retail location, customer traffic, sales distribution, type of manufacturing image required, or service. Maintain a projected advertising/publicity calendar to control your budget and expenditure results. Continuously monitor and analyze *promotion costs versus results* directly traceable to these efforts.

If you are applying for outside financing, your business plan needs to account for and detail your advertising investment. We prefer to call this line item an investment rather than an expenditure. The reason is purely psychological. Good advertising should return a profit on your investment.

Publicity is virtually cost-free, although publicity results may be unpredictable. It is also very much underused and misunderstood. If you are not familiar with publicity techniques, then discuss your situation with a professional or read a good book on the subject.

Your Marketing Strategy Worksheet

1. WHO are your customers? DEFINE your target market(s)

_____

_____

_____

2. WILL your markets continue growing? remain steady? decline?

_____

3. WILL your markets be large enough to expand; are there restrictions?

_____

_____

4. HOW will you attract, hold, increase your market share?

_____

_____

5. WHAT will be your strategy to promote sales?

_____

_____

_____

6. WHAT will be your pricing strategy?

_____

_____

7. WHAT will you do better than your competitors?

_____

_____

8. WHAT customer services will you offer?

_____

_____

9. WHICH benefits of your product line will you promote?

_____

_____

Step 10. Financial Information

This is the make-or-break section. It is the one a potential lender will understand best and will examine most closely for completeness, accuracy and realism. Even if you do not require outside capital, it is vital that you determine all of these figures accurately and realistically. It is sometimes better to err on the side of conservatism, than to be overly optimistic and be caught with your bank balance down (or your pants).

It would be wise, too, to look over some of the pitfalls mentioned elsewhere in this book. Uneducated predictions are of little use, but experience and networking can be immensely useful.

Economic circumstances beyond your control, catastrophies of nature, sudden obsolescence caused by shifting customer preferences, zoning and road pattern changes, recessions that affect sales and collections all demand that you factor in a good percentage for "unforeseens."

Financial Information includes six sections, plus a seventh one in case you are buying someone else's business, which requires special information.

10.1 Capital Requirements

Every business needs some capital. Even if you have zero expenses (for example, if you are a consultant working out of your home, you have to account for one major expense: your own living costs, especially until such time that your business can generate sufficient income to meet your personal expenses. However, bear in mind that:

• your own assets might provide you with sufficient working capital your family could pool its fiscal resources;

• friends who share your entrepreneurial enthusiasm may want to get in on your business;

• you might not need as much capital as you had thought;

• you can lease or rent equipment rather than buying it outright;

- you can hire part-time or per-job personnel rather than assuming a burdensome payroll;

- you might consider a monied partner to put up capital and share in potential profits;

- you could look into various methods of non-traditional, innovative funding such as a grant, an incubator (cooperative) association or supplier financing ("strategic alliances")

- you must not forget that money you borrow must be paid back, normally with interest, and that this money must be earned out of the proceeds of your business.

Should you still go out to a traditional money source, and you have carefully weighed all of the above nine considerations, match your capital requirement loan request with your current, negotiable collateral and start.

10.2 Depreciable Assets

In your business you have something of worth. It can be a building and the land on which it stands. It can be rolling stock, such as cars and trucks. It can be machinery used in an office or in production and warehousing. Or it could be inventory of merchandise destined for resale.

Most of these assets depreciate over a period of time, although some fixed assets, like real estate, could go up in value. The tax authorities may be most interested in your depreciable assets and they have fairly firm regulations about taking value reductions on them.

Most assets reduce in value due to obsolescence, wear and tear, accidental damage, and changes in consumer preferences. Such reductions in asset value are bookkeeping entries and do not represent any hard cash outlays. No funds need to be earmarked for such depreciation, though if such assets are pledged as collateral, depreciation might have to be supplemented with cash infusion in order to maintain your collateral's value.

In assessing value of real estate and land, the improvements upon the land and the land itself must be determined separately. For accounting purposes, two types of depreciation are used:

Straight Line Depreciation which is based on the estimated life of the item for bookkeeping purposes. Buildings might depreciate in 20 years, giving you a depreciation of five percent annually. A piece of machinery or truck might have a five-year depreciation, which allows you to reduce its value by 20 percent each year. Your country's tax guidelines need to be consulted annually.

Declining Balance Method of Depreciation is used when even quicker recovery of your investment is desirable. The tax authority may limit depreciation of the straight-line method. Example: If you choose to depreciate a truck costing 100.000f ($20,000 USD) in two years instead of five years, you could take an 50.000f ($10,000 USD) depreciation instead of the normal 20.000f ($4,000 USD) depreciation. However, it is always prudent to consult the authority, or your accountant, on what is safe and acceptable for the particular year in question.

10.3 Pro Forma Balance Sheet

[Note: The term "Pro Forma" refers to the fact that the item (in this case the balance sheet) is projected, or before-the-fact, rather than actual, which would necessarily be after-the-fact. This form displays the Assets, Liabilities and Equity of the business, which serves to indicate how much investment will be required by the business and how much of it will be used as Working Capital in its operation.]

10.4 Break-Even Analysis

An examination of the activity when your total revenue equals your expenses. This juncture is called the break-even point. You need to determine, realistically, when your business activity reaches that point and then plan to go beyond it in order to make a profit. You can determine the break-even point either in currency or in units of merchandise. You may either, let's say, do a gross dollar volume of 500.000f ($100,000 USD) in order to equal your expenses, or you can sell 10,000 items at 50f ($10

USD) apiece, equaling your 500.000 f ($100,000 USD) break-even point.

10.5 Projected Income Statement

The profit-and-loss statement for a specific length of time, usually monthly, if you're starting a new business, or for three years ahead if you have an established business. If you do not have specific and reasonably accurate figures based on your experience or past performance, then trade, industry or government figures can be consulted and adjusted for local conditions. At best, such a projection is reasonably accurate, rarely totally so. Its foundation is a number of educated guesses, but the more educated, the more accurate they will be. As we've said before, if you do err, let it be on the conservative side. Being overly optimistic could leave you with problems.

10.6 Cash Flow Projection and Analysis

Cash flow is the actual net income of a business. You cannot count money that is owed to you, because that money is only on your books, not in your pocket. However, for bookkeeping purposes, many businesses, especially corporations, will count depreciation, depletion, amortization and charges to reserves.

To be on the safe side, follow the old motto, *"Don't count your chickens 'til they're hatched."* Too many small businesses have troubles because they counted money that was coming in, supposedly, by the end of the month. When it did not, because customers were late, negligent, had troubles of their own, or other priorities, cash flow was diminished to dangerously low levels. In such cases, businesspeople had to resort to high-interest temporary loans, or had to factor their receivables by 70 to 80 percent.

Distorting cash flow figures can only hurt you. It will never fool the banker or lender. Your analysis needs to be ultra conservative, simply because it is in your own interest, even if you do not plan to borrow additional money.

> *Your analysis needs to be ultra conservative, simply because it is in your own interest, even if you do not plan to borrow additional money.*

Financial Information Checklist

___ 1. Balance sheet for the past three years if an established business; current balance sheet if this is a new business

___ 2. Operating statement same as (1)

___ 3. Project cash flow for three years (*month-by-month* if you're starting a new business; *quarterly* if you have an established business)

___ 4. Breakdown analysis same as (3)

___ 5. Financial statement for each principal, co-signor and/or guarantor of the business

___ 6. Personal or business tax returns for the three past years

___ 7. Capital equipment: if you need any, attach list of items, estimated cost or value of each

___ 8. Appraisal form from a bank-approved appraiser showing existence and current value of any real estate, vehicles, equipment and/or machinery owned by the business

___ 9. Assets that are owned or may own in the near future that should be disclosed.

Financial Information Worksheet
for Buying an existing Business

1. Who determined the acquisition price? How much is it? _____

   _____

   _____

2. How much will you pay for "goodwill" (this is the established-customer
   base that comes with the business, which is referred to as "goodwill"
   in some countries)? _____

   _____

   _____

3. Will the seller take back any portion of the purchase price as a loan?
   On what terms? _____

   _____

   _____

4. Attach a list of visible assets list of creditors and their terms, value and
   age of inventory, capital assets, any liabilities for which you will be
   responsible, appraisers' confirmations, photographs of building
   and/or location.

Step 11. Keeping Records

Records must be archived for some period of time, usually ranging from one to seven years. Full instructions may be obtained from the tax authority or your accountant. For the purposes of running a business adequately, accurately and efficiently, the following records must be considered and accounted for in your business plan:

• Day-by-day sales with weekly, monthly, quarterly and annual summaries

• *Perpetual inventory* to determine both availability and value of goods at hand, and re-ordering scheduling *(the term "perpetual inventory" refers to the maintenance of continuously-updated sales and inventory records, often with the implementation of computer barcode pricing and computerized reporting and reordering systems).*

• Sales taxes

• Cash Sales

• Credit sales

• Customer records (names, addresses, sales, payments, purchase patterns)

• Sales promotions and results

   -Detailed expenses, including:

   -Personnel costs—including taxes, withholdings, *et al.*

   -Equipment acquisitions through purchase or lease, including vehicles

   -Leases and lease terms/conditions

   -Loans and repayment schedules

In a projected or new business, many of the above figures will be estimates. For an established business these should be actual up-to-date amounts. If you plan to purchase an existing business, records should be provided to you for your analysis and your accountant's and/or attorney's study. Record-keeping requires discipline and timeliness. *The need will not go away; delay only makes record-keeping more difficult and less accurate.*

Executive Summary

We have left this part for last, although you'll put *The Executive Summary* up front in your business plan.

Here is why your *Executive Summary* goes up front:

Your *Executive Summary* is an overall view of your business. it includes what you plan to do with it, what its potential is, how much money you need and how much money the business will generate. It reveals the return on investment (ROI) and how and when the investor (including the entrepreneur) can expect to get his money back.

The importance of your *Executive Summary* cannot be overstated. Financial investors and bank loan officers will often skim through the business plan, reading only those parts that are of interest to them. However, these experts *always* read your *Executive Summary*. Thus it's vital that you present the essence of your business plan in this *Summary*.

Your *Executive Summary* should include:

1. Specifically what you plan to achieve with your business;

2. Objectives you intend to reach;

3. How you intend to reach these objectives;

4. Who will be responsible for meeting these objectives;

5. What capitalization will be required to achieve them including how such money, if borrowed, can be earned and repaid.

These five short paragraphs should occupy less than one page; if you make them complete and dramatic enough, they will open doors for you.

That, in brief, is your *Executive Summary* and the outline of your business plan.

Step 12. Miscellaneous Checklist (Appendix)

There are at least a dozen other considerations that could go into a business plan or matters that might be asked during a loan application process. They are listed here though you might have more.

Two reasons for providing as complete a series of documents as possible for the Plan are (1) so you will know exactly where you stand, and (2) so the financial officer to whom you may want to apply for a loan knows he is dealing with a professional.

Miscellaneous Checklist

1. If your business is a franchise, enclose the Franchise Agreement and disclosure statement

2. All pertinent contracts including lease

3. All business agreements

4. Management contracts

5. Maintenance agreements

6. Roster of major customers, annual purchases, terms

7. List of principal suppliers, annual volume, line of credit, terms

8. Credit card and credit system you use

9. Publicity that might have been generated

10. Annual report

11. Name of insurance carrier

12. Patents or copyrights owned

13. Other pertinent legal documents

You have now become acquainted with the various ingredients you'll use to create your business plan. It's time now for you to actually create one.

The importance of your Executive Summary cannot be overstated.

Let's continue...

Chapter III

Sample Business Plan: Retail Store

Your business plan should be "packaged" like a precious piece of jewelry or expensive perfume. In selling there is a saying: "When you want to make a good impression, put your best foot forward, and have your shoes well-shined."

The way you present the business plan can make a favorable first impression. That means: have a good cover on it. Use good stationery. Have it typed or word processed neatly and double check it for errors.

Most bankers and financial officers prefer a summary up front, rather than at the end. In this way they can tell immediately, without wasting their valuable time, whether they are interested in your proposition or not. This summary is not as easy to write as it might seem. Sometimes it is more difficult to say in a hundred or two hundred words what you might more easily say in one thousand.

The worked-out example of a business plan, which follows this outline, is about a typical retail store. Follow this outline step-by-step and you will be assured correct results for your own needs as well as for presentation to a potential lender.

> *When you want to make a good impression, put your best foot forward, and have your shoes well-shined.*

The 12 Steps

Step 1. Introduction to the Business Plan
Cover Letter
Cover Sheet for Business Plan
Table of Contents

Step 2. Business Identification

Step 3. Purpose
Statement of Purpose: why are you presenting this business plan

Step 4. Description of Business

Step 5. Market Research: Pinpointing Your Customer

Step 6. Competition: How Good are They?

Step 7. Management: Establishing credibility and establishing Goals;
Personnel

Step 8. Business Site: Location Location, Location

Step 9. Market Stategy

Step 10. Financial Information: Capital Requirement; Equipment;
Balance Sheet; Break-Even Analysis; Projected Income
Statement; Profit and Loss; Cash Flow Projection and
Analysis

Step 11. Keeping Records: 3 years of personal history, business history
and tax records

Step 12. Executive Summary:one page synopsis
(often placed up front)

Miscellaneous Checklist

Appendix:

- Copy of lease

- Contract, if business is purchased

- Franchise Agreement, if it's a franchise

- Partnership Agreement, if it's a partnership

- Articles of Incorporation, if it's a corporation

- Plan of location or property layout

- Agent Agreement if one or more are engaged

- Client Contracts, if such commitments exist

Sample Business Plan: Retail Store

There are millions of retail stores in the world. Many of them sell some form of women's clothes. We have chosen one particular store as an example for our business plan. It is an imaginary store, but typical of one owned and operated by a middle-aged person who has accumulated long, in-depth experience in women's clothes, is self-sufficient economically, accumulated fairly substantial cash reserves and equity, and has now arrived at a stage in life when he wants to become an entrepreneur independent of bosses and others' wiles and whims.

Our "sample" store will be a startup; that is, it will be a brand-new store, not a franchise or a store bought from a previous owner. This situation, too, is the most typical scenario, although more and more entrepreneurs are choosing the other two popular routes: buying an existing store or opening a franchise business. The reason for the latter trend: it is a short-cut to achieving a measurable stride of business volume and has a greater potential of survival and success. It also takes more up-front cash.

Our sample will stock and sell ladies' coats, raincoats, jackets, accessories. It might add additional related lines in the future, but initially, these are the principal clothing items for sale. They are ones the owner knows best from his prior experience; these are the items he feels will sell best and are the most-competition-proof at this time.

Your own Business Plan can be based upon this sample plan.

Your own business plan, whether for a startup, an established, or an expanding business, or whether planned as a tool for a business loan application, can be based upon this sample plan. Of course you might inject different elements to custom-tailor your own business plan to your particular situation. But this plan presents all the basic elements for a retail store of any type, as well as for most businesses.

Remember then: this sample business plan is only a guide to creating your own personal business plan; it is accurate only as an example of how to prepare your own business plan. The contents, figures, names, projections and entries are not authentic. You need to gather your own information for your business and corroborate it with appropriate market research.

US dollar amounts are shown in parenthesis as an example of other denominations only; these would not necessarily appear on an actual Business Plan.

Step 1 Introduction to Business Plan

1.1 Suggested Cover Letter

Imprinted business stationery on the very best paper you can buy, typewritten or word processed faultlessly.

Your Letterhead
Date
Name of Your Financial Officer
Name of Your Bank
Address
City

Dear _____ :

Thank you for seeing me last _____ and discussing my plans to start a retail business in _____.

Enclosed for you is our business plan for *La Belle Mode*. This confidential report is presented to you for your consideration of a 200.000 *francs* ($40,000 USD) loan.

The above loan is to be repaid monthly over a seven (7) year period, plus interest.

I will call you within a week for a follow-up appointment to discuss mutually-acceptable terms with you.

The proposed loan will be used for working capital, to back up my own investment of at least 300.000ƒ ($60,000 USD). You will note in my financials that our projected startup costs, including new inventory, amounts to 304.125ƒ ($60,825 USD).

As a long-time client of your bank, I am sure you will give your personal consideration to this loan proposal.

Sincerely yours,

Marie Bonhomme / *La Belle Mode*

1.2: Cover Sheet

Name and Address of Business
Name, Address and Phone Number
of the Preparer of this Document

Business Plan

La Belle Mode

100, avenue des Jongleurs

78100 Crespieres. France

Submitted by:

Marie Bonhomme

téléphone 30.54.80.30

20 janvier, 1997

Step 1.3

TABLE OF CONTENTS

This is optional, but desirable if the business plan is lengthy or if the enclosures (appendix) are numerous.

TABLE OF CONTENTS

Introduction

Statement of Purpose

Need in Community

Appropriateness of Location

Experience of Management

Equity Production

Executive Summary

Description of Business

Products

Primary Suppliers

Customer Services

The Market

Description

Marketing Strategy

Market Research and Demographics

Target Market

Sales Strategy

Pricing Policy

Promotion Plans: Opening and Continuing

Business Site

Use the very best stationery you can buy.

Location

Competition

Description

Strategy vs Competition

Management and Personnel

Proprietor's Personal Curriculum Vitae

Goals

Personal Advisors

Personnel

Legal Structure

Business Insurance

Capital Requirement

Return on Investment

Lender Equity

Equipment: Depreciable Assets

Balance Sheet: Assets and Liabilities

Starting Balance Sheet

Monthly Cost of Living

Initial startup Costs

Balance Sheet

Break-Even Analysis

Financial Management

Break-Even Point Worksheet

Ratios: 1st, 2nd, 3rd Year

Apparel and Accessory Stores, National Ratios

Projected Income Statement

Details, First Year

Period, Three Years

Cash Flow Projections

Monthly Cash Flow Projection

Annual Cash Flow Projection

Keeping Records

Appendix

Personal Resume(s)

Tax Returns, past three years

Lease Agreement

Store Floor Plan

Leasehold Improvement Agreement (if separate from Lease)

Fixture Purchase Quotations

Office Equipment Lease Agreement

Insurance Schedule and Quotations

Service Agreements: Accountant, Lawyer

Prime Suppliers' Correspondent, if pertinent

Demographics

Automobile Lease or Installment Purchase, if any

Mortgage Statement, if any

Advertising Contracts, if any already signed

Copies of Certificates, Diplomas, Honors

La Belle Mode

100, avenue des Jongleurs

78100 Crespieres. France

ID# 525-70-5874

Principal
Marie Bonhomme

Why are you preparing this Business Plan for someone else's eyes and requirements?

Accountant

Pierre Fleurs

téléphone 00.00.00.00

Attorney

Jacques Loies

téléphone 00.00.00.00

Banker

Rene X. Change

téléphone 00.00.00.00

Insurance

Mme C. Curie

téléphone 00.00.00.00

Consultant

Louis Conseilleur

téléphone 00.00.00.00

Step 3 Business Purpose

3.1 Statement of Purpose

This business plan is prepared (1) as a guide for management and (2) as supportive evidence that a business loan will be useful for the rapid growth of the business and can be repaid promptly out of projected cash flow.

Need in Community

The growth of Crespieres, based on state, municipal and Chamber of Commerce statistics, and the rise of a well-paid business and professional class of women shoppers, assures the concomitant growth of *La Belle Mode*. With very limited competition in the market for the merchandise proposed, this store is needed to round out the demand of the foregoing buying group. Advance marketing studies and examining of traffic in markets 15 or more km away, which now are magnets for local shoppers, indicate that *La Belle Mode* can help to round out market needs within the area and keep much business "at home."

Appropriateness of Location

The leased property at 100, avenue des Jongleurs is a high-traffic corner near convenient parking and an estimated customer base of at least 10,000 working women. The lease is a reasonable one and offers renewal options well into the future.

Experience of Management

The sole proprietor of *La Belle Mode* has had 20 years of experience in all facets of the women's fashion trade and store/department management. This is detailed in the section on Management.

Equity Production

Because of the need for this type of store, a growing customer base, and the experience of management, our projections indicate rapid equity production within a few months. Personal investment of owner is in excess of outside capitalization, assuring also that equity production will be of prime concern. Subsequent financials indicate that ample payback opportunity is assured by a healthy cash flow.

3.2 Executive Summary

Your synopsis of what the following business plan is all about, giving the lender a quick overview of your proposal.

Executive Summary

A significant market opportunity exists in the mid-town area of Crespieres for a business that caters to a growing number of professional women. These executives have special needs in the purchase of their outerwear.

Our intended audience is very busy with its professional life. Yet its members still need to maintain a home environment if single, or an extended home environment if married and with children. Purchasing the kind of wardrobe their multiple lives demand requires time and patience, and usually too little of either is available after professional and domestic demands are met.

La Belle Mode intends to satisfy the needs of this growing and profitable market. It is not being filled at this time in our city.

Crespieres has a growing number of business firms in the mid-town area, where many of our intended audience are working. Our planned store will attract considerable business during the middle of the day, when these women are on their lunch hours. One weekday, at least, the store will remain open until 9:00PM to accommodate evening shoppers from the suburbs. A Saturday store-opening from 9:00 to 5:00 will also be planned, and perhaps extended, as response dictates.

Our planned store location at 100, ave. des Jongleurs is on a convenient, well-lighted corner, accessible for day or evening traffic. Moderately-priced stores are located within a few blocks, such as *La Pharmacie, Gallerie Moliere, Les Messieurs, Le Bistro,* et *La Patisserie de Paris,* making for a good merchandise mix as well as for substantial foot traffic.

There is street parking on every adjacent street, a city parking lot one block away, and five bus routes, both local and long distance, on Main Street.

Give a quick overview of your proposal.

An estimated 37 percent return-on-investment worked out on the following financials make *La Belle Mode* a sound investment and much-needed contribution to our viable community.

The experience of the proprietor-manager, combined with local opportunities, assures the long-range success of this enterprise.

Step 4 Description of Business

Product or Service

Description of Business

La Belle Mode is a ladies' ready-to-wear shop located at 100, avenue des Jongleurs in Crespieres, a high-traffic corner that prior history has shown to enjoy optimum traffic of virtually any location in the mid-town area.

The nearest store that can be considered partially competitive is five blocks away. Ample municipal parking exists within a minute's walk. Display windows on two sides of the building offer excellent exposure of our merchandise to pedestrians. The following is a detailed description of planned merchandise:

Products

Description	Percent of Inventory
Group A—Coats	30%
Group B—Designer Coats—Off-Price	20%
Group C—Raincoats	20%
Group D—Jackets	20%
Group E—Handbags	7%
Group F—Gloves and Wallets	3%

Groups A, B and C will be 100% woolens or combinations of synthetics and will be no higher than 1.500*f* ($300 USD) retail.

Group B (designers' coats off-price), will be purchased for cash and be sample coats, discontinued styles or manufacturers' overcuts.

Group C (raincoats) will be 100% cotton or synthetic combinations or coated nylon, an all-year–round product group.

Group D (jackets) will be 100% wool or synthetic combinations for the fall season and will be lighter material and designed for the holiday, spring or summer season.

Group E and F (handbags, gloves and wallets) will be rotated in design, materials and purpose to sell throughout the year.

Inventory and open-to-buy (the amount of funds budgeted for new purchases) will be determined by the season and the unit and dollar sales. Adequate sales with be required for good turnover of the inventory in order to have open-to buy for new styles.

Primary Suppliers

Coats and Jackets:

> *Premiere Coat Manufacturer*
>
> *Studio Coats, Inc.*
>
> *Empire Outerwear, Inc.*

Designer Coats:

> *St. Guerre Design, Inc.*
>
> *Marie Modes, Inc.*

Raincoats:

> *Milano London, Ltd.*
>
> *Fleet Rainwear, Inc.*

Customer Services

Credit Cards—VISA, MasterCard and American Express

Lay-Away—⅓ down and ⅓ each for two months

Returns—three days with sales slip

Deliveries—Free for city, normal charges elsewhere

Guarantees—30 days on manufacturers' imperfections

Complaints—24 hour recorder with return call within one working day

Open—Weekdays from 10am to 6pm, Friday 10am to 9pm,
      Saturday 9am to 5pm; appointments on call

Step 5 Market Research—Pinpointing Customers

Crespieres' population: 75.000

Metropolitan area population: 200.000

Principal Industries: Professional and financial centers, local government offices, a number of "clean" industries primarily in the service, light chemical and electronic areas. All industries have proven to be remarkably stable and recession-proof. Because of the high-percentage of government and financial payrolls, the average income does not fluctuate with the seasons.

Customer Base: middle-income women in the 25-to-60–years age range earning between 50.000 and 200.000ƒ ($10,000 and $40,000 USD) annually. Fifty-five percent of trading area population is female. An equal percentage of women in the above age range is in the local workforce.

Outside assistance: the Chamber of commerce and the Economic Development Bureau have been immensely helpful in providing corroborating information and research material, providing training and advice, and are available for continuing counseling. The proprietor has attended a business startup workshop conducted by the University as well as a retail management workshop offered by the Chamber of Commerce. Considerable market research information was obtained from the above organizations.

Target Market

Primary: Women between ages 25 and 60, who are employed within a 10-block radius in professional positions, are our target market. Primary customers are anticipated to be the busiest, most-highly paid, professional women who seek better clothes, more personal service and assistance, and are reliable, repeat customers.

Secondary: Women working in offices, light industries and the five commercial-industrial parks and malls within a 15-km radius are our secondary market.

Tertiary: Visitors, tourists, and prospective customers from areas outside of the 15-km perimeter, including men purchasing for women on special occasions.

La Belle Mode will focus on professional and middle-income working women ages 25-to-60. Their estimated annual income is from 50.000 to 200.000*f* ($10,000 to $40,000 USD). The majority of prospective customers work within a 10-block area of the store and are considered walk-in traffic.

Within a 15-km radius of the store at *La Belle Mode* lie four industrial-and-office parks. Several hundred female prospects work in these facilities and efforts will be made to attract them to the store.

Considerable drive-by traffic also exists, adding to an estimated potential customer base of more than 10.000 women, of whom more than 30 percent are considered prime prospects.

Step 6 Competition

In the 5-km radius of our location, four stores have been identified as being partially or somewhat competitive:

La Printemps, well-established, 75-year-old company; large inventory of popularly-priced lines. Well-stocked on outerwear. Experienced sales help. Carries its own accounts (credit). More of a limited department store than a specialty operation.

La Femme Fantastique, in business for only two years; carries a very showy, not classic, line of styles, concentrating on dresses and sporty outfits. Limited selections, heavy turnover; youthful appeal.

Gallerie Lafayette, established three years ago as a mid-priced fashion store appealing to working and housekeeping women. Selections are not carried in depth, and inventory turnover does not appear to be fast enough to keep styles updated. Advertising reflects continuous sales. The store might present our most direct competition.

Strategy vis-a-vis Competition

Concentration on my specialty, quality outerwear for professional women; in-depth selections; middle-range pricing; exceptional personal service; unquestioned guarantees; convenient shopping hours and personal appointments are the advantages that will put *La Belle Mode* into the ranks of successful local businesses. Unlike chain stores, this store will always be personally managed.

Step 7 Management

Proprietor's Personal *Curriculum Vitae* and Goals:

I (Marie Bonhomme) am a retired buyer for *Capitol Stores* in Crespieres. I have 20 years of experience, principally in the ladies' coat department. During my two decades with the above company, I have learned all facets of buying, stocking, retail store management, and floor sales. I know the manufacturing and buying market, having made innumerable personal trips to the major fashion centers of France, Italy and England. I have continued excellent rapport with all major resources and received considerable encouragement to pursue an independent specialty business in this city.

A number of important vendors have agreed to set up moderate lines of credit. More details on expected credit lines and personal details are contained in the Appendix of this business plan.

Realizing the advantage of starting out with the best-available counsel to complement my pragmatic experience, I have assembled the following "team" to assure the success of *La Belle Mode*:

Attorney
Jacques Loies
Prince and Associates
100 Professional Plaza, Suite 00
78100 Crespieres
téléphone 00.00.00.00

Accountant
Pierre Fleurs
Able Accounting Corp.
100 Commerce Building, Suite 00
78100 Crespieres
téléphone 00.00.00.00

Banking
Rene X. Change
Banque Commerciale
Main and Keystone
78100 Crespieres
00.00.00.00

Insurance
Premiere Compagnie d'Assurance
Mme. C. Curie
100 de Securité Boulevard, Suite 00
78100 Crespieres
téléphone 00.00.00.00

Consultants
Crespieres Economic Development Agency
Louis Conseilleur, Director
78100 Crespieres
téléphone 00.00.00.00

Personnel

Personnel: During the foreseeable startup year, we plan to employ only part-time personnel, each working no more than 20 hours a week. A number of experienced saleswomen, seamstresses and interns are available to fill the needs of the store, depending on seasons and merchandising events that could require additonal help.

I do not presently contemplate having any partners.

Based on increase of business, my needs to make trips to the fashion markets, and availability of cash flow, permanent or full-time personnel will be considered in year two. It is expected that our experience with numerous part-time helpers will give us a pragmatic overview of the best individuals available.

Business Goals

The following is an anticipated schedule for the startup of *La Belle Mode*. The months between now and the opening will be devoted to buying and processing inventory; completing the fixturing of the store; continuing marketing and research observation; hirinig and training one or two assistants; and preparing promotion material. Meetings with my accountant and attorney will continue as necessary.

1. Announcements to local women's organizations mailed 7 July 1997.

2. Announcements placed inlocal newspaper previous to and following 7 August 1997.

3. Grand Opening 7 August 1997.

4. Review of operation by 1 October 1997 and analysis of sales, names signed in by customers and visitors, and merchandise turnover.

5. Filling in with new merchandise, especially small-ticket holiday and gift merchandise; order holiday decor, bags, and announcements for customer prospect list, during October 1997.

6. Begin decorating and change displays for holidays; special evening promotions; starting November 15.

7. Extend evening shopping hours (depending in part on plans of merchants' association), by December 14, 1997.

8. Plan post-holiday sales event, effective December 26.

Administratively, the business will begin as a single proprietorship. The planned loan of 200.000*f* ($40,000 USD). will re-invested in additional Spring lines, as our first five months of experience will dictate. Collateral on my condominium, with a market value of 700.000*f* ($140,000 USD), is expected to be 400.000*f* ($80,000 USD). and will be used as circumstances dictate.

Step 8 Business Location

Location, Location, Location

The store will be located in a four-story building occupied by offices, located at the corner of 1st and Boulevard Lafayette, in the downtown office section of Crespieres. Total leasable area is 100 sq. meters with a large display window flanking a recessed entrance door. The entrance is a revolving door which was left in place by a previous tenant. Display windows are in acceptable condition and each equipped with dual electric floor outlets and several ceiling high-hat outlets. Additional improvements in the interior are contemplated, and the landlord, the Crespieres Improvement Corporation, has agreed to contribute 15.000ƒ ($3,000 USD). toward leasehold improvements. This amounts to approximately 50 percent of improvements I expect to make, amounting primarily to dressing rooms (2), racks, one display case (used), furnishings, desk and chairs. Additional needed electrical connections and sanitary facility are already *in situ* and in acceptable condition.

Zoning permits only a frontage sign on the face of the building. Electric overhead connections are available on both sides of the corner store. Two elegantly-designed, painted signs, illuminated by existing fixtures, will be developed.

The lease calls for 100 sq. meters @ 1.000ƒ ($200 USD) per sq. meter, including utilities, which has been worked out with CIC, payable at 10.000ƒ ($2,000 USD) per month for five (5) years. A renewal option for an additional five (5) years has been negotiated at no more than ten (10) percent above current rental. (Please see copy of proposed lease in Appendix.)

Legal Structure

Marie Bonhomme, doing business as *La Belle Mode*, will be registered under this fictitious name and will operate as a single proprietorship. In the future, as the business grows and liability might increase, incorporation will be considered. An attorney's guidance will be sought to explore any such change in legal structure. An accountant will be consulted annually, at tax preparation time, to weigh advantages of corporate organization in relation to gross and net income.

Business Insurance

A discussion with a local insurance broker has already been held and his proposal is included in the Appendix. Insurance coverage will initially consist of three phases:

1. Fire and burglary coverage

2. Workers' Compensation

3. Customer liability coverage

Additional insurance coverage is under consideration. It will include glass breakage insurance, keyperson insurance, maintenance on electronic equipment, vehicle insurance upgrade.

Insurance is also in place for the building and external public areas, held by CIC.

Step 9 Market Strategy

Based on my 20 years of experience, outside counseling and current market research, the following sales strategies will be emphasized:

• We will introduce a new concept in outerwear specialization.

• Continual contacts with the fashion markets will assure advance styling, correct colors, top quality for value, and proper coordination of accessories.

• Our publicity and promotion will emphasize our professionalism and convenient city location.

• A discounted designer line will be maintained as a magnet and promoted widely.

• A newsletter to customers and signers of our guest book will be developed to maintain regular contact, no later than the first of the following year.

• The store's two corner windows will be changed weekly or more often, but decorated with only two or three selected items, dramatized with good "selling" signs and lights.

• Fashion show presentations will be explored during the six opening months, through contacts with local city and suburban women's groups, and planned for the following year.

• A system of rewards for bringing a friend or making repeat purchases will be devceloped for 1997 implementation.

• Pre-season trunk showings will be planned for selected customers and with the cooperation of representatives of our better resources. Advance orders will be taken.

Pricing requires special attention.

Pricing Policy

Normally, retailers in the fashion business "keystone" (*i.e.,* double the cost of an item) the first time it is offered to the public. Example: a garment costs 375f ($75 USD). from the manufacturer, plus 7,50f ($1.50 USD). delivery per unit. Thus the total delivered cost is 382,50f ($76 USD). Doubling the cost is 382,50f × 2 = 765f ($153 USD).

The retailer must take a number of expenses or "overhead" into consideration before recognizing a net profit. These expenses might include:

- Post-season markdowns

- Special sales and discounts

- Returns of Merchandise

- Theft

- Commissions or inventives to salespeople

Each store will have different expenses to the above. They can amount to 10 to 30 percent. Any realistic projections must take such potential reductions in profits into consideration.

In this "model store" we have set a policy of no carryover of merchandise from one season to the next. Such a policy allows the store to advertise that all fashion merchandise offered at the beginning of each season is fresh and up-to-date. The additional advantage of such a policy is that working capital will not be tied up in old inventory. It will permit the working capital to have a more favorable "open to buy" quota capital available to buy the new season's merchandise.

Promotion is a key element to a successful business.

Most retail fashion stores must have a net profit of 30 to 40 percent in order to pay for all normal overhead or expenses. Let's translate this all into a typical "retail shop" example:

Cost of merchandise	382,50ƒ ($76.50 USD).
40% overhead expense	153,00ƒ ($31 USD)
Total cost of merchandise	535,50ƒ ($107 USD)
Full price of merchandise	765,00ƒ ($153 USD)
Total cost of goods/expense	535,50ƒ ($107 USD)
Profit at full markup	229,50ƒ ($46 USD)

If the retailer makes a profit of 229,50ƒ ($46 USD) on full sale price of 765,00ƒ ($153 USD), a profit of 30 percent is earned.

However, there are those five other expenses which cannot always be determined in advance, but which must be taken into consideration. If no markdowns are taken, no discounts given, no merchandise stolen and only normal salaries or commissions paid to salespeople, then a 30 percent profit would result. But any one of these items can substantially reduce or even wipe out the profit. You can now see that pricing is a very difficult part of the business plan creation. Knowledgeable buying of merchandise (especially seasonal merchandise), tight management, shrewd promotion and advertising, and luck will effect the ultimate profit and the Cash Flow and Profit Projections.

Promotion Plans: Opening and Continuing

Grand Opening: Saturday, 7 August, 1997 is the projected opening date. Plans for this period are detailed under *Business Mods* in the *Management Section*. Promotional and advertising efforts will consist primarily of publicity releases to all local print and electronic media. The first will go out two weeks in advance of opening; and a different one a week prior to opening. Two opening announcements will be scheduled in the society section of the major daily newspaper on the previous Sunday and following Wednesday. Both windows will have attractive Grand Opening signs, and displays will be ready 3 to 7 days ahead of opening. Invitation-style announcements will be mailed First Class to the presidents of local women's professional and social groups, at least four weeks before opening, to allow time for information to be disseminated and announced. Because of summer time, these are not expected to have optimum effect, and will be supplemented by individual mailings to women executives and social leaders, teachers, businesses managed by women, in addition to editors, radio-TV personalities, *et al.*

Continuing Promotions: Since Grand Openings and holiday promotions usually demand a proportionately larger-than-average budget share, an investment of approximately 5.000*f* ($1000 USD). per month in total promotional costs will be used for these two major periods. 10.000*f* ($2,000 USD) remains to cover activities for the September–December segment (three months).

Our counselor will be of continuing guidance during this period. With the assistance of the Economic Development Bureau, two talented students have been recruited from the University to lend assistance in creating both advertisements and direct mail pieces. A weekly advertisement of current fashion merchandise will be run in the local newspaper, each one spot-lighting a sketch, prepared by the University's art department, under the heading "What's new....at *La Belle Mode*."

Direct mail promotions will continue with the start of a monthly fashion newsletter, which we will publish. The circulation of these newsletters will increase with the growth of our mailing list. Window signs will be changed weekly with the change in fashion displays. We will handle our

Study your competition.

own decorating as long as is feasible, but will have professional help in reserve. Holiday displays will be coordinated with the Crespieres Merchants' Council, affiliated with the Chamber of Commerce. Decorations will cover the front of our store. Two small, elegantly-decorated evergreen trees will be placed in the windows, an urn, and Christmas cookies will be available within the store for five weeks prior to Christmas.

Two invitation only "Men's Nights" will be planned for the first and second Friday evenings of December. Special holiday gift certificates will also be available at that time.

Seasonal promotions during gift-giving seasons and the promotion of executive gift certificates will also attract a select percentage of male customers.

Marketing Strategy

Time Scheduling Chart for 6 months Pre and Post Opening

1. Complete Fixturing

2. Inventorying, Marking

3. Sales Training

4. Displays, Signage

5. Produce Mailers, Ads

6. Mail Promotions

7. Place Ads, Publicity

8. Pre-Opening Reception

9. Grand Opening

10. Place Thank You Ads

11. Fill in Inventory

12. Review Sales, Selling, Personnel, Mailing List

13. Plan Holiday Ads, Promos, Decorations

14. Begin Holiday Promotion

15. Check Inventory, Plan Post-Holiday Sales

Particular emphasis will be placed on three (3) major functions:

1. Good training and observation of full and part-time sales personnel. Most employees at this time will be part-time employees.

2. Continual inventory auditing to assure full selections

3. Diligent collection of visitors' and customers' names and addresses for promotional mailing list.

Step 10 Financial Information

US dollar amounts are shown in parenthesis as a representative example of other denominations only; these would not necessarily appear on an actual business plan.

10.1 Capital Requirements

Proprietor's outside income from
     paid-up pension fund .... 50.000ƒ ($10,000 USD)

Current investment
     300.000ƒ ($60,000 USD) at 4% .... 12.000ƒ ($2,400 USD)

Expected annual salary from store .... 50.000ƒ ($10,000 USD)

Estimated first-year net profit before taxes,
     based upon 1.500.000ƒ ($300,000 USD)
     net sales and 4.0% net profit .... 60.000ƒ ($12,000 USD)

Estimated first-year earnings from operations .. 110.000ƒ ($22,000 USD)

Return on Investment

Total cash investment .... 300.000ƒ ($60,000 USD)

Estimated earnings .... 110.000ƒ ($22,000 USD)

Percentage earned (Return on Investment) ...... 37 percent

Compared to current income of 4% on investments, the income from my planned store operation is more than nine times as high. An additional benefit is that I feel I have closer control over my earnings.

I am in a position to build equity in a business that might some day be worth one-times gross or some other multiple of net income.

The above figures reflect first-year projections and are expected to rise year by year, until relative market saturation is reached and expansion plans would be appropriate.

Lender Equity

I project that a line of credit of 200.000ƒ ($40,000 USD), added to personal investment capital, will provide (1) current working capital after opening expenses, paid out of personal investments; (2) provide a cushion to cover unforeseen expenses; (3) allow for addition of merchandising lines that are either in demand or that will be offered by resources, usually at favorable discounts; (4) permit marketing activities that could lead to more rapid growth.

My details of projected operating statistics are attached.

10.2 Depreciable Assets

Equipment

This section can include:

> Leasehold Improvements
> Fixturing
> Signage
> Vehicles
> Store/Office Equipment

Upon advice of counselors and in order to preserve personal equity for the inventorying of current merchandise at all times, most depreciable assets will be leased rather than purchased.

Leasehold improvements to the premises of the 100 sq. meter store, especially window framing, entrance door, placement of electric outlets, improvements to floors and sanitary facilities, will be incorporated into the lease and amortized by the landlord over the terms of the five-year lease.

Fixtures will be purchased, but is limited to open, illuminated racks, free-standing display stands, one counter and one display case. A movable wall will separate sales floor from the stock room where mobile racks and tables are the only fixtures needed. Some fixtures will be purchased from bankrupt stock and all will be paid from my personal funds.

Signage will consist of two overhead illuminated signs which are being acquired on a lease-purchase-and-maintenance contract, payable in moderate monthly installments.

No vehicle will be purchased during the first month. If an additional vehicle is needed, it will be projected for the second year.

Store/Office Equipment consists of a computer which I presently own and which will be installed in the store for purposes of maintaining inventory and customer records. A cash register that will also maintain inventory control and cash flow will be leased. No other equipment is contemplated to be acquired or leased at this time.

10.3

Item 3: Starting Balance Sheet

Assets and Liabilities of Marie Bonhomme

as of 31 janvier 1997

Assets

Current Assets

Investment no. 1	8.125f	($1,625 USD)
Investment no. 2	31.375f	($6,275 USD)
Investment no. 3	300.000f	($60,000 USD)
Investment no. 4	200.000f	($40,000 USD)
Investment no. 5	107.500f	($21,500 USD)
Total Current Assets	797.000f	($159,400 USD)

Fixed Assets

Condominium	750.000f	($150,000 USD)
Furniture and decorations	80.000f	($16,000 USD)
Auto (*Peugeot* 1993)	50.000f	($10,000 USD)
Total Fixed Assets	850.000f	($170,000 USD)

Total Assets

	1.677.000f	($335,400 USD)

Liabilities

Current Liabilities

Condominium Mortgage	2.200*f*	($440 USD)
Condominium Tax Payment	600*f*	($120 USD)
Condominium Maintenance Fee	425*f*	($85 USD)
Credit cards	300*f*	($60 USD)
Total Current Liabilities	3.525*f*	($705 USD)

Fixed Liabilities

Mortgage Balance	325.000*f*	($65,000 USD)
Total Fixed Liabilities	325.000*f*	($65,000 USD)

Total Liabilities 828.525*f* ($165,705 USD)

Total Net Worth 1.348.475*f* ($270,000 USD)
(*i.e.*, Total Assets less Total Liabilities)

Total Net Worth + Liabilities 1.677.000*f* ($335,400 USD)

Monthly Budget
of Marie Bonhomme
as of (date) 31 janvier 1997

Fixed Monthly Expenses...

Mortgage Condominium	2.200ƒ	($440 USD)
Condominium Fee	425ƒ	($85 USD)
Condominium Taxes	600ƒ	($120 USD)
Health Plan	600ƒ	($120 USD)
Life Insurance	150ƒ	($30 USD)
Condominium Insurance	100ƒ	($20 USD)
Auto Insurance	250ƒ	($50 USD)
Auto Registration	30ƒ	($6 USD)
Estimated Taxes	1.000ƒ	($200 USD)
Total Fixed Monthly Expenses	5.355ƒ	($1,071 USD)

Controllable (*i.e.*, variable) Expenses

Telephone	150ƒ	($30 USD)
Gas & Electricity	225ƒ	($45 USD)
Food	600ƒ	($120 USD)
Credit Card Payments	400ƒ	($80 USD)
Restaurant & Outside Eating	250ƒ	($50 USD)
Auto Gas & Maintenance	210ƒ	($42 USD)
Laundry & Cleaning	100ƒ	($20 USD)

Dentists	125ƒ	($25 USD)
Newspapers & Publications	75ƒ	($15 USD)
Miscellaneous	250ƒ	($50 USD)
Gifts & Contributions	100ƒ	($20 USD)
Total Controllable Expenses	2.485ƒ	($497 USD)
Grand Total Expenses	7.840ƒ	($1,568 USD)

Income...

Pension	5.000ƒ	($1,000 USD)
Bank Account Interest (7.500ƒ @ 3%)	20ƒ	($4 USD)
Investment #1 (31.375ƒ @ 3.25%)	85ƒ	($17 USD)
Investment #2 (300.000ƒ @ 6%)	1.500ƒ	($300 USD)
Investment #3 (200.000ƒ @ 6.5%)	1.085ƒ	($217 USD)
Investment #4 (150.000ƒ @ 7.5%)	980ƒ	($196 USD)
Investment #5 (105.000ƒ @ 8.5%)	760ƒ	($152 USD)
Total Personal Income	9.430ƒ	($1,886 USD)
(less) Expenses	-8.120ƒ	($1,624 USD)
Net Personal Income	1.310ƒ	($262 USD)

10.4

Break-Even Analysis

Financial Management

Attached hereto are financials based on our projections for the fiscal year 1998. Figures are based on our educated estimates, national averages typical for our business, and consultations with both paid and volunteer professionals.

The figures are conservative.

I would like to point out that the Cash Flow Projected Statement shows a positive cash flow. These figures can be accomplished with existing financial resources and agreements with major resources to postpone billing (60-to-90–day dating).

However, the requested loan of 200.000ƒ ($40,000 USD) is necessary as a safeguard to cover unexpected and unforeseen operating expenses, to assure payment of Fall and Winter merchandise, to facilitate the cash purchase of designer fashion merchandise at advantageous prices, and to weather any possible volume decline after the holidays. An upswing in sales is expected traditionally during the Spring-and-Easter period to compensate for winter lulls and post-season markdowns.

The cost of carrying the loan, repayments and interest, will be assured by the traditional Spring–Easter sales increases. Also, it is expected that favorable holiday business will allow a healthy residue of assets to be present. The loan, however, is insurance for a progressive and profitable operation.

Company Name:
La Belle Mode

Break-Even–Point Worksheet
Period From 1 auguste 1997 to 31 juillet 1998

Fixed Expenses

1. Rent (15)*	120.000ƒ	($24,000 USD)
2. Insurance (16)*	25.500ƒ	($5,100 USD)
3. License/Tax	9.000ƒ	($1,800 USD)
4. Loan Payments	37.440ƒ	($7,480 USD)
5. Depreciation (23)*	7.020ƒ	($1,404 USD)
6. Interest Expense		
7. Professional Fees (Acctg/Legal, *etc.*)	13.500ƒ	($2,700 USD)
8. Owner's Salary (4)*	50.000ƒ	($10,000 USD)
9. Other		
10. Total Fixed Expenses	262.460ƒ	($52,492 USD)

Variable Expenses

11. Direct Material		
12. Direct Labor		
13. Overhead or other Costs		
14. Variable Expenses (2)* (cost of sales)	900.000ƒ	($180,000 USD)

Semi-Variable or Semi-Fixed

15. Sales Salaries (5)*	85.500ƒ	($17,100 USD)
16. Payroll Taxes (6)*	17.100ƒ	($3,420 USD)

17. Advertising (7)*   75.000*f*   ($15,000 USD)

18. Store Supplies (8)*   16.250*f*   ($3,250 USD)

19. Auto Expense (9)*   11,500*f*   ($2,300 USD)

20. Traveling (10)*   30.000*f*   ($6,000 USD)

21. Telephone (11)*   7.750*f*   ($1,550 USD)

22. Utilities (12)*   12.150*f*   ($2,430 USD)

23. Miscellaneous (14)*-line 7   19.500*f*   ($3,900 USD)
      (line 13 on income projection statement minus line 7 from page 102)

24. Other

25. Semi-Variable and Semi-Fixed   274.750*f*   ($54,950 USD)

Recapitulation of break-even point worksheet line numbers

26. Fixed Expenses—line 10   262.460*f*   ($52,492 USD)

27. 50% of Semi-Var—line 25   137.375*f*   ($27,475 USD)

28. Total Fixed Expenses   399.835*f*   ($79,967 USD)

29. Variable Expense—line 14   900.000*f*   ($180,000 USD)

30. 50% of Semi-Var—line 25   137.375*f*   ($27,475 USD)

31. Total Variable Expenses   1.037.375f   ($207,475 USD)
        (*i.e.,* line 29 + line 30)

32. Grand Total Expenses   1.437.110ƒ   ($287,422 USD)
            (*i.e.*, line 28 + line 31)

    33. Total profit before taxes (26)   62.790ƒ   ($12,558 USD)

    34. Net Sales (1)   1.500.000ƒ   ($300,000 USD)

    35. Percent of total sales revenue required to break even = 86.4%
            (*i.e.*, line 28 ÷ (line 28 + line 33)

Profit or (Loss) line 33

    36. Sales volume required to break even = 1.296.410ƒ ($259,282 USD)
            (*i.e.*, line 34 × line 35)

    37. Average *monthly* sales required to break even = 108.035ƒ ($21,607)
            (*i.e.*, line 36 ÷ 12 months)

*Note: Above numbers in parentheses (in left column) correspond to line numbers on the Income Statement.

Example in French Francs
LA BELLE MODE
INCOME PROJECTION STATEMENT
PERIOD: FISCAL YEAR August 1, 1997 to July 31, 1998

	Industry Average	La Belle Mode	1 Aug	2 Sep	3 Oct	4 Nov	5 Dec	6 Jan	7 Feb	8 Mar	9 Apr	10 May	11 Jun	12 Jul	TOTAL YEAR
1. Net Sales	100.0%	100.0%	150.000f	160.000f	190.000f	200.000f	150.000f	75.000f	75.000f	80.000f	90.000f	95.000f	110.000f	125.000f	1500.000f
2. Cost of Sales	59.1%	60.0%	90.000	96.000	114.000	120.000	90.000	45.000	45.000	48.000	54.000	57.000	66.000	75.000	900.000
3. GROSS PROFIT (1-2)	40.9%	40.0%	60.000	64.000	76.000	80.000	60.000	30.000	30.000	32.000	36.000	38.000	44.000	50.000	600.000
OPERATING EXPENSES Controllable Variable Expense															
4. Owner's Drawing	5%	3.3%	0f	0f	0f	5.555f	5.560f	5.555f	5.555f	5.555f	5.555f	5.555f	5.555f	5.555f	50.000f
5. Sales Salaries	8.9%	5.7%	9.000	9.000	9.000	9.000	7.500	6.000	6.000	6.000	6.000	6.000	6.000	6.000	85.500
6. Payroll Taxes	1.9%	1.1%	1.800	1.800	1.800	1.800	1.500	1.200	1.200	1.200	1.200	1.200	1.200	1.200	17.100
7. Advertising	2.2%	5.0%	10.000	6.000	6.000	6.000	5.000	6.000	6.000	6.000	6.000	6.000	6.000	6.000	75.000
8. Store Supplies	2.1%	1.1%	2.500	1.250	1.250	1.250	1.250	1.250	1.250	1.250	1.250	1.250	1.250	1.250	16.250
9. Auto Expense	0.8%	0.8%	1.500	1.000	1.000	1.000	750	750	750	750	1.000	1.000	1.000	1.000	11.500
10. Traveling	0.7%	2.0%	6.000	3.000	3.000	3.000	0	3.000	0	3.000	0	3.000	3.000	3.000	30.000
11. Telephone	0.5%	0.5%	1.000	750	750	750	750	750	500	500	500	500	500	500	7.750
12. Utilities	1.3%	0.8%	950	1.000	1.000	1.125	1.125	1.125	1.125	1.000	900	900	900	1.000	12.150
13. Miscellaneous	2%	2.2%	6.000	3.200	3.800	4.400	3.000	1.500	1.500	1.600	1.800	1.900	2.200	2.500	33.000
14. TOTAL VARIABLE EXPENSES (Sum of 4 to 13)	25.4%	22.6%	38.750	27.000	27.600	33.880	26.435	27.130	23.880	26.855	24.205	27.305	27.605	28.805	338.250
FIXED EXPENSES (OVERHEAD)															
15. Rent	8.9%	8.0%	10.000	10.000	10.000	10.000	10.000	10.000	10.000	10.000	10.000	10.000	10.000	10.000	120.000
16. Insurance	1.4%	1.7%	2.125	2.125	2.125	2.125	2.125	2.125	2.125	2.125	2.125	2.125	2.125	2.125	25.500
17. Taxes	0.6%	0.6%	900	960	1.140	1.200	900	450	450	480	540	570	660	750	9.000
18. TOTAL FIXED EXPENSES (Sum of 15 to 17)	10.9%	10.3%	13.025	13.085	13.265	13.325	13.025	12.575	12.575	12.605	12.665	12.695	12.785	12.875	154.500
19. TOTAL EXPENSES (14 + 18)	36.3%	32.9%	51.775	40.085	40.865	47.205	39.460	39.705	36.455	39.460	36.870	40.000	40.390	40.880	492.750
20. NET OPERATING PROFIT (3 - 19)	4.6%	7.2%	8.225	23.915	35.135	32.795	20.540	(9.705)	(6.455)	(7.460)	(870)	(2.000)	3.610	9.120	107.250
Other Income															
21. INTEREST INCOME	1.1%	0.0%													
Other Expenses															
22. Loan Payment		-2.5%	3.120	3.120	3.120	3.120	3.120	3.120	3.120	3.120	3.120	3.120	3.120	3.120	37.440
23. Depreciation	1%	0.5%	585	585	585	585	585	585	585	585	585	585	585	585	7.020
24. Interest Expense	0.5%														
25. TOTAL OTHER (21 - <22 to 24)	-0.4%	-3.0%	3.705	3.705	3.705	3.705	3.705	3.705	3.705	3.705	3.705	3.705	3.705	3.705	44.460
26. TOTAL PROFIT BEFORE TAXES (20- or +25)	4.2%	4.2%	4.520f	20.210f	31.430f	29.090f	16.835f	(13.410f)	(10.160f)	(11.165f)	(4.575f)	(5.705f)	(95f)	5.415f	62.390f
27. INCOME TAXES															
28. NET PROFIT OR (LOSS) AFTER INCOME TAXES (26-27)															

Example in French Francs
LA BELLE MODE
MONTHLY CASH FLOW PROJECTION

	Start-up Position	1997 1 Aug	2 Sep	3 Oct	4 Nov	5 Dec	1998 6 Jan	7 Feb	8 Mar	9 Apr	10 May	11 Jun	12 Jul	TOTAL Col. 1-12
1. CASH ON HAND	300.000f	317.875f	300.600f	333.475f	378.985f	410.985f	391.705f	332.330f	317.455f	308.440f	305.970f	299.635f	305.955f	317.875f
2. CASH RECEIPTS														
a. Cash Sales	0	60.000	64.000	76.000	80.000	60.000	30.000	30.000	32.000	36.000	38.000	44.000	50.000	600.000
b. Credit Card Collections	0	90.000	96.000	114.000	120.000	90.000	45.000	45.000	48.000	54.000	57.000	66.000	75.000	900.000
c. Loan or Other Cash In	200.000	0	15.000	0	0	0	0	0	0	0	0	0	0	15.000
3. TOTAL CASH RECEIPTS (2a+2b+2c=3)	200.000	150.000	175.000	190.000	200.000	150.000	75.000	75.000	80.000	90.000	95.000	110.000	125.000	1.515.000
4. TOTAL CASH AVAILABLE (1+3=4)	500.000	467.875	475.600	523.475	518.985	560.985	466.705	407.330	397.455	398.440	400.970	409.635	430.955	1.832.875
5. CASH PAID OUT														
a. Purchases (Merchandise)	55.000	145.000	90.000	96.000	114.000	120.000	90.000	45.000	45.000	48.000	54.000	57.000	66.000	970.000
b. Gross Wages (Excludes Withdrawals)	1.250	9.000	9.000	9.000	9.000	7.500	6.000	6.000	6.000	6.000	6.000	6.000	6.000	85.500
c. Payroll Expenses (Taxes)	250	1.800	1.800	1.800	1.800	1.500	1.200	1.200	1.200	1.200	1.200	1.200	1.200	17.100
d. Outside Services (Card %)	0	0	2.880	3.420	3.600	2.700	1.350	1.350	1.440	1.620	1.710	1.980	2.180	24.230
e. Supplies (Office & Store)	0	2.500	1.250	1.250	1.250	1.250	1.250	1.250	1.250	1.250	1.250	1.250	1.250	16.250
f. Repairs & Maintenance	0	0	0	625	0	500	0	750	0	0	1.125	0	0	3.000
g. Advertising	7.500	2.500	8.000	6.000	6.000	5.500	5.500	6.000	6.000	6.000	6.000	6.000	6.000	69.500
h. Auto Expense	1.500	1.500	1.000	1.000	1.000	750	750	750	750	1.000	1.000	1.000	1.000	11.500
i. Accounting & Legal	1.750	0	1.000	1.000	1.000	1.000	1.000	1.000	1.000	1.000	1.000	1.000	1.000	11.000
j. Rent	10.000	10.000	10.000	10.000	10.000	10.000	10.000	10.000	10.000	10.000	10.000	10.000	10.000	110.000
k. Telephone	0	1.000	1.000	750	750	750	750	750	500	500	500	500	500	8.250
l. Utilities	0	950	950	1.000	1.000	1.125	1.125	1.125	1.125	1.000	1.000	1.000	1.000	12.400
m. Insurance	0	2.125	2.125	2.125	2.125	2.125	2.125	2.125	2.125	2.125	2.125	2.125	2.125	25.500
n. Real Estate, etc.	0	900	900	900	900	900	900	900	900	900	900	900	900	10.800
o. Interest	0	0	0	0	0	0	0	0	0	0	0	0	0	0
p. Travel	10.000	0	4.500	3.000	3.000	1.500	1.500	6.500	1.500	1.500	3.000	3.000	3.000	27.000
q. Miscellaneous—Opening	13.875	0	4.600	3.500	3.900	3.500	2.250	1.500	1.550	1.700	1.850	2.050	2.250	28.650
r. Subtotal (5a thru 5q)	101.125	167.275	139.005	141.370	159.325	160.600	125.700	81.200	80.340	83.795	92.660	95.005	104.405	1.430.680
s. Loan Principal Payments	0	3.120	3.120	3.120	3.120	3.120	3.120	3.120	3.120	3.120	3.120	3.120	3.120	34.320
t. Capital Purchases (Name)	40.000	0	0	0	0	0	0	0	0	0	0	0	0	0
u. Other Start-Up Costs	30.000	0	0	0	0	0	0	0	0	0	0	0	0	0
v. Reserve or Escrow (Name)	11.000	0	0	0	0	0	0	0	0	0	0	0	0	0
w. Owner's Withdrawal	0	0	0	0	5.555	5.560	5.555	5.555	5.555	5.555	5.555	5.555	5.555	50.000
6. TOTAL CASH PAID OUT (5a thru 5w)	182.125	167.275	142.125	144.490	168.000	169.280	134.375	89.875	89.015	92.470	101.335	103.680	113.080	1.515.000
7. CASH POSITION (End of month) (4 minus 6)	317.875f	300.600f	333.475f	378.985f	410.985f	391.705f	332.330f	317.455f	308.440f	305.970f	299.635f	305.955f	317.875f	

Example in French Francs
LA BELLE MODE
ANNUAL CASH FLOW PROJECTION
Period: FISCAL YEARS 1998 thru 2000

	Year 1 FY 1998	Year 2 FY 1999	Year 3 FY 2000
1. CASH ON HAND	317.875f	317.875f	373.935f
2. CASH RECEIPTS			
a. Cash Sales	600.000	700.000	800.000
b. Credit Card Collections	900.000	1.050.000	1.200.000
c. Loan or Other Cash In	15.000	0	0
3. TOTAL CASH RECEIPTS (2a+2b+2c=3)	1.515.000	1.750.000	2.000.000
4. TOTAL CASH AVAILABLE (1+3=4)	1.832.875	2.067.875	2.373.935
5. CASH PAID OUT			
a. Purchases (Merchandise)	970.000	1.050.000	1.200.000
b. Gross Wages (Excludes Withdrawals)	85.500	95.000	110.000
c. Payroll Expenses (Taxes)	17.100	19.000	22.000
d. Outside Services (Card %)	24.230	31.500	36.000
e. Supplies (Office & Store)	16.250	16.750	17.500
f. Repairs & Maintenance	3.000	4.000	5.000
g. Advertising	69.500	80.000	90.000
h. Auto Expense	11.500	12.500	13.500
i. Accounting & Legal	11.000	12.500	15.000
j. Rent	110.000	120.000	120.000
k. Telephone	8.250	8.250	8.500
l. Utilities	12.400	13.000	13.500
m. Insurance	25.500	25.500	26.500
n. Real Estate, etc.	10.800	9.000	10.000
o. Interest	0	0	0
p. Travel	27.000	37.500	40.000
q. Miscellaneous—Opening	28.650	220.000	20.000
r. Subtotal (5a thru 5q)	1.430.680	1.556.500	1.747.500
s. Loan Principal Payments	34.320	37.440	37.440
t. Capital Purchases (Name)	0	0	5.000
u. Other Start-Up Costs	0	0	0
v. Reserve or Escrow (Name)	0	0	0
w. Owner's Withdrawal	50.000	100.000	150.000
6. TOTAL CASH PAID OUT (5a thru 5w)	1.515.000	1.693.940	1.939.940
7. CASH POSITION (End of month) (4 minus 6)	317.875f	373.935f	433.995f

Example in French Francs
LA BELLE MODE
INCOME PROJECTION STATEMENT

PERIOD: FISCAL YEARS August 1, 1998 to July 31, 2000

	Industry Average	Fiscal Year 1998		Fiscal Year 1999		Fiscal Year 2000	
1. Net Sales	100.0%	1.500.000f	100.0%	1.750.000f	100%	2.000.000f	100.0%
2. Cost of Sales	59.1%	900.000	60.0%	1.050.000	60.0%	1.200.000	60.0%
3. GROSS PROFIT (1-2)	40.9%	600.000	40.0%	700.000	40.0%	800.000	40.0%
OPERATING EXPENSES							
Controllable Variable Expense							
4. Owner's Drawing	5.0%	50.000	3.3%	100.000	5.7%	150.000	7.5%
5. Sales Salaries	8.9%	85.500	5.7%	95.000	5.4%	110.000	5.5%
6. Payroll Taxes	1.9%	17.100	1.1%	19.000	1.1%	22.000	1.1%
7. Advertising	2.2%	75.000	5.0%	80.000	4.6%	90.000	4.5%
8. Store Supplies	2.1%	16.250	1.1%	16.750	1.0%	17.500	0.9%
9. Auto Expense	0.8%	11.500	0.8%	12.500	0.7%	13.500	0.7%
10. Traveling	0.7%	30.000	2.0%	37.500	2.1%	40.000	2.0%
11. Telephone	0.5%	7.750	0.5%	8.250	0.5%	8.500	0.4%
12. Utilities	1.3%	12.150	0.8%	13.000	0.7%	13.500	0.7%
13. Miscellaneous	2.0%	33.000	0.8%	38.500	2.2%	40.000	2.0%
14. TOTAL VARIABLE EXPENSES (Sum of 4 to 13)	25.4%	338.250	22.6%	420.500	24.0%	505.000	25.3%
FIXED EXPENSES (OVERHEAD)							
15. Rent	8.9%	120.000	8.0%	120.000	6.9%	120.000	6.0%
16. Insurance	1.4%	25.500	1.7%	25.500	1.5%	26.500	1.3%
17. Taxes	0.6%	9.000	0.6%	9.000	0.5%	10.000	0.5%
18. TOTAL FIXED EXPENSES (Sum of 15 to 17)	10.9%	154.500	10.3%	154.500	8.8%	156.500	7.8%
19. TOTAL EXPENSES (14 + 18)	36.3%	492.750	32.9%	575.000	32.9%	661.500	33.1%
20. NET OPERATING PROFIT (3 - 19)	4.6%	107.250	7.2%	125.000	7.1%	138.500	6.9%
Other Income							
21. INTEREST INCOME	1.1%		0.0%		0.0%		0.0%
Other Expenses							
22. Loan Payment		37.440	-2.5%	37.440	-2.1%	37.440	-1.9%
23. Depreciation	1.0%	7.020	-0.5%	7.020	-0.4%	8.020	-0.4%
24. Interest Income	0.5%						
25. TOTAL OTHER [21 - (22 to 24)]	-0.4%	44.460	-3.0%	44.460	-2.5%	45.460	-2.3%
26. TOTAL PROFIT BEFORE TAXES (20- or +25)	4.2%	62.790f	4.2%	80.540f	4.6%	93.040f	4.7%
27. INCOME TAXES							
28. NET PROFIT OR (LOSS) AFTER INCOME TAXES (26-27)							

Example in U.S. Dollars
LA BELLE MODE
INCOME PROJECTION STATEMENT
PERIOD: FISCAL YEAR August 1, 1997 to July 31, 1998

#	Item	Industry Average	La Belle Mode	1 Aug	2 Sep	3 Oct	4 Nov	5 Dec	6 Jan	7 Feb	8 Mar	9 Apr	10 May	11 Jun	12 Jul	TOTAL YEAR
1.	Net Sales	100.0%	100.0%	$30,000	$32,000	$38,000	$40,000	$30,000	$15,000	$15,000	$16,000	$18,000	$19,000	$22,000	$25,000	$300,000
2.	Cost of Sales	59.1%	60.0%	18,000	19,200	22,800	24,000	18,000	9,000	9,000	9,600	10,800	11,400	13,200	15,000	180,000
3.	GROSS PROFIT (1-2)	40.9%	40.0%	$12,000	$12,800	$15,200	$16,000	$12,000	$6,000	$6,000	$6,400	$7,200	$7,600	$8,800	$10,000	$120,000
	OPERATING EXPENSES Controllable Variable Expense															
4.	Owner's Drawing	5%	3.3%	$0	$0	$0	$1,111	$1,112	$1,111	$1,111	$1,111	$1,111	$1,111	$1,111	$1,111	$10,000
5.	Sales Salaries	8.9%	5.7%	1,800	1,800	1,800	1,800	1,500	1,200	1,200	1,200	1,200	1,200	1,200	1,200	17,100
6.	Payroll Taxes	1.9%	1.1%	360	360	360	360	300	240	240	240	240	240	240	240	3,420
7.	Advertising	2.2%	5.0%	2,000	1,200	1,200	1,200	1,000	1,200	1,200	1,200	1,200	1,200	1,200	1,200	15,000
8.	Store Supplies	2.1%	1.1%	500	250	250	250	250	250	250	250	250	250	250	250	3,250
9.	Auto Expense	0.8%	0.8%	300	200	200	200	150	150	150	150	200	200	200	200	2,300
10.	Traveling	0.7%	2.0%	1,200	600	600	600	0	600	0	600	0	600	600	600	6,000
11.	Telephone	0.5%	0.5%	200	150	150	150	150	150	100	100	100	100	100	100	1,550
12.	Utilities	1.3%	0.8%	190	200	200	225	225	225	225	200	180	180	180	200	2,430
13.	Miscellaneous	2%	2.2%	1,200	640	760	880	600	300	300	320	360	380	440	500	6,600
14.	TOTAL VARIABLE EXPENSES (Sum of 4 to 13)	25.4%	22.6%	$7,750	$5,400	$5,520	$6,776	$5,287	$5,426	$4,776	$5,371	$4,841	$5,461	$5,521	$5,601	$67,650
	FIXED EXPENSES (OVERHEAD)															
15.	Rent	8.9%	8.0%	$2,000	$2,000	$2,000	$2,000	$2,000	$2,000	$2,000	$2,000	$2,000	$2,000	$2,000	$2,000	$24,000
16.	Insurance	1.4%	1.7%	425	425	425	425	425	425	425	425	425	425	425	425	5,100
17.	Taxes	0.6%	0.6%	180	192	228	240	180	90	90	96	108	114	132	150	1,800
18.	TOTAL FIXED EXPENSES (Sum of 15 to 17)	10.9%	10.3%	$2,605	$2,617	$2,653	$2,665	$2,605	$2,515	$2,515	$2,521	$2,533	$2,539	$2,557	$2,575	$30,900
19.	TOTAL EXPENSES (14 + 18)	36.3%	32.9%	$10,355	$8,017	$8,173	$9,441	$7,892	$7,941	$7,291	$7,892	$7,374	$8,000	$8,078	$8,176	$98,550
20.	NET OPERATING PROFIT (3 - 19)	4.6%	7.2%	$1,645	$4,783	$7,027	$6,559	$4,108	($1,941)	($1,291)	($1,492)	($174)	($400)	$722	$1,824	$21,450
	Other Income															
21.	INTEREST INCOME	1.1%	0.0%													
	Other Expenses															
22.	Loan Payment		-2.5%	$624	$624	$624	$624	$624	$624	$624	$624	$624	$624	$624	$624	$7,488
23.	Depreciation	1%	0.5%	$117	$117	$117	$117	$117	$117	$117	$117	$117	$117	$117	$117	$1,404
24.	Interest Expense	0.5%														
25.	TOTAL OTHER (21 - <22 to 24)	-0.4%	-3.0%	$741	$741	$741	$741	$741	$741	$741	$741	$741	$741	$741	$741	$8,892
26.	TOTAL PROFIT BEFORE TAXES (20- or +25)	4.2%	4.2%	$904	$4,042	$6,286	$5,818	$3,367	($2,682)	($2,032)	($2,233)	($915)	($1,141)	($19)	$1,083	$12,478
27.	INCOME TAXES															
28.	NET PROFIT OR (LOSS) AFTER INCOME TAXES (26-27)															

Example in U.S. Dollars
LA BELLE MODE
MONTHLY CASH FLOW PROJECTION

	Start-up Position	1997 1 Aug	2 Sep	3 Oct	4 Nov	5 Dec	1998 6 Jan	7 Feb	8 Mar	9 Apr	10 May	11 Jun	12 Jul	TOTAL Col. 1-12
1. CASH ON HAND	$60,000	$63,575	$60,120	$66,695	$75,797	$82,197	$78,341	$66,466	$63,491	$61,688	$61,194	$59,927	$61,191	$63,575
2. CASH RECEIPTS														
a. Cash Sales		12,000	12,800	15,200	16,000	12,000	6,000	6,000	6,400	7,200	7,600	8,800	10,000	120,000
b. Credit Card Collections		18,000	19,200	22,800	24,000	18,000	9,000	9,000	9,600	10,800	11,400	13,200	15,000	180,000
c. Loan or Other Cash In	40,000		3,000											3,000
3. TOTAL CASH RECEIPTS (2a+2b+2c-3)	$40,000	$30,000	$35,000	$38,000	$40,000	$30,000	$15,000	$15,000	$16,000	$18,000	$19,000	$22,000	$25,000	$303,000
4. TOTAL CASH AVAILABLE (1+3=4)	$100,000	$93,575	$95,120	$104,695	$115,797	$112,197	$93,341	$81,466	$79,491	$79,688	$80,194	$81,927	$86,191	$366,575
5. CASH PAID OUT														
a. Purchases (Merchandise)	$11,000	$29,000	$18,000	$19,200	$22,800	$24,000	$18,000	$9,000	$9,000	$9,600	$10,800	$11,400	$13,200	$194,000
b. Gross Wages (Excludes Withdrawals)	250	1,800	1,800	1,800	1,800	1,500	1,200	1,200	1,200	1,200	1,200	1,200	1,200	17,100
c. Payroll Expenses (Taxes)	50	360	360	360	360	300	240	240	240	240	240	240	240	3,420
d. Outside Services (Card %)			576	684	720	540	270	270	288	324	342	396	436	4,846
e. Supplies (Office & Store)	500		250	250	250	250	250	250	250	250	250	250	250	3,250
f. Repairs & Maintenance				125		100		150			225			600
g. Advertising	1,500	500	1,600	1,200	1,200	1,100	1,100	1,200	1,200	1,200	1,200	1,200	1,200	13,900
h. Auto Expense	300	300	200	200	200	150	150	150	150	200	200	200	200	2,300
i. Accounting & Legal	350		200	200	200	200	200	200	200	200	200	200	200	2,200
j. Rent	2,000		2,000	2,000	2,000	2,000	2,000	2,000	2,000	2,000	2,000	2,000	2,000	22,000
k. Telephone		200	200	150	150	150	150	150	100	100	100	100	100	1,650
l. Utilities		190	190	200	200	225	225	225	225	200	200	200	200	2,480
m. Insurance		425	425	425	425	425	425	425	425	425	425	425	425	5,100
n. Real Estate, etc.		180	180	180	180	180	180	180	180	180	180	180	180	2,160
o. Interest														
p. Travel	2,000		900	600	600	300	300	300	300	300	600	600	600	5,400
q. Miscellaneous—Opening	2,775		920	700	780	700	450	300	310	340	370	410	450	5,730
r. Subtotal (5a thru 5q)	$20,225	$33,455	$27,801	$28,274	$31,865	$32,120	$25,140	$16,240	$16,068	$16,759	$18,532	$19,001	$20,881	$286,136
s. Loan Principal Payments			$624	$624	$624	$624	$624	$624	$624	$624	$624	$624	$624	$6,864
t. Capital Purchases (Name)	8,000													
u. Other Start-Up Costs	6,000													
v. Reserve or Escrow (Name)	2,200													
w. Owner's Withdrawal			1111	1111	1111	1112	1111	1111	1111	1111	1111	1111	1111	10,000
6. TOTAL CASH PAID OUT (5a thru 5w)	$36,425	$33,455	$28,425	$28,898	$33,600	$33,856	$26,875	$17,975	$17,803	$18,494	$20,267	$20,736	$22,616	$303,000
7. CASH POSITION (End of month) (4 minus 6)	$63,575	$60,120	$66,695	$75,797	$82,197	$78,341	$66,466	$63,491	$61,688	$61,194	$59,927	$61,191	$63,575	

Example in U.S. Dollars
LA BELLE MODE
ANNUAL CASH FLOW PROJECTION
Period: FISCAL YEARS 1998 thru 2000

	Year 1 FY 1998	Year 2 FY 1999	Year 3 FY 2000
1. CASH ON HAND	$63,575	$63,575	$74,787
2. CASH RECEIPTS			
a. Cash Sales	120,000	140,000	160,000
b. Credit Card Collections	180,000	210,000	240,000
c. Loan or Other Cash In	3,000	0	0
3. TOTAL CASH RECEIPTS (2a+2b+2c=3)	303,000	350,000	400,000
4. TOTAL CASH AVAILABLE (1+3=4)	366,575	413,575	474,787
5. CASH PAID OUT			
a. Purchases (Merchandise)	194,000	210,000	240,000
b. Gross Wages (Excludes Withdrawals)	17,100	19,000	22,000
c. Payroll Expenses (Taxes)	3,420	3,800	4,400
d. Outside Services (Card %)	4,846	6,300	7,200
e. Supplies (Office & Store)	3,250	3,350	3,500
f. Repairs & Maintenance	600	800	1,000
g. Advertising	13,900	16,000	18,000
h. Auto Expense	2,300	2,500	2,700
i. Accounting & Legal	2,200	2,500	3,000
j. Rent	22,000	24,000	24,000
k. Telephone	1,650	1,650	1,700
l. Utilities	2,480	2,600	2,700
m. Insurance	5,100	5,100	5,300
n. Real Estate, etc.	2,160	1,800	2,000
o. Interest	0	0	0
p. Travel	5,400	7,500	8,000
q. Miscellaneous—Opening	5,730	4,400	4,000
r. Subtotal (5a thru 5q)	286,136	311,300	349,500
s. Loan Principal Payments	6,864	7,488	7,488
t. Capital Purchases (Name)	0	0	1,000
u. Other Start-Up Costs	0	0	0
v. Reserve or Escrow (Name)	0	0	0
w. Owner's Withdrawal	10,000	20,000	30,000
6. TOTAL CASH PAID OUT (5a thru 5w)	303,000	338,788	387,988
7. CASH POSITION (End of month) (4 minus 6)	$63,575	$74,787	$86,799

Example in U.S. Dollars
LA BELLE MODE
INCOME PROJECTION STATEMENT

PERIOD: FISCAL YEARS August 1, 1998 to July 31, 2000

	Industry Average	Fiscal Year 1998		Fiscal Year 1999		Fiscal Year 2000	
1. Net Sales	100.0%	$300,000	100.0%	$350,000	100%	$400,000	100.0%
2. Cost of Sales	59.1%	180,000	60.0%	210,000	60.0%	240,000	60.0%
3. GROSS PROFIT (1-2)	40.9%	120,000	40.0%	140,000	40.0%	160,000	40.0%
OPERATING EXPENSES							
Controllable Variable Expense							
4. Owner's Drawing	5.0%	10,000	3.3%	20,000	5.7%	30,000	7.5%
5. Sales Salaries	8.9%	17,100	5.7%	19,000	5.4%	22,000	5.5%
6. Payroll Taxes	1.9%	3,420	1.1%	3,800	1.1%	4,400	1.1%
7. Advertising	2.2%	15,000	5.0%	16,000	4.6%	18,000	4.5%
8. Store Supplies	2.1%	3,250	1.1%	3,350	1.0%	3,500	0.9%
9. Auto Expense	0.8%	2,300	0.8%	2,500	0.7%	2,700	0.7%
10. Traveling	0.7%	6,000	2.0%	7,500	2.1%	8,000	2.0%
11. Telephone	0.5%	1,550	0.5%	1,650	0.5%	1,700	0.4%
12. Utilities	1.3%	2,430	0.8%	2,600	0.7%	2,700	0.7%
13. Miscellaneous	2.0%	6,600	0.8%	7,700	2.2%	8,000	2.0%
14. TOTAL VARIABLE EXPENSES (Sum of 4 to 13)	25.4%	67,650	22.6%	84,100	24.0%	101,000	25.3%
FIXED EXPENSES (OVERHEAD)							
15. Rent	8.9%	24,000	8.0%	24,000	6.9%	24,000	6.0%
16. Insurance	1.4%	5,100	1.7%	5,100	1.5%	5,300	1.3%
17. Taxes	0.6%	1,800	0.6%	1,800	0.5%	2,000	0.5%
18. TOTAL FIXED EXPENSES (Sum of 15 to 17)	10.9%	30,900	10.3%	30,900	8.8%	31,300	7.8%
19. TOTAL EXPENSES (14 + 18)	36.3%	98,550	32.9%	115,000	32.9%	132,300	33.1%
20. NET OPERATING PROFIT (3 - 19)	4.6%	21,450	7.2%	25,000	7.1%	27,700	6.9%
Other Income							
21. INTEREST INCOME	1.1%		0.0%		0.0%		0.0%
Other Expenses							
22. Loan Payment		7,488	-2.5%	7,488	-2.1%	7,488	-1.9%
23. Depreciation	1.0%	1,404	-0.5%	1,404	-0.4%	1,604	-0.4%
24. Interest Income	0.5%						
25. TOTAL OTHER [21 - (22 to 24)]	-0.4%	8,892	-3.0%	8,892	-2.5%	9,092	-2.3%
26. TOTAL PROFIT BEFORE TAXES (20- or +25)	4.2%	12,558	4.2%	16,108	4.6%	18,608	4.7%
27. INCOME TAXES							
28. NET PROFIT OR (LOSS) AFTER INCOME TAXES (26-27)		$12,558		$16,108		$18,608	

Step 11: Record Keeping

My existing personal computer will be used to utilize an accrual book-keeping system. My experience in computer operation will enable me to perform all day-by-day bookkeeping tasks on a weekly basis. An accountant will prepare quarterly and annual taxes. A cash register, which I am able to acquire at a reasonable price, will maintain perpetual inventory, allow at least eight (8) group entries, separate sales tax, cash sales, and credit card sales. I expect that a large percentage of sales will be made by personal credit cards. While this method adds a few percentage points to the cost of doing business, it will enable me to recoup cash more quickly, eliminate the need for credit sales (except layaways), and avoid collection costs and potential losses.

Credit card sales: Prior to opening I will work with the bank to set up Credit Card Merchant Account arrangement, as a mutually-beneficial and profitable element of our business.

I will keep meticulous records of all sales, noting customers' names, addresses, phone numbers, and other vital particulars. Such records will enable us to make follow-up contacts and develop a valuable mailing list, as well as personalize our relations with each customer.

Step 12: Executive Summary

The planned retail store described in this business plan fulfills a need in this market. This need, the lines of fashion merchandise offered, and the personal service rendered, is not currently available in this market area.

Thorough personal research and assistance by prominent and reliable counselors confirms our premise that this business will be successful, and that any working capital obtained from outside sources can be repaid promptly and profitable.

The location for the proposed business is a premium location; lease terms are reasonable; and leashold improvements are minimal.

Management of the business is seasoned during more than 20 years of direct experience in this field. Advisors in supporting services have been consulted and will be available in the continuing operation of the business.

Our market strategy has been carefully planned, taking into consideration our realistic market area, our competition, and our capital availability.

All financial projections have been verified by professional and independent counsel, all identified herein. Based on thorough market research and in-depth experience, we have made conservative projections that could well exceed our figures.

Chapter IV

Secrets of Financing

- **How to Get a Loan**

- **What to Do if You are Turned Down**

Using Your Business Plan to Get a Loan

The most brilliant and professional business plan remains a bunch of printed papers unless you understand the nature of the person who is going to look it over and make a judgment, and decide or recommend that a loan is extended to you. The psychology of getting a loan, if this is the principal purpose of your business plan, is virtually as important as its physical proposal.

Let us take a look at that loan officer and examine what he or she will be looking for.

Bear in mind that *The Lender* is a fellow human being whose business it is to lend money at a specific interest rate, and to assure that he or his company is repaid with interest. His livelihood depends on the successful conclusion of your loan application. The only brake he has on okaying the loan is the possibility that his institution's loan might not be repaid. With thousands of bank and savings & loan bankruptcies occurring yearly loan officers are especially cautious. It puts additional strain on your business plan's credibility. Conversely, it emphasizes the importance of your plan's expertness, realism, and credibility.

> *The loan officer's livelihood depends upon the successful conclusion of your loan application.*

Once you have completed your business plan and checked it for accuracy in spelling and figures, you need to sit back and think of yourself once more. Let's critique your request.

Question number one: Is the amount of your loan request (or credit line) sufficient to accommodate all possible reverses, unexpected slowdowns or expansions? Or is it too much? Perhaps you do not need as much as you are asking. Remember that you must earn the money you will need to pay back the loan—plus interest.

Question number two: while you are thoroughly steeped in your business, does your business plan reflect this conviction and enthusiasm? The lender on the other side of the desk does not share your knowledge about your enterprise, nor your conviction that it will succeed, nor your belief that your business is unique and everyone will beat a path to your door. The lender (1) wants to know every minute detail about your business until he knows almost as much about it as you do, (2) needs to catch your excitement until he, too, believes in its unequivocal success, and (3) has seen all kinds of other business plans and might not share your viewpoint of its exclusivity.

Consider all of these probabilities and then proceed to the "psychology" of making your business plan presentation.

The management of your new business or expanding business is of primary importance to the success of the enterprise as well as your loan application. We have offered pointers on this topic elsewhere in this book, but we cannot reiterate this importance too often: you are the creator; you are the reason for the business's being and continuance; you are the bearer of the business plan and loan application; and you are the one who is charged with the payback of the loan. So here is a quick 10-point check list again to use as a last-minute review before you enter the bank or financial institution with your business plan in hand:

1. **Your Appearance:** The way you look during your interview is the way you are likely to be judged. The lending officer is very likely to be conservatively dressed. He will feel more comfortable with someone of peer appearance. Remember that first appearances are important.

> **You must earn enough to pay back your loan—plus interest.**

2. Documents: Check and double-check to make sure all needed documents are available quickly and easily. It will show your thoroughness, your organizing ability, and eliminate any nervousness on your part.

3. The Interview: For most of us, being interviewed by a bank or financial officer is not an everyday experience. It can be a strain. Be confident, and you will be if you have prepared yourself thoroughly. Remember that you are the customer. The banker needs you, too.

4. Questions and Answers: Hopefully all of the bank officer's questions will be answered by your business plan. If verbal answers are necessary, give the answers with confidence and candidness. If you do not have a rational answer or are unsure, it will be better to say so and request that you can send or bring the answer back shortly.

5. Leading the Interview: Do not be afraid to ask questions of your own, or to fill in any gaps in the presentation. Let your own comments reflect your own enthusiasm and knowledge, without being overbearing or pompous. After all, the banker should know that you are an entrepreneur and not a messenger boy.

6. Ask for the Loan: Just like a sales situation should always end in a request for the order or signature, the purpose of making the presentation is to get a loan or line of credit. End your presentation with *"Do you feel that your bank can make the xxx.xxx loan to my business?"*

7. The Negative: Bankers, particularly during these times, are just as likely to say 'no' as 'yes.' The banker might not be comfortable or able to tell you the reason for a refusal. But if you ask a direct question in a friendly way, ask him if there was a specific section in your business plan that led to the refusal. If you cannot correct the problem with this lender, then at least you can make a correction when seeing another financial institution.

8. The Positive: Should you be lucky the first time around and get a 'yes' from the banker, it will be your turn to assure that this loan is indeed in your best interest. Consider the amount of the loan, the interest

> *Reflect your own enthusiasm and knowledge without being overbearing or pompous.*

rate, the payback period, any restrictions, the requested collateral or any other detail in the small print. Request that you take the loan agreement with you for 24 hours in order to study it or go over it with your accountant or attorney. Then if it meets with your needs sign it and return it.

9. **Friends and Family:** Many loans are made with people close to you. This does not eliminate or reduce the responsibility that you are assuming, nor the payback. Make sure everything is in writing and is understood by both parties. It is not just the businesslike and legal way to do it, but the ethical way. Losing a friend or the support of family could be worse than not getting the money.

10. **Persistency:** In the final analysis, a certain doggedness must be part of the loan process. Like a salesman, you need to be persistent in your efforts. The better your business plan, the more likely your success. But in case a lender, friend or family member turns you down, don't be downcast. Know and understand why you are turned down by putting yourself in the other person's shoes and try another one.

> ## Nothing can defeat persistence.

> Getting a loan is a form of combat. In combat you must 1) have the proper ammunition; 2) aim at the correct target, and 3) have a cause you believe in fervidly.
>
> In this analogy, 1) your ammunition is the data you gather for your business plan; 2) the correct target is your own objectives you condense into your business plan, which should simultaneously take into account the objectives and psychology of your lender, and 3) you must believe in your cause just as fervidly.

Everything You've Always Wanted to Know About Your Bank But Were Afraid to Ask

Getting a loan or a line of credit is fully 50 percent of the reason for the business plan. The financial section of the business plan is, of course, for your own guidance, but it is absolutely mandatory if your own cash reserves are inadequate to launch, operate and expand your business.

Elsewhere we have offered various hints on how to produce the "financials" necessary for the Plan, and pointed to numerous problems that can crop up and how to avoid them. In this chapter we take a look inside the banking business, listen in on what bankers say, and what their customers have done to cope with the banks' traditional intransigence.

The banking crises of the past decade must be borne in mind, as a partial explanation, in order to understand banks' traditional reluctance to lend money carelessly, or on terms that we feel are acceptable and digestible. Still, there is always more than one way to reach a goal.

From these examples we can learn that techniques exist (call them "psychological warfare") that can either overcome traditional banking objections or get around them with more innovative methods. As one banker said: *"We're not like venture capitalists. We're like a car rental company. When they rent you a car, they charge you for usage, and they expect to get the car back. When we give you a loan, we charge interest, and we expect to get our money back."*

Communicating with Your Bank before, during and after a financial transaction, you need to communicate with your bank on all levels. Financial transactions are not always cut-and-dried. From the bank president to the assistant loan officers, these men and women are human. Plan periodic get-togethers with them, either at your business or the bank. Candidly advise them on what you are doing, and especially on how you are using the money you have borrowed. Find out, too, how the bank's portfolio is changing from period to period. It might affect your next transaction to know fiscal or physical changes that are about to take place.

Banking Hints

The New Failure Syndrome. The profusion of and bank failures around the world has indubitably spooked the banking industry. But the same goes for the customer. If your business is blessed with a sound cash position, never put all your eggs into one basket. If you have more liquid assets than that at any one time, be sure to spread it around into different banking institutions. Before depositing large amounts, either you or your accountant should check the bank's past four statements. Check to see whether the bank was profitable during the past year, carries a three percent or better ratio of net worth to assets, and a satisfactory report about who the bank is loaning major money to.

A Worst-Case Scenario. It shouldn't happen, but occasionally it does: your bank may go bankrupt. You've got money in the institution. What about the loan you have with this bank? Can you walk away from your debt? No. The Government will probably take over and you will have to pay back everything, just as before, to the new management. In fact, the situation could get worse. The government agency may not know you as well as your former banker does. A review by some bureaucrat might lead him (or her) to conclude that your collateral is inadequate and you will be asked for additional collateral, a co-signer, or to accelerate your payments. Dealing with the government agency is no picnic. As Gertrude Stein said, *"A debt is a debt is a debt . . ."*

Expanding Your Credit. We hope this will happen to you: your business expands; your present banking resource is limited, especially the credit your current bank has allocated to you. What to do? Expand by exploring an additional banking relationship. As your business expands and your credit needs increase, this should be part of your planning. Remember that the more you need to borrow to accommodate your expanding business, the greater the possibility of a turn-down from your present resource and the longer the review process. Send your financials to the loan officers of other banks, as your needs expand. Get acquainted with them before your need becomes acute.

Personal Asset Protection. Unless it is absolutely necessary to obtain needed opening or expansion capital, never pledge your personal assets, such as your residence. There is an alternative, however: get a separate loan on your private assets. Let's say you own a home with a substantial equity in it. You have business property or equipment that can back a business loan. However, you need another long-term loan for additional money. Using your home equity, you could make a personal or equity loan for up to 30 years. Whereas a business loan would be written for one, two or three years, with a correspondingly high monthly payback, a personal or home equity loan, payable over a long period of time, is a much more comfortable transaction. First, second or equity home loans to support a business venture make your personal residence at risk, of course, but you are the best judge as to your chances for success. Because it is unlikely that your commercial loan officer will suggest such a split arrangement, you need to be apprised of this possibility. At this specific point in time, the reduction of monthly payments by stretching out the loan might be just what you need, at least until the business develops and generates the needed profits.

Key Executives to the Front. If yours is the kind of business that has several key executives or partners, you might consider taking turns talking to, and negotiating with, the bank's loan officers. Perhaps this will reduce your ego a bit, make you less important with the banker, but the psychology is useful. By alternating discussions and contacts, you show the bank that you have a team, and that the business is not in jeopardy if something should happen to you. Show that your business has several key players, all singing the same tune.

Other Banking Services. When dealing with a bank, you need to consider that this institution has many other services on which they make money. One of the questions your loan officer will no doubt ask you, *"Do you have any other accounts in this bank?"* He will be looking at other income opportunities from you. Do you have a safety deposit box? Do you use any of the bank's personal services? Do you have a mortgage or auto loan with the bank, any deposits or a trust arrangement? Consider what other services the bank offers you and act upon them before you consider asking for a business loan.

Get acquainted with your banker before your need becomes acute.

Play the Field. Dealing with one bank officer might be putting all your eggs into a leaky basket. Bank officers, like so many other executives, tend to play musical chairs with their jobs. The man with whom you have established a great relationship, after many months of cultivating him, has suddenly been shifted to another office out-of-town, or joined another bank. However, his former assistant is still there and has, perhaps, been moved up into the number one slot. But the assistant knows you only as a name, and perhaps as a face. You have to become acquainted with him or her all over again unless, of course, you take the time and trouble to have become friendly with the number two person ahead of time. Like making a political contribution, spread your attention around. You never can tell…

Educating the Loan Officer. It would be impossible to assume that the banker who is considering your loan application will be intimately familiar with your specific business or profession. Perhaps a little personal education is appropriate. Bring him a pamphlet about your company, a publicity clipping about you or your product, a sample of whatever you produce. If something is printed about your business in the local newspaper or a recognizable trade journal, it immediately assumes the nature of gospel truth. Why not take advantage of this, especially if the publicity might cost only one postage stamp? If you have something to blow your horn about, make sure the banker hears it too.

Hedging Your Bet. One executive proposes that if your collateral and reputation allow a loan or credit line of, let's say, 500.000ƒ, take this credit but never use more than half or three-quarters of it (unless, of course, you need it all). The psychology is that the banker, looking at your record, will see that you have not taken all you could take and he'll be asking you why you don't want more. Or offer you a larger credit line or loan. That's the way it is in banking. Similarly, if you have adequate cash flow and can reduce the loan balance ahead of time, the banker will wonder if you don't need more money. Business people who are in such an enviable position admit that they will occasionally play this game deliberately. Psychology plays as important a part in the loan process as accounting.

Banking is a Business. A moderate-size contractor had expanded after a number of years and was ready to make a major move, requiring a temporary infusion of cash. Because the business had a sound operating and credit history, the owner was able to come up with an impressive business plan. He submitted it to four local banks with a specific loan request. A cover letter was attached to each business plan that contained a brief postscript: *"The best bid wins."* The owner had the confidence of his convictions and told the prospective lenders up front that his business was worthwhile getting. When all "bids" were in, he selected the lowest bidder and saved thousands of dollars.

Belt-and-Suspenders. Sometimes it will appear to you that loan officers want too much security especially when they ask for personal assets to secure the business loan. It's the same mentality that wears a belt, then secures his pants further with suspenders. You must realize that it is the bank officer's job to secure as much collateral as possible. This is especially true during the past few years. However, it is your job to try and negotiate a loan most favorable to your business—particularly a loan that you can live with, pay for, and that does the job your business plan says it should. Alternatives to such bank demands could be (1) come up with more collateral; (2) reduce the amount of money you actually need or switch it to a staged line of credit; (3) offer key-man insurance that will assure the lender that, should anything happen to you, your policy will pay off the balance immediately; and (4) document your own investment in the business and your willingness to increase your equity.

Just as your business plan will tell everything about you, your business and your plans for the future, so will certain information that you can gather about the bank. Don't be afraid to ask for it. Much of it is open to the interested public. And the more you know about the bank, the better your chance for swinging a loan that you can live with.

If Your Loan Application is Rejected

Large banks have a bad habit of turning down many loans they deem too small, too risky, inadequately collateralized or because they don't know you well enough.

Smaller banks are often more eager to do business with you, especially if they know you better, and are satisfied with smaller loans because of their lower overhead.

There is still another option: one of the hundreds of foreign-owned banks. These foreign banks sometimes have not been as hard hit as your local banks on bad loans, low returns on loans from big borrowers, and stringent new regulatory constraints. This situation may create opportunities for many banks that are seeking expanding their commercial banking operations.

You might want to consider taking your business plan to the officer of such a foreign bank. It is unlikely that you will need an interpreter, just the kind of credible, complete business plan you should be able to compile with the help of this guidebook.

Recent Developments
on Dealing With Banks

One of the primary purposes of the business plan is to use it as leverage for a business loan or line of credit.

Dealing with banks in the final years of this millennium is a whole different situation than it was during the previous score of years. You need to know the ins and outs of the banking business before you even go through the door of the first lending institution. Here are some hints from inside the banking profession:

1. Not all banks are born alike. To find the right one that will work with you and most likely authorize a loan, ask around. Question other business people in town, at the chamber of commerce, in your civic club, especially friends in the same business or profession.

2. The people who will look over your business plan and talk to you are individuals, not institutions. They represent institutions, but they still have their own personalities, idiosyncrasies, and standards. If you cannot get anywhere with one, for whatever reason, try another one, preferably at another bank. Besides, bankers are on "career tracks" and move around to different jobs. The one you talk to today might not be one who is there tomorrow.

3. Large banks are notoriously conservative. Perhaps that is why they have grown large and fat. You might be better off to make applications with small to medium-size banks.

4. Banks render services beyond money lending. If you find a bank or lender who will suggest other services, or respond constructively to your inquiry, grab him as a golden resource. Some of the collateral service might include alternative methods of financing, lending and factoring advice.

5. If you get a turndown, find out why. Chances are that your accounting data is inadequate, or your collateral appears insufficient, or a nearby competitive or other challenging situation exists, known to the banker

The more you know about your bank, the better your chances for a loan.

but perhaps unknown to you, that could affect the health of your loan. The closer your relationship with the bank and the banker, the better your chances. Although your business plan evidences your Know-How, you still need Know-Who to complete the deal.

6. Be visible to your banker. Not all banking and lending relations can be reduced to dollars-and-cents. If you have dealt with the bank for some time, have other accounts there, and get to know some other employees of the institution, you'll smooth the way to the loan application and approval.

7. Lending standards in the '90s are much tougher than they were in the '80s and before. However, the two basic questions that bank officers ask remain the same: Can the business generate the cash to pay back the loan? Does the loan need collateral, and if so, is it available? Your business plan can go a long way in answering these two concerns.

Underscoring all advice from the banking industry is the need for persistency, supported by a realistic, updated business plan.

Commenting on personal guarantees expected of small businesses, both proprietorships and closely-held corporations, a senior VP stated:

> *"If a principal isn't willing to give his personal guarantee as an act of faith in the company, we certainly are not going to do business with him."*

A loan applicant's record of accomplishments, reputation and managerial skills are paramount criteria in evaluating the loan request, regardless how brilliant the business plan. One chief financial officer expressed it this way:

> *"The first thing our bank does is to look at the character, reputation and past performance of the individual. Character, for me, is honesty and reliability... A person who can't handle his personal finances is unlikely to be much better at business finance."*

Smaller banks are often easier to do business with.

3 Different Loans and How Best to Get Them

Not all loans are alike. There are at least three different types and each must be the focus of your business plan especially if you are approaching a loan officer specifically for that purpose.

Business Expansion Loan: Get a bank loan because you will have collateralizable property or capital equipment to secure at least a major portion of the anticipated loan.

Research & Development (R&D) Loan: If your company is trying to get money to finance research and development, a new marketing effort or a new product or process, those loan proceeds will be quickly consumed. Little or no collateral is realized and the traditional bank loan will be difficult to obtain. The best way to go in such a case is through equity funding.

Seasonal Loan: For limited-time money requirements, the traditional bank loan might be too costly. Ask the loan officer for a short-term line of credit. Interest rate is usually lower and collateral requirements easier.

How to Finance Short-Term Debt

Recent interest rates and the realization that if you do borrow, no matter how low the interest, it still costs money, have created a shift in capital borrowing. An accounting firm surveyed a number of businesses to find out how they handled cash flow problems. While bigger businesses optioned to sell their stock in order to raise capital, smaller firms had more limited options for such capital. Here is how they handled it:

Operating profit and company cash flow	64.7%	71.4%
Short-term bank loans	38.2%	58.9%
Long-term bank loans	41.2%	35.7%
Private placements	32.4%	21.4%
Individual lenders	29.4%	12.5%
Public equity capital	5.9%	7.1%
Venture capital	5.9%	5.4%

Raising Capital Through the "Other People's Money" Method

If the reason for the "other half" of your business plan is to raise money from other people, then a few words about the other people's money method will be appropriate.

Of course the best way to raise business capital is with your own savings and assets. But if this is not sufficient or is not the way you feel you want to go, then the next "touch" might be your own immediate or even extended family. Even then, if you want to make sure you will remain persona grata in your family, you will have to put any family loans or investments on a business-like basis. Your business plan, plus your good family relationships and enthusiasm, will stand you in good stead. Of course, showing that Uncle John can expect some material rewards from your proposal will also cement relationships.

For the sake of this chapter, however, we will look into sources beyond the family or even your own bank account. Here are a few real-life cases that can give you both direction and inspiration.

One man wanted to start a specialty magazine. He figured that it could take as much as 10.000.000ƒ to get it running smoothly. One problem with publication financing always has been that banks consider them almost equivalent to restaurants. They are highly vulnerable; they come and go with regularity. Yet they are glamorous, too, and promoters will always find angels who will support a bright idea. This man had such an idea and a great portfolio of past achievements. He also was a shrewd psychologist, knowing full well that to know *who* is as important as to know how. He shared his proposal with his fishing buddies and was able to raise more than 3.000.000ƒ of his necessary capitalization by casting his bait among his fellow fishermen.

He got 50 investors to participate with 10.000ƒ to 1.000.000ƒ each by selling convertible debentures that pay regular interest and can be converted into stock. In addition to his fishing buddies, this entrepreneur surveyed managers in the field in which his magazine would be a major player.

Nearly 30 years ago one of the authors of this book followed a similar technique. He invited local people in his immediate area whom he, or his attorney and accountant knew, to a briefing. They were all interested in the product—a newspaper—and a number of them subscribed to investment packages matching his own investment, and thus getting the publication off the ground. It is still being published.

Private placement of loans can also be achieved through advertising for local investors in the business or "business opportunities" columns of the local newspaper. One man raised 3.500.000*f* for a real estate development by this method. If you have maintained strong school ties, your ex-college mates might be interested in participating in your venture. Other business people in the community if they know you and want to see your new venture succeed, are also likely prospects .When a major industry in a town goes bankrupt, the community knits together, especially if a strong Chamber of Commerce gets behind a money-raising drive. "Other people's money" can then be raised rather quickly to prevent local consumers becoming unemployed and creating a ghost factory or retail building in the town, if the bankrupt business closes shop. In one particular case state development agencies lent a hand, and between them and numerous investors who were impressed and convinced by the new entrepreneurs' presentation, a large amount was raised just in time to prevent the product line from becoming history.

Other people's money includes venture capital funds. This is a rather tricky and often uncertain source, but if you are going into a fast-track, high-growth product business, and you have a convincing story of high-profit expectations, then venture capitalists will listen to you.

Because of the rather avaricious possibilities of such money lending, it should be approached with caution and knowledge of what you are letting yourself in for. If these money providers guess right, the borrower will get his money along with a lot of advice and supervision, and at the end of a few years—let's say three to five years—the venturers prefer a sellout at a high initial-growth rate. You might not desire to sell, but remember that you have your deal. This is one of the handicaps of other people's money.

Another innovative method of funding is the "Big Brother" method. Example: A small computer company developed a special design application. To market it would take more capital than the firm had available. The owners started their financing search by going for the top: IBM. Their idea and presentation struck a welcome chord in the minds of IBM executives and they agreed not only to finance the small company innovation, but to help in the marketing of it. It was a perfect hand-holding symbiosis that was helped in no small measure by a personal contact at IBM. Again, such financing depended on a combination of Know-Who and Know-How.

It is impossible to overestimate the importance of Know-Who. It imparts a degree of credibility that is impossible to obtain otherwise. Another case history to prove this point; A young business needed an infusion of funds for a short period.

All normal attempts to borrow from local banking sources were in vain. Asset-based lenders including banks shied away from the assumed high-risk investment in a small, developing company. But one of the other members of the incubator group had dealt successfully with a bank, and established close rapport with the institution and the county's development center. Literally holding the other business's hand, he took him to the bank and introduced him to the banker, serving also as a needed reference. In short order, the loan was approved, another proof that financing often starts and ends with other people's influence.

He shared his proposal with his fishing buddies and raised the start-up money.

131

Six Rules to Remember
When You Try to Borrow Money

1. Seller-financing beats bank-financing. Never go to a bank until you have explored the seller first; never borrow until you have received the final NO from the seller.

2. Bank lenders are like fingerprints. No two are alike, even though their forms are alike. Shop around until your deal and needs dovetail with those of the lender.

3. Know what the lender is looking for: the 4 C's (credit, cash flow, collateral and character). If you come up short on any of them, find another way; ask your mother.

4. There is a right way and a wrong way to borrow. Make sure first of all that the structure of the loan is for your benefit. Then triple-check your application for accuracy and completeness. You cannot look anything less than a professional the first time.

5. If you really know how to structure the deal, you might even borrow 100 percent of the purchase price or need. Read the right books; ask the right people for advice before you hand in that loan application. But remember: the more you borrow, the more you need to prove that you will have the cash flow to pay it back.

6. Don't undervalue yourself; you might be worth more than you think. Research every nook and cranny of your worth. Your own assets might very well cover the down payment or collateral.

10 Financing Questions to Ask Yourself:

1. How much do I really need to start my business?

2. How long will it realistically take to break even?

3. How much volume do I need to produce to reach that point?

4. What should my gross and net profit be?

5. What should my fixed and variable expenses be?

6. How do my figures compare with industry figures?

7. Can I adapt this information for my operating budget?

8. Will my business earnings be sufficient to pay off any loan?

9. Can I make adjustments in my budget so I can reach necessary profit goals?

10. Do these figures show that I can develop a profitable business? Or am I premature to gamble my life savings?

Understanding Cash Flow

To be competitive, small business owners must plan and prepare for all future events and market changes. Possibly the most important aspect of preparation is effective cash-flow planning. Failure to properly plan cash flow is one of the leading causes for small business failures. In planning and achieving a positive cash flow, you must have a sound plan.

Cash reserves can be increased by:

- Collection of receivables

- Tightened credit requirements

- Price of products or services

- Loans, both long term and short term

- Increased sales

- Reduced overhead

- Budgeting your operating expenses

- Purchasing at better prices and longer terms

Chapter V

Introduction to International Business Opportunities

1. Financial Assistance

A. The first thing you do is to look at your personal financial resources and if that is not enough then go to your family and then friends with your business plan. Borrow on a loan basis rather than as an investment in your business from these people. Be sure and pay at least current market interest rates to your benefactors.

B. Check with your government agencies to determine if they have a loan program for entrepreneurs. They may also have an Economic Development Agency for financial assistance. For example: the Federal Republic of Germany has a Federal Office of Foreign Trade Information. The credit programs of the European Recovery Program (ERP) special fund and the promotional institutes, especially the Kreditanstalt für Wiederaufbau (KfW), are important components of economic development. The program of special government grants to set up new businesses is handled by the Deutsche Ausgleichsbank (DtA). Low-interest credits from the ERP special fund are granted to private individuals, small and medium-sized enterprises, as well as members of professions, these credits are used to finance the setting up of new businesses and investment in the new Federal States.

C. The Inter-American Development Bank (IDB): The IDB was established in 1959 by 19 countries. Its membership includes 40 regional organizations and member states. The primary goals of the bank are to encourage investment (or to supplement existing funds) in development projects and provide technical assistance for preparation, financing and implementation of development plans and projects in Latin and South America.

One IDB program is The Bolivar Program which is a "match-maker for businesses." The program's central mechanism is its network of business alliances, known as ENLACE. Through ENLACE, Latin American companies—*preferably small- and medium-sized and technologically innovative ones*—can find partners in other countries.

To date, The Bolivar Program has received nearly 1,000 requests to locate business partners, 38 percent of which has been successfully met. More than 170 institutions have signed letters of intent to set up companies or to form business alliances.

Secretaria Ejecutiva del Programa Bolivar, Av. Francisco de Miranda, Edificio Parque Cristal, Torre Oeste, Oficina 13-4, Caracas, Venezuela. Tel: 582-283-2867; Fax: 582-285-7113. Internet access at http: //www.iadb.org/

D. The International Bank for Reconstruction and Development (BRD): The IBRD is the principal member of the World Bank Group, the others being the Multilateral Investment Guarantee Agency (MIGA), the International Finance Corporation (IFC), and the International Development Association (IDA). The IBRD lends funds, provides advice, and investment in most countries. IBRD, 1818 H Street NW, Washington, D.C. 20433 USA. Tel: 202-477-1234; Fax: 202-477-6391. Internet access at http: //www.worldbank.org/

E. The European Bank for Reconstruction and Development
    (EBRD): The EBRD formally opened on 15 April 1991, and was
    initially capitalized with over $12,000,000,000 USD. The purpose
    of the EBRD is to aid the countries of Central and Eastern Europe
    in the transition toward market oriented economics and to
    promote private and entrepreneurial initiative in the region.
    EBRD, 1 Exchange Square, Broadgate, London EC2A2EH
    England. Tel: 0171 338 6372; Fax: 0171 338 6690.

F. The Asian Development Bank (ADB): The ADB is an interna-
    tional development finance institution which fosters economic
    growth and coordinates development policies. The ADB is owned
    by 52 member states. ADB, 6 ADB Avenue, Mandaluyong, 0401
    Metro Manila, Philippines. Tel: 632 632 4444;Fax: 632 636 2444.
    Internet access at http: //www.asiandevbank.org

G. The African Development Bank (AfDB): The AfDB promotes the
    integration of African economies through progressive extension of
    national markets. It has a Board of Governors comprised mostly of
    financial economic planning ministers from the AfDB's member
    countries. AfDB, BP V316 Rue Joseph Anoma, Abidjan, La Cote
    d'Ivoire. Tel: 225 20 426; Fax: 225 20 4206.

H. The Overseas Private Investment Corporation (OPIC): OPIC is a
    U.S. government agency that was established to mobilize and
    facilitate the participation of U.S. capital and skills in the
    economic development of developing countries. OPIC
    accomplishes its purpose through three principal programs by:

    • Insuring investment against political risk,

    • Financing investment projects with direct loans and loan
      guarantees, and

    • Providing a variety of pre-investment services to the U.S. firms.

I. The U.S. Agency for International Development (AID): AID is a U.S. government agency that provides assistance to less-developed countries. AID operates in over 70 countries through field missions and representative offices.

K. Foreign Chambers of Commerce in your country may have economic development and financial assistance programs.

J. Contact the Commercial Trade Attaché of foreign embassies and consulates for any assistance programs they have in your country.

K. U.S. Chambers of Commerce as well as your local city Chamber of Commerce should be contacted.

2. Minority Enterprise Development

Many countries have minority programs for assistance in developing new businesses. Check with your city or federal government to determine if this is available and who to contact.

3. Business Counseling and Training

A. The U.S. Department of Commerce has a "SABIT Program" in some countries whereby a mid-management person can apply for a short intern program in the U.S. with a U.S. company. Most of the expenses are paid for the selected intern. He or she must speak English to be eligible. Contact your nearest U.S. Embassy, Foreign Service Officer.

B. Volunteers in Technical Assistance (VITA), 1815 North Lynn St., Suite 200, P.O. Box 12438, Arlington, Virginia, 22209-8438 USA, has set up a training program for entrepreneurs in Nairobi, Kenya. Contact Harun N. Baiya, Country Representative, VITA, P.O. Box 34336, Nairobi, Kenya, Tel: 721872.

C. The U.S. Peace Corp does some small business counseling in many countries. Contact your U.S. Embassy.

D. Contact your own government economic or trade office for counseling and training programs they have for starting and operating small businesses.

4. International Franchises

A. Franchises are established businesses which sell their operational and marketing strategies to licensed franchisees. A royalty fee is charged to purchase the franchise and approximately 5 percent of the total gross sales of the new franchise is paid to the franchisor periodically. There may be additional charges for advertising or marketing. Check out your franchise contract with a lawyer.

The franchisor may furnish initial training, help in location selection, initial market research, help to set-up bookkeeping, personnel, costing, and marketing. They may sell necessary equipment and supplies to the new business. There are a number of international franchises, primarily in fast food such as *McDonald's, Pizza Hut, Dairy Queen, et al.,* as well as thousands of others.

B. The International Franchise Association (IFA), 1350 New York Avenue NW, Suite 900, Washington, DC 20005, USA tel: 202-628-8000, publishes a complete list of its franchise members and information on costs and type of operation.

C: Info Franchise News, Inc. 728F Center St., P.O. Box 550, Lewiston, New York 14092, USA tel: 716-754-4669, publishes a Franchise Annual Directory which describes 5,329 Franchisors. Its Handbook section tells you what you need to know before investing.

D. FRANDATA Corp. 1155 Connecticut Ave., NW, Washington, DC 20036, USA tel: 202-659-8640 offers Uniform Franchise Offering Circulars (UFOCs) data on franchises via fax. Telephone inquiry within the USA can be made by phone 800-800-4553 and franchise information, up to three pages, can be supplied by fax for a small charge.

E. Franchising around the world

Country	Number of Franchise Systems	Number of Franchise Outlets
France	600	30,000
United Kingdom	432	18,600
Germany	390	17,000
Italy	387	19,000
Netherlands	309	11,005
Spain	213	22,700
Sweden	200	6,800
Austria	170	2,700
Norway	125	3,500
Belgium	90	3,200
Portugal	55	800
Denmark	42	500

(Source International Franchise Association, Washington)

5. International Nonprofit Consulting Organizations

A Citizens Democracy Corps (CDC), 1735 I St., NW, Suite 720, Washington, DC 20006 USA. (*In the USA you can dial the toll-free 800-394-1945*) Tel: 202-872-0933 Fax: 202-872-0923

Provides volunteer business consultants at a minimal shared charge to established firms in the former Soviet republics.

B. International Executive Service Corps (IESC), P.O. Box 10005, Stamford, Connecticut 06904 USA, (*in the USA you can dial the toll-free 800-243-4372*) Tel: 203-324-2531 Fax: 203-324-2531

Volunteer consultants provide business assistance at a minimal shared charge to established firms business assistance. IESC volunteers provide technical and managerial assistance for client companies and for public and private sector organizations during short and long-term projects. The widest range of assistance can be provided from the volunteer talent bank of 13,000 skilled business executives.

IESC has 67 field offices overseas in 50 countries. Check with your country's U.S. Embassy for contact with IESC. World wide service provided in developing countries.

C. Volunteers in Overseas Cooperative Assistance (VOCA)
50 'F' St., NW, Suite 1075, Washington, DC, USA
Tel: 202-626-8750 Fax: 202-783-7204

Provides volunteer technical assistance to cooperatives, agriculturalists and agribusiness in developing countries at a minimal shared cost. VOCA send hundreds of U.S. specialists annually to provide short-term, voluntary technical assistance abroad.

D. Volunteers in Technical Assistance (VITA)
1600 Wilson Blvd., Suite 500, Arlington, VA 22209, USA
Tel: 703-276-1800 Fax: 703-243-1865 VITA provides the following:

a. Information Services through its Inquiry Service, has responded to more than 200,000 requests for technical information. VITA distributes over 200 manuals and papers. It's available through Internet and BITNET and broadcasts a weekly *Voice of America* program—all of which focus on technical issues related to international development.

b. Communications Technology is used by VITA in a variety of mechanisms for providing communications services, including space technology. VITA also utilizes computer-to-computer communications without dependence on telephone lines or satellites.

c. Field Projects of collecting, testing, and disseminating information crucial to development that promotes economic growth and respect for environment.

d. The CONNECT Program utilizes the new information age by allowing people to improve the quality of their lives by accessing resources which will help to reduce poverty, overcome hunger and disease, and mitigate natural disasters.

e. Volunteer consultants are available for field projects throughout the developing world at a minimal shared cost.

5. Peace Corps
1990 'K' Street N.W.
Washington, DC 20526 USA

800-254-8580 toll-free number *(from within U.S. only)*
202-606-3010 local and overseas dialing number
202-606-3110 local and overseas Fax number

The Peace Corps currently has 6,500 Volunteers in more than 90 countries. Of the many Environmental and Educational Programs conducted worldwide, the Vocational Education program teaches small business skills and workplace behavioral skills and facilitates apprenticeship opportunities. Help in starting a business is also available.

6. There are many other programs available from religious organizations and other non-profit firms from the USA, European Community, Japan *et al.* Contact with the embassies of these countries will enable you to take advantage of their services.

Entering any marketplace, whether it is within your country or into a foreign country presents the same areas of concern for success. Remember that a business must offer something to sell and find someone to buy it. This is very basic and yet many people entering their own business do not follow this basic business premise. You must be able to satisfy a need or a want or create a desire to buy your product or service. To accomplish this objective a business plan is needed as a way to determine what your goals are and what you have to do to realize your dream. *The International Instant Business Plan* is the basis for writing your plan and it applies to all the countries.

Appendix 1:
North and South America

BRAZIL

Business Opportunities: Brazil has made efforts to improve the foreign investment climate as it attempts to create a more market-oriented economy. International businesses are free to pursue direct investment with prior approval of the Central Bank. Foreign-controlled companies that are public corporations may raise capital through public subscriptions or debenture issues.

Government policy discourages or prohibits foreign investment in certain sectors of the economy such as petroleum production and refining, basic telecommunications services, mining, hydraulic energy resources and most public utilities.

Incentives: The granting of investment incentives is contingent on the approval of the federal government agencies SUDENE and SUDAM. These two agencies examine the proposed projects for their technical and economic merits, and their suitability in the overall economic development of the region.

In the Northeast and Amazon regions, the investment incentive plans administered by SUDENE and SUDAM offer the following fiscal benefits to companies operating approved projects:

- Exemption from all or part of federal taxes and charges on imported equipment for new industries.

- Exemption from income tax for a period of 10 to 15 years for all new industrial investments that are the first of their kind.

- Reduction of 50 percent in income tax for industries already operating or that are new to the region but do not qualify for the above exemption.

The Industrial Development Council (CDI) encourages import substitution by authorizing reduction in taxes on importation of raw materials to industries, whether controlled by local or foreign capital, that undertake to achieve nationalization targets for their products. Financing with lower-than-market interest rates from government sources may also be granted for related capital expenditures. The CDI may also grant exemptions or reductions in taxes and duties on imported plant and equipment for approved industrial projects considered to be of a national interest, whether controlled by local or foreign capital.

Exports: $38.8 billion commodities: iron ore, soybean bran, orange juice, footwear, coffee, motor vehicle parts. partners: EC 27.6%, Latin America 21.8%, U.S. 17.4%, Japan 6.3%

Imports: $25.7 billion commodities: crude oil, capital goods, chemical products, foodstuffs, coal. partners: U.S. 23.3%, EC 22.5%, Middle East 13.0%, Latin America 11.8%, Japan 6.5%.

Industries: textiles and other consumer goods, shoes, chemicals, cement, lumber, iron ore, steel, motor vehicles and auto parts, metal working, capital goods, tin.

Agriculture: accounts for 11% of GDP; world's largest producer and exporter of coffee and orange juice concentrate and second largest exporter of soybeans, other products-rice, corn, sugarcane, cocoa, beef, self-sufficient in food, except for wheat.

Business Organizations: The most common forms of business entities are corporations (*sociedade por anonima*-denoted *SA*) and limited liability companies (*sociedade por quotas de responsabilidade limitada*-denoted *Ltda*). *SA*s are similar to European corporations, while *Ltdas* incorporate features of both partnerships and corporations and are similar to European limited liability companies. Joint ventures, a common method for U.S. firms to penetrate the Brazilian market, may be established as either *SA*s or *Ltdas*.

Taxes

Corporate Taxes: Income tax rate is 30%, effective rate on profits is approximately 50.5 percent, capital gains are taxed at 25%, but acquisition price is adjusted for inflation.

Personal Income Taxes: Non-residents are taxed only on income derived from Brazilian sources. They pay a 25% personal income tax.

Other Taxes: Value-added taxes (VATs) are levied on both the state and federal levels. Federal VAT (IPI) varies between zero and 365.6 percent. Exports are exempt. The state VAT (ICMS) rates vary from nine to 17%. In Rio de Janeiro and San Paulo, the basic VAT rate for imports and goods shipped to a final consumer is 18%. All imports and exports are controlled by DECEX, the Foreign Trade Department of Ministry of Economy. All companies engaged in foreign trade must register with this agency.

BRAZIL

Useful Contacts

• Check for a Brazilian embassy, chamber of commerce or trade development agency in your country.

• **Brazilian Government Trade Bureau**, 551 Fifth Ave., Suite 210, New York, NY 10010
  Tel: (212) 916-3200 Fax: (212) 573-9406

• **Secretariat for Health Surveillance**, Romero Claus,
  Tel: (55 61) 226-9169

• **Directorate of International Trade (DECEX)**, Lucia Maldonado,
  Tel: (55 21) 216-0372 Fax: 223-1235

• **U.S. Consulate in Rio de Janeiro**, Avenida Presidente Wilson 147, 20030 Rio de Janeiro, RJ, Brazil
  Tel: (55 21) 292-7117 Fax: (55 21) 220-0439

• **The American Chamber of Commerce for Brazil**, Praca Pio X-15, 5th Floor, Caixa Postal 916, 20-040, Rio de Janeiro, RJ
  Tel: (55 21) 203-2477 Fax: (55 21) 4477

CANADA

Business Opportunities: The Government of Canada welcomes foreign investment in the expectation that such investment will provide benefits to the country and its citizens. Both federal and provincial governments offer a wide range of industrial incentive programs and tax incentives.

Foreign investors usually conduct business in Canada through Canadian corporations. Foreign investors may participate in partnerships carrying on business in Canada. Individuals or corporations may also establish a joint venture.

There is a number of statutory restrictions which apply to foreign ownership in certain Canadian industries. Industries involved include communications and financial services, although most restrictions in the latter category were removed for U.S. investors under CFTA.

Foreign acquisitions of a Canadian business under the Investment Canada Act (ICA), generally requires that non-nationals submit an application to Investment Canada for review when the value of the assets involved exceeds C$ 5 million or the business relates to Canada's cultural heritage or national identity.

Under the CFTA , the thresholds for review for direct acquisitions by U.S. investors was raised to C$ 150 million in 1992, and review of indirect acquisitions by U.S. investors was eliminated.

Provincial statues also impose certain requirements on foreign investors, including:

- A majority of the members of the board of directors of companies incorporated in Alberta, British Columbia, Manitoba, Ontario, Saskatchewan, and federally incorporated must be resident Canadians.

- Foreigners registering ownership of land in certain provinces must disclose their citizenship.

- Most provincial securities acts provide that an applicant may be refused registration as a securities dealer if the applicant has not been a resident of Canada for at least one year prior to the date of application.

Incentives: Government programs provide direct assistance in the form of repayable or non-repayable cash grants or loan guarantees to encourage investment in less-developed regions. Tax incentives are another type of incentive program. Although neither tax nor direct incentives are aimed at attracting foreign investment, many of the incentives are available to foreign investors.

Tax incentives for investment take many forms, including:

- Investment Tax Credits (ITC) which give special treatment to certain taxpayers, certain regions and specific types of investment.

- Tax reductions for qualifying income derived from certain manufacturing and processing activities. Reductions are generally available to subsidiaries and branches of foreign corporations.

CANADA

Manufacturing and processing deductions against profits derived from manufacturing and processing activities carried out in Canada include:

- Small business tax credits for the first C$200,000 of annual active business income of a Canadian-controlled private corporation.

- A film industry tax benefit which provides a 30 percent rate of capital cost allowance for certified film productions.

- Tax incentives for certain research and development expenses.

- Federal legislation has named Montreal and Vancouver as international banking centers. This allows prescribed financial institutions (including foreign banks that carry on international banking business from a designated branch or office in Vancouver or Montreal) to operate free of federal income tax for income on loans to non-residents.

Exports: $133.9 billion. Commodities: newsprint, wood pulp, timber, crude petroleum, machinery, natural gas, aluminum, motor vehicles and parts, telecommunications eqpt. Partners: U.S., Japan, UK, Germany, South Korea, Netherlands, China.

Imports: $125.3 billion commodities: crude oil, chemicals, motor vehicles and parts, durable consumer goods, electronic computers, telecommunications and parts. partners: U.S., Japan, UK, Germany, France, Mexico, Taiwan, South Korea.

Industries: Processed and unprocessed minerals, food products, wood and paper products, transportation equipment, chemicals, fish products, petroleum and natural gas.

Agriculture: Accounts for about 3% of GDP; one of the world's major producers and exporters of grain (wheat and barley); key source of U.S. agricultural imports; large forest resources cover 35% of total land area; commercial fisheries provide annual catch of 1.5 million metric tons, of which 75% is exported.

This is an important industry with all year-round activities in all provinces. Contact Tourism Canada—listed as Useful Contacts with offices in other cities in Canada.

Business Organizations: Forms of business enterprises in Canada include corporations, partnerships and sole proprietorships. Corporations, whether public or private, and whether federally or provincially incorporated, are legal entities distinct from their shareholders. Partnerships are generally not treated as legal entities distinct from their members. Sole proprietorships are owned by an individual and may be carried on under their own name or a trade name.

CANADA

Taxes

Corporate: Corporations must pay 28% federal income tax on taxable income earned in Canada. A recent five percent reduction for manufacturing and processing income cuts the effective rate to 23%. There is also a three percent surtax on corporate tax payable and a variety of capital taxes. A federal Goods and Services Tax (GST) has been created as a multi-stage tax on consumption and is charged at a rate of seven percent on most transactions in Canada. Since the GST is a value-added tax, manufacturers and businesses in the distribution chain pay tax only on the value added to the product or service.

Useful Contacts

Check for a Canadian embassy, chamber of commerce or trade development agency in your country.

- **Canadian Direct Marketing Association**, 1 Concorde Gate, Suite 607, Don Mills, Ontario M3C 3N6
  Tel: (416) 391-2362 Fax: (416) 441-4062

- **Industry, Science and Technology Canada (ISTC)**,
  Business Service Centre, C.D. Howe Building, 235 Queen St., Ottawa, Ontario K1A OH5
  Tel: (613) 952-4782

- **U.S. Consulate General—Halifax**, U.S. and Foreign Commercial Service, Cogswell Tower, Scotia Square, Suite 910,
  Halifax, Nova Scotia B3J 3K1
  Tel: (902) 429-2482 Fax: (902) 423-6861

- **Montreal, U.S. and Foreign Commercial Service**,
  Place Felix Martin, 455 Rene Levesque Blvd, W, Montreal, Québec H2Z 1Z2.
  Tel:(514) 398-0673 Fax: (514) 398-0711

- **Toronto, U.S. Foreign and Commercial Service**, 480 University Ave., Suite 602, Toronto, Ontario N5G 1V2.
  Tel: (416) 595-5414 Fax: (416) 595-5419

CHILE

Business Opportunities: In general, the Chilean government takes a liberal attitude toward, and imposes few restrictions upon, foreign investment. One hundred percent foreign ownership is permissible and Chilean partners need be secured only if the investor deems it advantageous. There are no restrictions on foreign ownership of buildings or other forms of real estate, however, ownership restrictions apply in the broadcasting, fishing, shipping, and hydrocarbons sectors. In addition, coastal trade is reserved for Chilean nationals except in certain cases involving small vessels.

The Chilean Foreign Investment Committee (CFIC) is the institution authorized to accept the inflow of foreign capital and to stipulate the terms and conditions of the corresponding contract. Foreign investors in Chile have the same rights and obligations as Chileans. Foreign investment is subject to the same legislation as local investment, and no discrimination is allowed.

The following general rules affect foreign investment in Chile:

- For investments made under Decree Law (DL) 600, capital must remain in the country for three years before it may be remitted. (This may be reduced to one year). Capital may be remitted only with proceeds from the sale or liquidation of the investment. Profit remittances on dividends are freely remitted.

- Foreign exchange for profit and capital remittances will be available under the same conditions applicable to Chilean nationals purchasing foreign exchange to cover general imports. The local market provides exchange insurance and dollar-denominated deposits to cover exchange risks.

- The netting of trade-related payments is not allowed. However, when some goods are imported and then re-exported, the Central Bank can approve the netting of the respective prices. Foreign investments exceeding US $50 million can obtain authorization to net export proceeds with remittable profits or repatriable capital directly abroad.

- Foreign investments are not subject to time limits, but the Chilean government requires that 30 percent of all external credits be placed in a non-interest bearing reserve account held at the Central Bank for a period of one year. This requirement (known locally as the "*encaje*") applies equally to foreign investors and Chileans. Alternatively, the recipients of external credits may pay the Central Bank an amount equivalent to the interest of such a deposit. This alternative enables the investor to avoid tying up part of his working capital with the Central Bank.

- Foreign investors are never required to sell part or all of their operations or investment to Chilean nationals or at any time phase out their operations in Chile.

- Residents and non-residents can maintain accounts in U.S. dollars in Chile or aboard.

- The Central Bank of Chile handles all terms, commissions, and other charges for foreign credits associated with foreign investments.

- The CFIC must examine and approve all investments exceeding US$ 5 million or involving the public service sector.

- Investments in export generating projects that exceed US$ 5 million receive additional benefits such as: the use of offshore accounts to maintain export proceeds for payments, including principal and interest on loans.

CHILE

Incentives: The Chilean government does not differentiate between Chilean and foreign investors when offering investment incentives. The Foreign Investment Act permits foreign capital to enter the country in various ways as agreed upon by the investor and the CFIC. A system of debt-equity swaps that requires the approval of the Central Bank is also in effect.

The Income Tax Law favors capital investment and the reinvestment of profits, and acts as an incentive in the following fashion: Domestic and foreign corporations are subject to a 15 percent first category income tax rate applied to new taxable income for commercial, industrial, mining, fishing and real estate investment.

Services rendered abroad by a foreign corporation to a resident entity are subject, as a general rule, to a 40 percent additional withholding tax. This rate is reduced to 20 percent in the case of engineering and technical assistance services rendered exclusively outside Chile. Payments abroad for freight, loading and unloading, commissions and international communications are exempt. Foreign branches operating in Chile are taxed only on their Chilean source income.

A foreign investor, when contracting with the CFIC, may select one of two options for Chilean income tax purposes— the General Tax Regime (applicable to all Chilean businesses) or the Special Tax regime for foreign investors.

The General Tax Regime currently has a corporate tax rate of 15 percent on accrued income. If the remaining corporate profits are to be repatriated abroad, however, there is an additional tax of 35 percent. This tax, using the total accrued income as its basis, authorizes a tax credit on the amount of corporate tax paid. The Special Tax Regime is more costly than the General Tax Regime, but provides more certainty. The Chilean Congress can change the corporate tax rate under the General Tax Regime, but the Special Tax Regime for foreign investors remains fixed.

To be eligible for the Special Tax Regime, the investor must specifically request this Regime when applying for a contract with the CFIC. Failure to make such an application is interpreted to mean a foreign investor has elected the General Tax Regime.

The process for taxation under the Special Tax Regime has two tax rate options, one of 49.5 percent, and one of 40 percent. The 40 percent rate also includes a variable surcharge ranging from zero to 30 percent. Consequently, the 40 percent tax on repatriated profits can escalate to as high as 70 percent, when maximum 30 percent surcharge is included.

Exports: $10 billion. Commodities: Copper 41%, other metals and minerals 8.7%, wood products 7.1%, fish and fishmeal 9.8%, fruits 8.4%. Partners: EC 29%, Japan 17%, US 16%, Argentina 5%, Brazil 5%

Imports: $9.2 billion. Commodities: Capital goods 25.2%, spare parts 24.8%, raw materials 15.4%, petroleum 10%, foodstuffs 5.7%. Partners: EC 24%, US 21%, Brazil 10%, Japan 10%.

Industries: Copper, other minerals, foodstuffs, fish processing, iron and steel, wood and wood products, transport equipment, cement, textiles.

CHILE

Agriculture: Accounts for about 7% of GDP (including fishing and forestry); major exporter of fruit, fish, and timber products; major crops-wheat, corn, grapes, beans, sugar beets, potatoes, deciduous fruit; livestock products-beef, poultry, wool, self sufficient in most foods; 1991 fish catch of 6.6 million metric tons; net agricultural importer.

Business Organizations: Chilean law allows for a variety of different business enterprises. The three types of business operations generally used by foreign investors are corporations, limited liability companies, and branches. Tax treatment of the three entities is basically equal in Chile, and thus consideration of taxation in the investor's country of origin is important. While the cost of incorporation is inexpensive for all three entities, a limited liability partnership is usually the simplest to establish. According to the law, corporations and limited liability companies in Chile are considered to be separate legal bodies, unlike branch operations. There is no minimum requirement for local participation in the foundation or operation of a foreign enterprise and thus the decision is strictly a commercial consideration. However, the presence of a local legal entity is essential from a liability standpoint.

Taxes

Corporate Taxes: Companies in Chile are taxed in two stages. Initially they are assessed a flat rate of 10 percent on their income derived from within Chile. Secondly, dividends remitted to non-residents abroad are subject to additional taxes, bringing the total effective tax rate to 35 percent. Capital gains, with few minor exceptions, are considered income and taxed at the according rate. Deductions are granted for: depreciation and depletion of assets, net operating losses, payments to foreign affiliates, general business expenses, and taxes imposed by law, except for income and real estate taxes.

Other Taxes: The primary indirect tax is the Value-Added Tax (VAT), which is set at 18 percent and expected to decrease to 16 percent. All imports (except capital goods), general sales of merchandise, and services are subject to the VAT, while exports are exempt from payment. Other indirect taxes include: a 0.1 percent stamp tax on most financial and credit transactions; annual real estate taxes of two percent of the property's total appraised value; a 50 percent tax on the importation of specific luxury items such as gold, silver, ivory, and furs; and a progressive tax rate from one to 25 percent on the value of gifts and inheritances.

Useful Contacts

•**AV. Americo Vespucio Sur 80**, 9th Floor, P. O. Box 82, Correo 34, Santiago
  Tel: (562) 208-3451, 6830, 04 4140 Facsimile: (562) 206-0911

•**National Tourism Board of Chile**, Av. Providencia 1550, P. O. Box 14082, Santiago
  Tel: (562) 696-7141 Facsimile: (562) 969-0981

•**U. S. Embassy in Chile**, Codina Building, 1343 Augustinas, Santiago
  Tel: (562) 671-0133 Facsimile: (562) 699-1141 Telex: 240061-USA-CL

MEXICO

Business Opportunities: Certain sectors of the Mexican economy are unavailable to foreign investors. For example, all investments in the following sectors are reserved for the state: oil and other hydrocarbons, basic petrochemicals, the mining of radioactive minerals, nuclear energy, electricity, communications satellites, the mining of certain minerals from the national reserves, railroads, and telegraphic communications. In addition, Mexican citizens have the exclusive right to invest in such areas as radio and television; land, air, and sea transport; forestry, stockbrokerage and exchange houses; credit unions; and satellite operations. Implementation of the NAFTA agreement would eliminate many of these restrictions.

Specific restrictions on foreign direct investments have been greatly reduced and it is not difficult (and in many cases not necessary) for foreigners to gain permission to own a majority interest in a Mexican enterprise. Non-nationals may own, without prior approval, a minority interest in a business engaged in the following activities: banking, mining, auto parts, fishing, explosives and firearms, telecommunications, and financial leasing. Investors who wish to own a majority share of a Mexican business must first obtain approval from CNIE. However, due to the 1989 investment law revisions, CNIE must automatically approve all foreign investments in unrestricted sectors which meet the following criteria:

- The investment must have a value of under US$ 100 million.

- The investment must be funded entirely from sources external to Mexico, intermediated by Mexican financial institutions.

- The investment must not be located in metropolitan Mexico City, Monterrey, or Guadalajara.

- The operation must balance foreign exchange outlays for its first three years of operation.

- The investment must create permanent jobs and training for workers.

- The enterprise must utilize adequate technology which meets environmental regulations.

- Foreigners may not own land, water or mineral rights in Mexico. Under certain conditions, they may lease a 30-year fee trust for property located along the ocean or national borders.

Incentives: In order to be eligible for certain tax incentives, a company must be at least 51 percent Mexican-owned. However, both national (majority capital owned by Mexican citizens) and foreign (majority capital owned by foreigners or foreign-controlled management) companies qualify for accelerated depreciation benefits on fixed assets and this often serves as an important investment incentive.

Special incentives are also available for investors in certain priority development zones. Most of these zones are near national borders, seacoasts, or ports, thus facilitating Mexican exportation. The major population centers of Mexico City, Monterrey, and Guadalajara are specifically excluded from these priority zones.

Moreover, various industries are eligible for special tax credits. Industries that receive the most incentives are those involving agriculture and specific categories of capital goods. Industries that receive these tax incentives include nondurable consumer goods, electric household appliances, equipment for transportation and service industries, construction materials, pharmaceuticals, and intermediate petrochemical and metallurgical products.

MEXICO

Secretariat of Commerce and Industrial Development (SECOFI) oversees foreign investment in Mexico. The Maquiladora program was created by the Mexican government in 1965 to boost employment in the border zones through the establishment of foreign export-producing businesses. These Mexican subsidiaries of foreign corporations may be 100 percent foreign owned and combine the use of cost-efficient Mexican labor and materials with foreign capital, components, and technology in order to produce exports. Under the maquiladora program, a U.S. company will often export the necessary capital equipment and raw materials to its Mexican subsidiary, which will then complete the assembly process and re-export the finished product to the United States, where the product is only taxed on the value added while in Mexico. All machinery, parts, raw materials, equipment, and other components necessary for assembly are granted exemptions from all Mexican import duties. There are currently over 1,900 maquiladora plants owned by Mexican, U.S. and other nations throughout Mexico, employing over 450,000 Mexicans and generating US$ 12.4 billion in products each year.

Exports: $50.5 billion includes in-bond industries. Commodities: crude oil, oil products, coffee, silver, engines, motor vehicles, cotton, consumer electronics. Partners: U.S. 74%, Japan 8%, EC 4%

Imports: $65.5 billion. Commodities: metal-working machines, steel mill products, agricultural machinery, electric equipment, car parts for assembly, repair parts for motor vehicles, aircraft, and aircraft parts. Partners: U.S. 74%, Japan 11%, EC 6%

Industries: food and beverages, tobacco, chemicals, iron and steel, petroleum, mining, textiles, clothing, motor vehicles, consumer durable, tourism.

Agriculture: accounts for 9% of GDP and over 25% of work force; large number of small farms at subsistence level; major food crops—corn, wheat, rice, beans; cash crops—cotton, coffee, fruit, tomatoes.

Business Organizations: Mexican law recognizes corporations (*sociedades anonimas*—denoted SA), corporations with variable capital (*sociedad anonima de capital variable*—denoted SA de CV), limited liability companies, branches of foreign corporations, general and limited partnerships and joint ventures. All corporations must register with the Secretariat of Commerce and Industrial Development (SECOFI) and, in some cases, prior approval of the National Foreign Investment Commission (CNIE) is required.

MEXICO

Taxes

Corporate taxes: The official rate is 35 percent. Residents are taxed on income from all sources; non-residents are taxed on income from Mexican sources. The majority of dividends, royalties, and fees paid to foreign shareholders of a Mexican business are subject to a 35 percent withholding tax. Capital gains are included in a corporation's gross taxable income and are assessed at the normal rate.

Personal income taxes: are assessed on a sliding scale ranging from three percent to 35 percent. Tax brackets are adjusted quarterly according to Mexico's inflation rate. Mexican residents are required to pay income tax on their worldwide income while non-residents pay taxes only on their income derived from Mexico.

Other taxes: Mexico has a value-added tax (VAT) that is levied on the sales of most goods, services, and certain imports. Generally, the VAT is paid by the consumer. Their are four general rates and categories of VAT payments: zero per cent for basic foodstuffs, agricultural equipment, and all exports; six percent for medicines and the majority of other than basic foodstuffs; 15 percent basic rate for all transactions not placed under other categories; and 20 percent for certain luxury goods, such as planes, certain motorcycles, caviar, champagne and large televisions. All corporations are required to share 10 percent of their pre-tax profits with employees. All employers are expected to pay a one percent payroll tax on employees.

Important: Mexican firms, whose capital is more than 25,000 pesos, are obliged to belong to an official chamber organized in accordance with the Law of Chambers of Commerce and Industry. Mexico's national business organizations are divided between those that are established under federal law with mandatory membership and voluntary associations. Contact for information on Mandatory Membership:

MEXICO

Useful Contacts

•**Consejo Coordinador Empresarial** (CEE), (Businessmen's Coordinating Council), Homero 527-6 Piso, 11570 Mexico, D.F.
Tel: 5/531-7636, 531-1590.

•**Confederacion de Camaras Industriales de Los Estados Unidos Mexicanos** (CONCAMIN), (Confederation of the National Chambers of Industry), Manuel Maria Contreras 133,8 Piso, 06500 Mexico, D.F.
Tel: 5/546-9053, 566-7822 Fax: 535-6871

•**American Chamber of Commerce in Mexico,**
A.C., Lucerna No. 78, 3er Piso, Colonia Juarez, 06600 Mexico, D.F.
Tel: (52 5) 724-3800 Fax: (52 5) 703-3908

Specialized chambers of commerce and associations represent particular sectors in commerce, industry and services and have the same objective: to promote the interests of their membership. Membership is compulsory.

Check for a Mexican embassy, chamber of commerce or trade development agency in your country.

PERU

Business Opportunities: Peru enacted broad investment legislation which accords national treatment, opens almost all sectors to foreign investment, guarantees free currency convertibility and eliminates monopolies. At the same time the general investment laws were implemented, Peru also enacted a large number of sectorial specific anti-monopoly decrees.

Incentives: Incentives are offered to companies that establish operations in the following zones: export processing free zones, tourist free zones, special commercial treatment zones, and special development free zones.

Export processing free zones offer investors exemptions from customs duties for imports and exports, exemption from any Peruvian tax for 15 years, temporary labor agreements, and accounting in foreign currency. Free zones for tourists offer similar benefits.

Special commercial treatment zones are generally located on the jungle frontier. They extend the following benefits to companies operating inside their borders: exemption from Value-Added Taxes; a reduced 10 percent customs duty; and accounting is permitted in foreign currency.

Exports: $3.7 billion. Commodities: copper, zinc, fishmeal, crude petroleum and byproducts, lead, gold, refined silver, coffee, cotton. Partners: U.S. 25%, Japan 9%, Italy, Germany.

Imports: $4.5 billion. Commodities: machinery, transport equipment, foodstuffs, petroleum, iron and steel, chemicals, pharmaceuticals

Industries: mining of metals, petroleum, fishing, textiles, clothing, food processing, cement, steel, shipbuilding, metal fabrication

Agriculture: accounts for 13% of GDP, about 35% of labor force; commercial crops—coffee, cotton, sugarcane; other crops—rice, wheat, potatoes, asparagas, plantains, coca; animal products—poultry, red meats, dairy, wool; not self-sufficient in grain or vegetable oil; fish catch of 6.9 million metric tons

Business Organizations: The corporation (*sociedad anonima* or SA) is the most common form of business for foreign-owned businesses. Other business organizations permitted: private limited company S.R.L. (*sociedad comercial de responsabilidad limitada*), limited partnerships with or without shares (*sociedad en comandita simple* and *sociedad en comandita por acciones*), unlimited partnership (*sociedad colectiva*) and sole proprietorship (*persona natural*).

PERU

Taxes

Corporate Taxes: Taxation is based on financial statements adjusted for inflation. The minimum income tax is equivalent to 2 percent of net assets adjusted for inflation. Royalties, exchanges, losses and interest paid to foreign affiliates are fully deductible. Dividends are subject to withholding tax of 10 percent. No income tax on saving accounts or stock market gains until year 2000.

Personal Income Taxes: is based on sliding scale ranging from six to 37 percent. Domiciled individuals living in Peru for more than two years regardless of nationality pay tax on worldwide income. Non-domiciled individuals pay tax only on Peru income.

Other Taxes: An 18 percent value-added tax (VAT) is levied on individuals and businesses that sell taxable goods and imports. This tax also includes services rendered by companies and can be used as a tax credit. 97% of imports pay 15% duty 3% pay 25%.

Useful Contacts

Check for a Peru embassy, chamber of commerce or trade development agency in your country.

- **U.S. Embassy-Lima,** Foreign Commercial Service,
  Tel: (511) 434 3000 Fax: (511) 434 3040

- **American Chamber of Commerce,** Avenida Ricardo Palma 836, Lima 18, Peru
  Tel: (5114) 47-9349 Fax: (5114) 47-9352 or (5112) 41 4317

UNITED STATES

Business Opportunities: The US is the most technologically advanced economy in the world, with a per capita GDP of $24,700, the largest among major industrial nations. The economy is market oriented with most decisions made by private individuals and business firms and with government purchases of goods and services made predominantly in the marketplace. Economic challenges for the remainder of the 1990s include needed investment in economic infrastructure, rapidly rising medical costs and sizable budget and trade deficits.

A highly skilled and successful manufacturer from the Netherlands decided to sell its equipment in the U.S.A.. Because of the firm's proximity to Europe and the sophistication of its population, it was decided to invest the equivalent of $100,000, to open a warehouse and office in Baltimore, Maryland, suburbs (it was cheaper than in the Washington area and closer to shipping facilities), and start here to penetrate this potentially most lucrative of all world markets.

For two years good progress was made and enough equipment was sold—so that the company wanted to expand into the U.S. west coast. It took three months for the move, three months to start making contacts, and three more months to realize that the company had neither the resources nor the personnel to survive here. Within a year they went bankrupt and sold the remaining inventory at a fraction of the original cost.

What this Netherlands company had discovered is that the United States is as large and as diverse as Europe. Each of the 50 states is unique, has different marketing problems, different customer needs, different state administrations. Distances are enormous, competition is fierce both from domestic companies as well as overseas exporters. Advertising costs are both high and necessary. In addition, the U.S. government regulatory agencies are often stricter than those in other countries.

As in other countries of the world, each state and each region has its own characteristics. It is more than 4,000 km from the east coast of the U.S. to the west coast; there are more than 260,000,000 customers with different needs and wants. Even though the U.S.A. is the richest big nation and a very magnetic market, superior skills and investments are required to penetrate it.

As in many other nations, the way to do business in the U.S. is often to make a "strategic alliance" with an American firm. Do not try to invade the local distribution system with your own methods. The easiest, cheapest, and fastest marketing method is the enter the existing distribution system. Any foreign business that wishes to enter the gigantic U.S. market, needs to study four broad areas and gather as much information, either through its own resources or by employing an American consultant or organization. These four areas are:

1. Determine how your product or service can enter the U.S. market distribution system.

2. What are the methods with which you can enter this U.S. market for long-term success; what money is needed.

3. Get all the latest market and industry information possible. The U.S. government and all 50 State governments' business development agencies publish much useful material at low costs—but you must know how to find it.

4. Determine the latest consumer and industry trends in the U.S.A., including what your local competition is doing.

Assessing your chances of success cannot be done by looking from the outside in, but must be done within the U.S.A.. Some information can be obtained in your country from the resident U.S. bureaus; some as referenced in this book as Useful

UNITED STATES

Contacts. If you fail to find satisfactory answers, you may want to write the publisher of this book for low-cost by-mail counsel: Puma Publishing, 1670 Coral Drive, Santa Maria, CA 93454, USA.

Exports: $449 billion commodities: capital goods, automobiles, industrial supplies and raw materials, consumer goods, agricultural products partners: Western Europe 24.3%, Canada 22.1%, Japan 10.5%

Imports: $582 billion commodities: crude oil and refined petroleum products, machinery, automobiles, consumer goods, industrial raw materials, food and beverages partners: Canada 19.3%, Western Europe 18.1%, Japan 18.1%

Industries: leading industrial power in the world, highly diversified and technologically advance; petroleum, steel, motor vehicles, aerospace, telecommunications, chemicals, electronics, food processing, consumer goods, lumber, mining

Agriculture: accounts for 2% of the GDP and 2.8% of the labor work force; favorable climate and soils support a wide variety of crops and livestock production; world's second largest producer and number one exporter of grain; surplus food producer; fish catch of 4.4 million metric tons

Business Organizations: Sole Proprietorship is the simplest form of conducting business. It is a non-corporate form which is easy to start and to terminate although tax saving opportunities are limited. No formal organization documentation is necessary. Owner must procure all necessary licenses and permits before commencing business. The owner is liable for all liabilities of the business. Partnership is the association of two or more persons to carry on as co-owners of a business for profit. An agreement for partnership is usually entered into and all partners are equally responsible for all liabilities of the business. Limited Partnership is composed of "general" partners and "limited" partners. General partners run the business and are unlimited in potential liability. A limited partner is essentially an investor whose liability is limited to their financial investment. Corporation is an artificial, fictitious entity created for the purpose of conducting business. The C or the S corporation must file in a state to be legally recognized by filing articles of incorporation, adopting corporate bylaws, and holding an organizational meeting. One or more officers and shareholders as required by the state corporation laws. Liability is the responsibility of the assets of the corporation. The officers are employees of the corporation and not liable for liabilities.

The only difference between the S corporations and C corporations arise primarily in the areas of taxation. S corporations are taxed only once as an individual while C corporations are taxed as a corporation and also as individual share owners. Limited Liability Company is a hybrid entity possessing both corporate and partnership characteristics. Like a corporation, it shields all its owners from debts and liabilities of the entity. The limited liability company is treated as a partnership form tax purposes, however, thereby allowing the owners pass thru tax benefits.

UNITED STATES

Taxes

Corporate Taxes: Are on a graduated scale basis depending on taxable income.

Personal Income Taxes: Are on a graduated basis contingent upon taxable income, marital status and other factors.

Other Taxes: Sales taxes of the city or state, licensing taxes, user taxes and other taxes depending on the city, county, state, or federal government.

UNITED STATES

Useful Contacts

Check for a United States embassy, chamber of commerce or trade development agency in your country.

- **U.S. Small Business Administration (SBA)**, 409 Third St. S.W., Washington, DC 20416
  Tel: 202 205-6720 Fax: 202 205-7272
  Offers small business development assistance and guaranteed loans obtained through lenders. SBA sponsors the Service Corps of Retired Executives (SCORE) who counsel and train entrepreneurs with volunteer experienced business owners or professionals at no cost to the client. They present business seminars and workshops at minimal fees throughout the entire country, with over 800 counseling locations. SBA also sponsors the Small Business Development Centers (SBDC) who perform similar services as SCORE but their paid staff is generally located at university or college centers, with about 800 locations.

- **U.S. Department of Commerce**, 14th & Constitution Ave., N.W., Washington, DC 20233 Tel: 202 482-1936—
  Information Clearing House—Specifically set up to help guide small businesses.

- **Department of Agriculture**, Independence Ave., between 12th and 14th Sts., SW, Washington, DC 20250
  Tel: 202 720-4323. Provides farm operating and other loans through network of regional offices.

- **U.S. Foreign Commercial Services, Export Counseling Center,**
  14th & Constitution Ave, Room 1066, Washington, DC 20230
  Tel: 202 377-3181. Export business counseling on the mechanics of exporting and on all phases of international trade.

- **National Technical Information Service**, 5285 Port Royal Rd., Springfield, VA 22161
  Tel: 703 487-4600. Technical data/reports, magnetic tapes, CD-ROMs, periodicals

- **Government Printing Office (GPO)**, 710 N. Capital St., DC 20402
  Tel: 202 783-3238. Sale, distribution of government publications

- **Department of Treasury, Internal Revenue Service,**
  1201 E. Street, N.W., room 703, Washington, DC 20004
  Tel: 800-829-1040 (toll-free). Taxpayer service for new businesses, information, and assistance for federal taxes

- **U.S. Customs Service**, Customs District Director and Customhouse, Dulles International Airport, P.O. Box 1723,
  Washington, DC 20041. Collection of revenues from imports, enforcement of customs and related laws. Customs specialists.

- **U.S. Department of Commerce**, Minority Business Development Agency,
  14th St. and Constitution Ave., N.W. Washington, DC 20230
  Tel: 202 482-1936

VENEZUELA

Since 1990, the Venezuelan government has enacted economic and investment reforms which have liberalized, though not completely eliminated, the majority of restrictions on foreign investment. The reforms have opened up most areas of the economy to foreign participation, except for certain strategic industries.

The following regulations affect foreign investment in Venezuela:

- Although official approval is no longer required, foreign investment must be registered with the Superintendency of Foreign Investment (SIEX) after being established in the country.

- For most sectors, 100 percent foreign ownership is allowed.

- All repatriation restrictions have been eliminated. The only exception applies to debt-to equity exchanges, which is governed by special rules.

- Foreign enterprises may remit royalty payments for technical assistance, trademarks and royalties, to parent companies up to a maximum of five percent of net technological sales. Profits remitted in excess of this percentage must be approved by SIEX.

- Special Spanish language restrictions apply to operations and professional services.

- Foreign investment in the area of petroleum exploration, productions, and refining is encouraged by the government but proposals for such projects must receive governmental approval.

Incentives. The Venezuelan government has formed free-trade zones, and established a series of tax incentives for foreign companies doing business in the country. In addition, many of the investment incentives available to domestic companies are also available to foreign firms, Tax investment incentives include tax holidays, usually lasting for five years, and tax rate reductions of between 25 and 100 percent.

There are also a number of industry incentives, including tax holidays, according to the following schedule:

- 100 percent tax exemption for coal and petrochemical products, agricultural products, publishing and transport companies;

- 75 to 100 percent tax exemption for hotels, tourist center, schools and public housing;

- 50 to 100 percent tax exemption for new industrial companies processing iron ore, aluminum, steel, cement, and other resource-related products; and

- Up to 15 percent tax exception for equipment manufactured in Venezuela related to pollution control, decontamination, and toxic waste disposal.

Exports: $14.2 billion. Commodities: petroleum 77%, bauxite and aluminum, steel, chemicals, agricultural products, basic manufactures. Partners: U.S. and Puerto Rico 42%, Japan, Netherlands, Italy.

VENEZUELA

Imports: $11 billion commodities: raw materials, machinery and equipment, transport equipment, construction materials. Partners: U.S. 50%, Germany, Japan, Netherlands, Canada.

Industries: petroleum, iron-ore mining, construction materials, food processing, textiles, steel, aluminum, motor vehicle assembly

Agriculture: accounts for 6% of GDP and 16% of labor force.
Products: corn, sorghum, sugarcane, rice, bananas, vegetables, coffee, beef, pork, milk, eggs, fish. Not self-sufficient in food other than meat.

Business Organizations: There are three primary forms of business enterprises which include corporations, joint ventures, and branches of foreign companies.

Taxes

Corporate Taxes: set in a two-tiered system: 20 percent for firms with taxable income up to 2 million *Bolivars* (*B*), 30 percent less *B*200,000 for companies with taxable income over *B*2 million. Petroleum companies typically pay a flat rate of 67.7 percent. However, other specific taxes result in an effective tax of about 82 percent. Capital gains are taxed as normal income. A five percent tax is withheld at the source on interest paid to non-residents. Rates for royalties vary depending the types of product transactions.

Personal Income Taxes: Non-residents are subject to tax of 20 percent on Venezuelan source wages and 30 percent on professional fees. Residents are subject to progressive tax rates ranging from 10 percent to 30 percent on Venezuelan income.

Other Taxes: Minor excise taxes exist on liquor, tobacco, cigarettes and petroleum products. A 3 percent transferral tax is applied to the transferral of ownership of particular items. A municipal tax is bases on gross receipts or sales.

Useful Contacts

Check for a Venezulean embassy, chamber of commerce or trade development agency in your country.

• **Corporacion de Turismo de Venezuela**, Lecuna Parque Central Torre Oeste Piso 37, P.O. Box 50-200, Caracas 1010
   Tel:(58 2) 2 574-1513 or 507 8815 Fax: 573-8989

• **U.S. Chamber of Commerce**, Torre Credival, Piso 10, 2da. Ave de Campo Alegre, Apdo. 5181, Caracas, 1010-A
   Tel: (58 2) 263 0833 Fax: (58 2) 263 182

Appendix 2:
Europe

BELGIUM

Business Opportunities: The government actively encourages foreign investment and treats foreign investors on an equal basis with Belgian nationals. In fact, foreign corporations in Belgium account for one-third of all employment in the country. Only a few select areas (involving national security concerns) require pre-approval of investment. In some cases, acquisitions of shares must be reported to the Ministry of Economic Affairs, the Ministry of Finance and the Ministry of Regional Affairs.

Incentives: General investment incentives include interest subsidies and capital grants. The interest subsidy is a discretionary reduction on interest payment, where a particular project received funding through an approved credit institute. Capital grants are available in place of, or in addition to, the interest subsidy. Although both the interest subsidy and the capital grant are available all over the country, the rates of award differ depending on the area. In depressed areas, the maximum rate of award can be between 21 and 24 percent of the investment. This rate can be reduced to 12 percent. The payment of the subsidies usually is spread over a period of years. Firms in development areas (also known as "reconversion zones") receive special tax incentives, including accelerated depreciation on equipment, real estate tax exemption and exemption from the company registration tax.

The government has also established special tax regimes for "coordination centers" and "distribution centers". Entities which meet the financial and legal requirements set forth in the relevant laws benefit from greatly reduced tax burdens.

Exports: $117 billion commodities: iron and steel, transportation equipment, tractors, diamonds, petroleum products partners: EC 75.5%, U,S. 3.7%, former Communist countries 1.4%

Imports: $120 billion (c.i.f., 1992) Belgium-Luxembourg Economic Union. Commodities: fuels, grains, chemicals, foodstuffs. Partners: EC 73%, U.S. 4.8%, oil-exporting less developed countries 4%, former Communist countries 1.8%

Industries: engineering and metal products, motor vehicle assembly, processed food and beverages, chemicals, basic metals, textiles, glass, petroleum, coal

Agriculture: accounts for 2.0% of GDP; emphasis on livestock production-beef, veal, pork, milk; major crops are sugar beets, fresh vegetables, fruits, grain, tobacco; net importer of farm products.

BELGIUM

Business Organizations: The principal forms of business organizations are limited liability companies, partnerships and branches. Corporations: Most limited liability companies are either public companies (*societes anonymes/Naamloze Vennootschap*—denoted SA/NV or private companies (*societes privees a responsabilite limitee/beolotenvennootschap met beperkte aansprak-elijkheid*—denoted SPRL/BVBA). Limited liability companies may also take the form of a "cooperative company" (SC/SV). Other Forms of Incorporation: the SPRL/BVBA is the most widely used of the other corporate forms. In general, the same formation requirements apply to SPRL/BVBA as to SA/NVs. the minimum paid-in capital is *BF* 750.000. Additional forms may include simple partnerships, partnerships limited by shares and "cooperative companies." Licensing and Franchising: there are no specific franchising laws.

Taxes

Corporate Taxes: The basic corporate tax rate is 38 percent. The following tax rates are applicable to taxable revenue which do not exceed *BF* 14.8 million:

• Up to *BF* 1.0 million—28 percent. This rate applies to revenue up to *BF* 2.0 million (non-distributed).

• Between *BF* 1.0 million and 3.6 million—36 percent

• Between *BF* 3.6 million and 14.8 million—41 percent

Personal Income Taxes: The maximum personal income tax is 55 percent and is reached for income above *BF* 2.4 million.

Other Taxes: A value-added tax (VAT) is charged on the sale of all goods and services at the standard rate of 19.5 percent. A reduced rate of six percent is applied to basic necessities, with an interim rate of 12%.

Useful Contacts

Check for a Belgian embassy, chamber of commerce or trade development agency in your country.

• **The American Chamber of Commerce in Belgium**:
  Avenue des Arts 50, Bte 5, B-1040 Brussels, Belgium
  Tel: (32 2) 513 67 70/9 Fax: (32 2) 513 79 28

• **The National Investment Corporation** is an autonomous state-owned operation which aids in the establishment of new companies, provides venture capital for private investment and serves to rehabilitate lagging industries in Belgium.

CZECH REPUBLIC

Business Opportunities: The Government of the Czech and Slovak Federal Republic has committed itself to building a western-style market economy, and an integral part of the government's economic reform program is privatization and the solicitation of foreign investment and capital. The Privatization Act and other legislation has made it possible for foreign investors to circumvent the traditional administrative, regulatory and legal restrictions. Investment projects generally must be cleared by the governments of the two republics, rather than by the federal government. Investment in "green" projects requires no government approvals, except the regular requirements to establish a business in the country.

In order to do business in the CSFR, international business executives must seek approval from the Federal Ministry of Finance, the Czech or Slovak Ministry of Finance, Prices and Wages, and (if the proposed venture will engage in foreign trade activities) the Federal Ministry of Foreign Trade. The Federal Ministry of Finance requires a minimum investment of Kcs 100,000 for a foreign joint venture, with at least 30 percent of the initial capital investment (a minimum of Kcs 50,000) deposited with a local bank. If the proposed venture meets the following conditions, ministerial approval is waived:

- The company is 100 percent foreign owned and operated;

- The venture does not deal with banking or commercial finance services;

- One of the partners to the joint venture is considered to be a "natural person" rather than a legal entity; and

- The local partner is a cooperative founded after July 1, 1988

Restrictions on Foreign Investment: U.S. companies can invest in domestic companies either through a privatization venture or by purchasing shares in a company already privately owned. The new commercial code of January, 1992 provides a framework for business entities and contracts. Government approval of most foreign investment will no longer be required, except for direct sale of government equity under privatization. In addition, 25 percent of major banks may be foreign-owned, but no more than 10 percent of the bank may be owned by a single investor. Foreign investment in insurance companies is limited to 45 percent of the property, capital and equity. Tax holidays for joint ventures have been removed.

Investment Incentives: Fewer incentives for investment exist in the CSFR than in most other East European countries. However, the U.S. granted permanent most-favored-nation (MFN) status to Czechoslovakia in 1992.

Exports: $12.6 billion. Commodities: manufactured goods, machinery and transport equipment, chemicals, fuels, minerals and metals. Partners: Germany, Slovakia, Poland, Austria, Hungary, Italy, France, U.S., UK, CIS republics

Imports: $12.4 billion. Commodities: machinery and transport equipment, fuels and lubricants, manufactured goods, raw materials, chemicals, agricultural products. Partners: Slovakia, CIS republics, Germany, Austria, Poland, Switzerland, Hungary, UK, Italy

Industries: fuels, ferrous metallurgy, machinery and equipment, coal, motor vehicles, glass, arms & armaments

Agriculture: largely self-sufficient. Diversified crop and livestock production, including grains, potatoes, sugar beets, hops, fruit, hogs, cattle and poultry; exporter of forest products

CZECH REPUBLIC

Business Organizations: joint stock companies, limited liability companies, general commercial partnerships, partnerships with corporate sponsors, limited commercial partnerships, partnerships limited by shares, silent partnerships, consortia, associations, representative offices, and sole proprietorships. Joint Stock Companies (*akciova spolecnost*—denoted AS): capital stock must be at Kcs 1 million and at least 30 percent of this subscribed cash amount must be paid-in upon incorporation. Limited Liability Company (*spolecnost srucenim omezenyn*—denoted SSRO): this type of company combines certain elements of the joint stock company and the partnership, but is not regulated as is the AS. The SSRO exists independently of its members, who are not liable for the debts or obligations of the company. Partnerships: There is a variety of different partnership arrangements available for foreign businesses.

Taxes

Corporate Taxes: A flat tax rate of 45 percent for all companies. The individual republics may levy an additional tax of up to five percent. The general payroll tax rate is 50 percent, although some service-oriented organizations pay a reduced rate of 20 percent.

Personal Income Taxes: are levied on individuals for all sources of income outside of employment. Presently, a revised federal income tax structure is being formulated. The Czech and Slovak republics however, retain the right to charge an additional tax of up to five percent.

Other Taxes: a value-added tax (VAT) rates are broken down as follows: zero percent for all exports, five percent for basic foodstuffs, fuels, oil, minerals and other necessities; 23 percent on most products and services such as catering, tourism, and maintenance. Postal charges, broadcasting, education, medical services and products, financial services, lotteries, and business sales are exempt from the VAT.

Useful Contacts

Check for a Czech embassy, chamber of commerce or trade development agency in your country.

•**U.S. Embassy in the CSFR:** Trziste 15, 125 48 Prague Tel: (42 2) 536641/9

•**American Chamber of Commerce:** Karlovo Namesti 24, 129 89 Prague 2, Czech Republic
  Tel: (42 2) 299-887 Fax: (42 2) 291-481

FRANCE

Business Opportunities: The French government welcomes foreign investment in France, particularly when it creates new jobs, involves a transfer of technology and training, increases export capacity, or is located in under developed areas. The government does not require (but does encourage) French participation in investment enterprises. Investments in state-owned industries, such as broadcasting and petroleum extraction are prohibited, while investment in other "sensitive" industries (*e.g.,* aerospace and banking) requires special authorization.

The following summarizes several specific provisions applicable to foreign investment in France:

- All proposals for investment by foreign parties must be submitted to the Ministry of Finance which is required to register any objections to the investment within two months. If the Ministry fails to disapprove of the proposal within a two-month period, the proposal will be deemed acceptable.

- Foreign enterprises may purchase up to 20 percent of the capital of a publicly-listed French company without having such purchase be considered a direct investment, and thus subject to applicable restrictions.

- Under the Treaty, American investors may acquire any interest in real or personal property of any kind (except ships), and are entirely free to dispose of such property interests.

- French enterprises owned or controlled in whole or in part by American nationals or enterprises are subject to no French management or ownership obligations.

Incentives: France is divided into four investment zones with varying degrees of incentive priority for each zone. Investments in Zone A receive the highest priority. This zone includes the majority of western, central, and southwestern France, as well as Corsica and certain sections of the northeast. The number of incentives decreases incrementally until Zone D, containing the Paris region and Lyon, where very few, if any, incentives are offered. A variety of incentives are offered by the regions themselves and a prospective investor should compare offers from different regions. In order to receive incentives, investors must apply either to the Territorial Planning and Regional Development Agency (*Delegation l'Amenagement du Territoire et l'Action Regionale*—DATAR) or to the prefecture of the specific area in which the prospective investment is to be made.

Cash grants are a common form of investment incentive. These grants may be given either at the national level, by DATAR, or at the regional level, by local government authorities. The main grants are as follows:

- A regional development grant (*Prime d'Amenagement du Territoire*—PAT) is financed by DATAR and is available to industrial businesses which create local jobs. The amount of the grant varies, up to ƒ50,000 for each job created.

- Regional authorities award regional employment grants (*Prime Regionale l'Emploi*—PRE). The local council sets the guidelines and specific award levels for these grants.

- The Regional New Enterprise Grant (*Prime Regionale pour la Creation d'Entreprise*—PRCE) is given by regional councils and is a grant not in excess of ƒ150,000 to be used for the cost of capital equipment. Prospective grantees must be new enterprises, existing for less than 12 months before application, and must create new jobs.

FRANCE

- Agriculture-based grants (*Prime d'Orientation Agricole*) are also local grants offered to enterprises which improve the quality of agricultural and food products as well as the farming sector in general.

- Various tax holidays are also available for new enterprises:

- A new enterprise involved in commercial or industrial business, including companies with not more than 50 percent external ownership of capital, may be exempt from all income tax for its first two years, decreasing to a 75 percent level for the third year, 50 percent the fourth, and 25 percent for the fifth year.

- A two-year income tax exemption is offered to a new company which takes over a failing company.

- The government allows tax losses during a new enterprise's tax holiday to be carried forward for five years after the year in which the loss occurred.

- A plant that has been in operation for less than five years may receive immediate reimbursement for all VAT expenses from the purchase of equipment.

Various regional tax incentives are available for investors in specified areas. These include: a reduction in transfer taxes, reduction of capital gains tax from the sale of real estate holdings, the accelerated depreciation of construction costs and the reduction or exemption from taxes on local business licenses and real estate for not more than three years.

The government has designated certain regions as enterprise zones to combat especially high rates of unemployment and economic depression. The areas of Dunkerque, on the northern coast, and La Ciotat, La Seyne, and Toulon, on the Mediterranean, are currently designated as enterprise zones. A company that is created with five years of a zone's designation will be exempt from all corporate income taxes for its first 10 years of operation. There are various restrictions and qualifying factors to receive this incentive. A prospective enterprise must create at least 10 new jobs within three years and must have its French headquarters and operations within the zone. Certain fields of business may not participate in these zones or receive other government grants or low-cost loans.

Exports: $207.5 billion. Commodities: machinery and transportation eqpt., chemicals, foodstuffs, agricultural products, iron and steel products, textiles and clothing. Partners: Germany 18.6%, Italy 11.0%, Spain 11.0%, Belgium/Luxembourg 9.1%, UK 8.8.%, Netherlands 7.9%, U.S. 6.4%, Japan 2.0%, former USSR 0.7%

Imports: $250.2 billion. Commodities: crude oil, machinery and equipment, agricultural products, chemicals, iron and steel products. Partners: Germany 17.8%, Italy 10.9%, U.S. 9.5%, Netherlands 8.9%, Spain 8.8%, Belgium/Luxembourg 8.5%, UK 7.5%, Japan 4.1%, former USSR 1.3%

Industries: steel, machinery, chemicals, automobiles, metallurgy, aircraft, electronics, mining, textiles, food processing and tourism.

FRANCE

Agriculture: Accounts for 4% of GDP (including fishing and forestry); one of the world's top five wheat producers; other principal products inclue beef, dairy products, cereals, sugar beets, potatoes, wine grapes; shortages include fats, oils and tropical produce. Overall net exporter of farm products; fish catch of 850,000 metric tons ranks France among the world's top 20 seafood producers.

Business Organizations: Corporation (denoted SA): similar to a U.S. corporation, must have a minimum of seven shareholders, minimum capital of FF 250,000, and at least 25% of corporate shares must be paid-in at time of subscription with balance in five years. Payment of registration tax, publication of certain legal announcements, filling of certain documents with the commercial court and commercial Registar must be fulfilled upon formation. Limited Liability Company: (denoted SARL) The SARL must have a minimum of FF 50,000, and must have a minimum of one but not more than 50 shareholders. All shares must be subscribed to and paid-in, at time of formation. Other Forms of business organizations in France include General partnerships, Limited partnerships, and Stock partnerships.

Taxes

Corporate Taxes: Are assessed at the flat rate of 34 percent on retained earnings and 42 percent on distributed profits. All enterprises subject to corporate tax must make an advance non-refundable minimum tax payment of between FF 5,000 and 21,500 (depending upon the firm's gross income for the previous fiscal year) by March 15th of the applicable tax year. Certain enterprises may be exempted from this advance payment for the first three years of operation. Withholding: French companies are required to withhold 25 percent on all distributions made to non-resident shareholders. Under special circumstances for U.S. firms this may be further reduced.

Personal Income Taxes: French residents are taxed on their worldwide income, while non-residents are taxed only on their French-source income. Tax rates range from zero to 56.8 percent.

Other Taxes: Include a tax on real property owned by foreign companies; social security taxes; local taxes; registration taxes, and the value-added tax (VAT). The ordinary VAT tax is currently 18.6 percent, with special rates ranging from 2.1 percent for certain medications to 25 percent on automobiles.

FRANCE

Useful Contacts

Check for a French embassy, chamber of commerce or trade development agency in your country.

- **U.S. Embassy Commercial Section**, 2 Avenue Gabriel, 75382 Paris Cedex 08 France

  Tel: (33 1) 42-66-48-27

- **U.S. Consulate General** in Bordeaux, Marseilles, and Strasbourg

- **U.S. and Foreign Commercial Service** in Lyon

- **American Chamber of Commerce**, 21, Avenue George V, 75008 Paris

  Tel: (33 1) 47-23-70-28 Fax: (33 1) 47-20-18-62

GERMANY

Business Opportunities: Germany offers an attractive investment climate. Foreign firms are generally treated as equals to national firms when investing. There is no limit on the percent of equity foreigners may own, or on the size of their investment.

No license in required for any type of investment, although certain large-scale investments, and other investments that may affect national security, are precluded. Certain investments must be reported for statistical purposes. Investments are not subject to foreign-exchange controls. Profits and dividends may be freely repatriated without restrictions of any kind. Germany has a well-established system of arbitration of commercial disputes, and enforces (through it courts) arbitral awards. Germany is also a signatory to the UN Convention on Recognition and Enforcement of Foreign Arbitral Awards.

Investors should be aware of certain requirements when investing in Germany. For example, German antipollution laws are stringent. The Ministry for the Environment enforces existing laws and will soon implement decrees and laws pertaining to a 1986 water-pollution law. A series of recycling programs started with a packaging decree of 1991. These restrictions will apply to manufacturing and the impact of the legislation should be considered when investing in manufacturing (new or existing). Finally, special attention should be paid to EC environmental restrictions.

Incentives: Germany has introduced a number of incentives and other special conditions to encourage investments in eastern Germany. Substantial investment grants and tax incentives will be available for investors in eastern Germany through the end of 1993. Investors should also consider the following:

- Accelerated tax depreciation may be available in certain cases;

- In many cases municipal trade taxes in eastern Germany are not in effect until target dates; and

- The European Recovery Program (ERP) has provided credit for investments in eastern Germany if they meet relevant guidelines.

Germany will continue to offer other programs as it seeks to develop eastern Germany. Interested parties should contact the *Treuhandanstalt* (Trust Agency), which is the holding company assigned to privatize state-owned assets and firms in eastern Germany. The Treuhandanstalt has signed an agreement with the EC to computerize information, making it more readily available to foreign investors, and has an office in New York City.

Investors should recognize that certain challenges may exist with eastern German enterprises, and that Treuhandanstalt's mission to privatize businesses in eastern Germany takes the nature of tendered bids as well as the size of such bids into account. This has caused some confusion among potential investors, but it also reflects Germany's dedication to encourage serious investment and avoid speculation on properties. Characteristics of former state-owned firms include: heavily depreciated and obsolete capital stock; labor intensive production processes; environmental problems; and decline in sales revenue due to shocks of the open market.

Exports: $392 billion. Commodities: manufactures 89.0% (including machines and machine tools, chemicals, motor vehicles, iron and steel products), agricultural products 5.4%, raw materials 2.2.%, fuels 1.3%. Partners: EC 51.3 (France 11.1%, Netherlands 8.3%, Italy 8.2%, UK 7.9%, Belgium/Luxembourg 7.5%), EFTA 13.3% U.S. 6.8%, Eastern Europe 5.0%, OPEC 3.3%

GERMANY

Imports: $374.6 billion. Commodities: manufactures 74.9%, agricultural products 10.3%, fuels 7.4%, raw materials 5.5.% (1992). Partners: EC 49.7 (France 11.0%, Netherlands 9.2%, Italy 8.8%, UK 6.6%, Belgium & Luxembourg 6.7%) EFTA 12.7%, U.S. 5.9%, Japan 5.2%, Eastern Europe 4.8%, OPEC 2.6%

Industries: *western region:* among world's largest producers of iron, steel, coal, cement, chemicals, machinery, vehicles, machine tools, electronics, food and beverages; *eastern region:* metal fabrication, chemicals, brown coal, shipbuilding, machinery, food and beverages, textiles, petroleum refining

Agriculture: *western region:* accounts for 2% of GDP (including fishing and forestry); diversified crop and livestock farming (principal crops and livestock include potatoes, wheat, barley, sugar beet, fruit, cabbage, cattle, pigs and poultry); net importer of food; *eastern region:* accounts for 10% of GDP (including fishing and forestry); principal crops (wheat, rye, barley, potatoes, sugar beets, fruit), livestock products include pork, beef, chicken, milk, hides and skins; net importer of food.

Business Organizations: Corporations: principal are the *Aktiengesellschaft* (stock corporation); and the *Gesellschaft mit beschränkter Haftung* (limited liability company). Stock Corporations (AG): The stock corporation (*Aktiengesellschaft*)—denoted AG) is a legal entity whose shares are freely transferable in German stock exchanges. The corporate form is designed for large enterprises with an indefinite number of private stockholders. Limited Liability Companies (*GmbH*): Due to the flexibility offered, the closed corporation (limited liability company, *Gesellschaft mit beschränkter Haftung*—denoted *GmbH*) is particularly popular. The company may have as few as one shareholder, with a minimum capitalization of *DM*50,000. Branches and Subsidiaries: In contrast to a subsidiary, a branch is not a separate legal entity distinct from the parent company. Branches can be dependent or independent. This foreign corporation is fully liable for branch obligations. Partnerships: various types include: general commercial partnership (*offene Handelgesellschaft*—denoted OHG) and the limited commercial partnership (*Kommanditgesellschaft*—denoted KG) are roughly analogous to general and limited partnerships in the United States. The liability of partners for the debts of the partnership is determined by the nature of the partnership and the partnership agreement itself.

GERMANY

Taxes

Corporate Taxes: 36 percent on distributed profits and 50 percent on undistributed profits. Resident corporate entities are taxed on their worldwide income, however income of foreign parents is excluded. Branches of foreign corporations are taxed only on German income at a flat rate of 46 percent.

Personal Income Taxes: German residents are taxed on their worldwide income while non-residents are taxed only on German income. Based upon a progressive scale that ranges from 19 to 53 percent, minus the personal deduction.

Other Taxes: A value-added tax (VAT) is levied at 15 percent. A reduced rate of seven percent applies to specific goods such as food items, books, newspapers, and antiques. There is no special tax for luxury goods.

Additional taxes applying to commerce include a municipal trade tax ranging from 11.1 to 20 percent and an annual assets tax of 0.6 percent on 75 percent of taxable assets over *DM* 125,000.

Useful Contacts

Check for a German embassy, chamber of commerce or trade development agency in your country.

- **U.S. Embassy in Germany:** Deichmanns Alle 29, 5300 Bonn 2, Germany
  Tel: (49 228) 339-2895 Fax: (49 228) 3334-649

- **American Chamber of Commerce in Germany:** Roßmarkt 12,
  Postfach 100 162, D-60311 Frankfurt am Main 1, Germany
  Tel: 49-69-929-1040 Fax: 49-69-929-10411

- **American Chamber of Commerce in Germany—Berlin**, Budapesterstraße 29, D-10787 Berlin, Germany
  Tel: 49-30-261-55-86 Fax: 49-30-262-26-00

ITALY

Business Incentives: Italy's investment incentive programs correspond with massive capital and employment needs, or with newer, high-priority industries in markets where import substitution is desired. Investment incentives include a 10-year total exemption from corporate income tax (for companies formed for undertaking new industrial initiatives in the Mezzogiorno region), low interest loans, capital grants, and rebates on social security payments.

Other benefits are available from regional authorities and from national transportation agencies on shipment by rail and sea to incentives areas. In addition, government purchasing preferences for firms located in underdeveloped areas in Southern Italy have been established.

Exports: $178.2 billion. Commodities: metals, textiles and clothing, production machinery, motor vehicles, transportation equipment, chemicals, other. Partners: EC 58.3%, OPEC 6.1%, U.S. 5.5%

Imports: $188.5 billion. Commodities: industrial machinery, chemicals, transport equipment, petroleum, metals, food and agricultural products. Partners: EC 58.8%, OPEC 6.1%, U.S. 5.5%

Industries: machinery, iron and steel, chemicals, food processing, textiles, motor vehicles, clothing, footwear, ceramics

Agriculture: accounts for 4% of GDP and about 9.8% of the work force; self-sufficient in foods other than meat, dairy products, and cereals. Principal crops: fruits, vegetables, grapes, potatoes, sugar beets, soybeans, grain and olives; fish catch of 525,000 metric tons in 1990

Business Organizations: Apart from sole proprietorships, the forms of independent business entities may be grouped into two general categories: partnerships and joint-stock corporations. Three types of business relationships are also of interest: branches of foreign corporations, joint ventures and agencies and distributorship. The three types of partnerships authorized are as follows: unlimited partnerships (*societa innome collecttivo*); limited partnerships (*societa in accomandita semplice*); and limited partnerships with shares (*societa in accomandita per azioni*). There are two types of Italian joint-stock corporations: limited liability companies (*societa a resonsabilita limitata*—denoted SRL), and corporations (*societa per azioi*, denoted SpA).

ITALY

Taxes

Corporate Taxes: Subject to local income tax (ILOR) at 16.2 percent and corporate income tax (IRPEG) at 36 percent. Since 75 percent of ILOR is deductible the taxable income for IRPEG purposes, the global income rate applicable to companies is 47.8 percent. Corporate income tax is levied on the total net income. Income includes inventory valuation, dividends income, foreign source income, capital gains, assets revaluation reserve, exchange differences. Deductibles are given for depreciation and interest paid. A corporate rate of 36 percent applies to national and foreign entities alike. A 56.25 percent tax is applied to dividends.

Personal Income Taxes: Residents are taxed on income from all sources; non-residents are taxed only on Italian-source income. Italy employs a progressive tax scheme with rates ranging from 10 to 50 percent. Taxable income includes salary and capital gains. Withholding provisions are subject to different circumstances.

Other Taxes: Italy levies a number of indirect taxes, including stamp taxes, mortgage taxes, inheritance taxes and government concession taxes. From time to time, "one time" taxes are levied on property ownership, bank deposits and capital investments.

Useful Contacts

Check for a Italian embassy, chamber of commerce or trade development agency in your country.

- **U.S. Embassy in Italy,** Via Veneto 119A, 00187-Rome, Italy
  Tel: (39 6) 46741 Fax: (39 6) 46742

- **American Chamber of Commerce in Italy**, Via Cantu 1, 20123 Milan, Italy
  Tel: (39 2) 86-90661 Fax: (39 2) 80-57737

NETHERLANDS

Business Opportunities: The Dutch government actively promotes direct investment and economic policies provide a wide range of tax and non-tax incentives to encourage investors. With the exception of certain public-sector activities (military production, aviation, shipping, telecommunications and postal services, distribution of electricity, gas, and water; railways, radio and TV broadcasting and public bus transport), foreign firms are able to invest in any sector.

Incentives: A broad range of subsidies, premiums, guarantees, and tax holidays are offered by the government to promote trade and investment in the Netherlands. Numerous incentives are available in the form of cash grants, low-interest loans, government capital participation, and export guarantees. The Dutch Investment Premium Regulations offers a variety of incentives for the development of businesses in the Northern provinces of the Netherlands. Tax breaks are provided on a case-by-case basis and should be discussed with the local Dutch authorities. Other incentives exist for investments bringing new technology to the Netherlands.

Exports: $139 billion. Commodities: metal products, chemicals, processed food and tobacco, agricultural products. Partners: EC 77% (Germany 27%, Belgium/Luxembourg 15%, UK 10%), U.S. 4%

Imports: $130.3 billion. Commodities: raw materials and semi-finished products, consumer goods, transportation equipment, crude oil and food products. Partners: EC 64% (Germany 26%, Belgium/Luxembourg 14%, UK 8%), U.S. 8%

Industries: agro-industries, metal and engineering products, electrical machinery and equipment, chemicals, petroleum, fishing, construction, microelectronics

Agriculture: accounts for 4.6% of GDP; animal production predominates; crops (grains, potatoes, sugar beets, fruits, vegetables); shortages of grain, fats, and oils**Travel in the Netherlands:** Tourist Arrivals: 5,843,000. Tourist Receipts: $3,074,000,000. Tourist attractions: Amsterdam (Anne Frank house, canals, Van Gogh Museum, Rijksmuseum, Historical Museum, Keukenhof Gardens); The Hague (Music and Ballet festival, Madurodam miniature village); Rotterdam (cruises, Euromast panorama), scenic countryside, windmills.

Business Organizations: Corporations are distinguished between two forms, the *naamloze vennootschap* (NV), and the *besloten vennootschap met beperkte aansprakelijkheid* (BV). The main difference between the NV and BV relate to capital structure and share transferability. For example, the minimum issued and paid-up capital for NV is *Hfl* 100,000, and for the BV is *Hfl* 40,000. In addition, NV shares are freely transferrable, while BV's articles of association must contain certain restrictions on transferability. Partnerships are recognized as both general and limited. These forms of business organization are regulated under the *Dutch Commercial Code*.

NETHERLANDS

Taxes

Corporate Taxes: Both resident and non-resident corporations are subject to the same tax rules. The corporate tax rate is 40 percent on the first *Hfl*250,000 in taxable income and 35 percent on amounts over that sum. The Dutch corporate rate is among the lowest in the EC, second only to the United Kingdom.

Personal Income Taxes: For residents are on worldwide income, levied on a progressive scale up to 60 percent. Non-residents are only subject to tax on Dutch-source income. Currently, expatriates temporarily working in the country may deduct 35 percent of their Dutch-source employment income from their taxable income.

Other Taxes: Include : a transfer tax on real (*i.e.,* immovable) property, insurance tax, capital tax, and stock exchange tax. The six percent transfer tax is levied on acquisition of immovable property situated in the Netherlands. The capital tax of one percent is levied on the issuing of share capital by corporate bodies. Value-added Tax (VAT) is six percent on basic necessities such as food, medicine, and transportation goods. Most goods are subject to the 18.5 percent general rate.

Useful Contacts

Check for a Dutch embassy, chamber of commerce or trade development agency in your country.

- **U.S. Embassy in the Netherlands**, Lange Voorhuut 102, The Hague, Netherlands
  Tel: (31 70) 310-9417 Fax: (31 70) 263-2985

- **U.S. Consulate in Amsterdam**, Museaumplein 19, Amsterdam, Netherlands
  Tel: (31 20) 664-8111 Fax: (31 20) 675-2856

- **The American Chamber of Commerce in the Netherlands**,
  Van Karnebeklaan, 14, 2585 BB The Hague, The Netherlands
  Tel: (31 70) 365-9808 Fax: (31 70) 364-6992

NORWAY

Business Opportunities: The Government of Norway is generally supportive of foreign private investment, particularly in three major areas: the petroleum industry, high-technology projects, and projects in remotely-populated regions.

The following rules currently apply to foreign investment in Norway:

- A company is considered foreign if a foreigner is a member of the board of directors and if more than 20 percent of its share capital is held by foreigners.

- Concessions related to industrial activity are granted by the Ministry of Industry, and by the Ministry of Agriculture for agricultural projects.

- No prior approval is necessary for investing in the share of capital of a wholly-owned subsidiary.

- The government permits 100 percent foreign ownership of investments.

- No registration is required for license, royalty, and technology agreements.

Foreign Investment is restricted under the following circumstances:

- Foreign as well as domestic investors are prohibited from directly investing in public sector industries (postal services, railways, broadcasting, production of alcohol and drugs). Furthermore, foreign investors are restricted from owning or controlling natural resources.

- International executives are not generally allowed to own more than 10 percent equity in Norwegian financial/leasing companies. In special cases, they may own up to 25 percent with government approval.

- Foreign companies are required to obtain special approval for the purchase of certain types of real estate. However, it is not necessary to obtain concessions to rent real estate, provided the contract does not exceed 10 years.

- Foreign investors must obtain approval to acquire more than one-third of the voting shares in listed Norwegian companies.

The Government of Norway has established a liberal repatriation policy. Dividends, profits from business activities in Norway, interest and contractual amortization on loans, and repatriation of invested capital are freely and fully remittable. Ordinary payments from within Norway to foreign entities are not subject to significant restrictions, provided they are made through a Norwegian commercial bank. In contrast, some transfers of capital into Norway require foreign exchange licenses.

Incentives: Norway generally encourages all investments that will stimulate growth and development. No national investment incentive scheme exists (although some local agencies offer grants). The government also supports the growth of export-oriented industries with non-tax incentives such as loans at favorable rates and direct assistance for penetrating foreign markets.

A reduced payroll tax schedule is applied to businesses operating in less populated regions of Norway. For businesses operating in the northernmost part of Norway, the reduction can be as high as 16.7 percent. Foreign personnel who intend to work in Norway for less than 4 years are entitled to a 15 percent standard reduction on their income tax.

NORWAY

Exports: $32.1 billion. Commodities: petroleum and petroleum products 40%, metals and products 10.6%, fish and fish products 6.9%, chemicals 6.4%, natural gas 6.0%, ships 5.4%. Partners: EC 66.3%, Nordic countries 16.3%, developing countries 8.4%, U.S. 6.9%, Japan 1.8%

Imports: $24.8 billion. Commodities: machinery and equipment 38.9%, chemicals and other industrial inputs 26.6%, manufactured consumer goods 17.8%, foodstuffs 6.4%. Partners: EC 48.6%, Nordic countries 25.1%, developing countries 9.6%, U.S. 8.1%, Japan 8.0%

Industries: petroleum and gas, food processing, shipbuilding, pulp and paper products, metals, chemicals, timber, mining, textiles and fishing

Agriculture: accounts for 3% of the GDP and about 6% of the labor force; among world's top 10 fishing nations; livestock output exceeds value of crops; over half of food needs are imported; fish catch of 1.76 million metric tons

Business Organizations: For Foreign corporations operating in Norway, the joint stock corporations and the branch are the most popular business forms. Other types of common business forms are partnerships, single proprietorships, cooperative societies and limited-stock partnerships. Foreigners may own up to 100 percent of a joint stock company and have limited liability. Franchising is growing rapidly in Norway and opportunities exist in areas such as fast food restaurants and motels. Licensing is also a common practice. The Bank of Norway approves licensing arrangements between foreign licensor and Norwegian licensees.

Taxes

Corporate Taxes: are levied at a flat rate of 50.8 percent on undistributed income. There is an investment tax of seven percent on goods acquired by enterprises, but exceptions are granted in certain areas. Dividends, interest and royalties from foreign subsidiaries are generally taxed as foreign income. Dividends paid to non-resident shareholders, excluding stock dividends, are subject to a withholding tax of 25 percent at the source. Foreign-owned firms domiciled in Norway are subject to taxes on their global incomes.

Personal Income Taxes: Persons who reside in Norway (a stay beyond six months) are subject to tax on their worldwide income and assets. Non-residents are taxed only on their Norwegian source income.

Other Taxes: is the 20 percent value-added tax (VAT) on domestic and imported goods. The VAT is assessed as a percentage of the value added at each sales transaction along the production and distribution chain. On imported goods, the VAT is payable to Norwegian custom at the time of entry. There are also levies of excise taxes on items such as alcoholic beverages, tobacco, chocolate, cosmetics, electric power, mineral oil, gasoline and motor vehicles. Also, certain document are subject to a stamp tax.

NORWAY

Useful Contacts

Check for a Norwegian embassy, chamber of commerce or trade development agency in your country.

- **U.S. Embassy of Norway**, Drammensveien 18, N-0244, Oslo, Norway
  Tel: (47) 2-44-85-50 Fax: (47) 2-55-88-03

- **Oslo Chamber of Commerce**, Drammensveien 30, N-0225, Oslo, Norway
  Tel: (47) 2-56-36-20

- **Federation of Norwegian Importers and Distributors,**
  Norge Grossistforbund, Drammensveien 30, Oslo, Norway
  Tel: (47) 2-56-73-90

POLAND

Business Opportunities: As part of the government's economic development privatization programs, restrictions on foreign investment have been relaxed to attract new investment to Poland. Firms are still restricted from ownership of certain strategic industries including seaports and airports, real estate, defense industries, legal services, and wholesale trade of imported consumer goods. Permits to conduct economic activity are needed for activities in operation of harbors, airports, real estate brokerages or legal service providers.

Incentives: As part of its incentive program, the Government of Poland has established investment laws which allow for tax holidays, repatriation of profit shares, and guarantees against expropriation of profits, investment, or capital equipment.

Special incentives and liberal tax holidays are available for corporations which increase Polish export potential, introduce new technologies, or invest in areas with high structural unemployment.

Ethnic divisions: Polish 97.6%, Germans 1.3%, Ukrainian 0.6%, Byelorussian 0.5%

Exports: $13.5 billion. Commodities: machinery 24%, metals 17%, chemicals 12%, fuels and oil 11%, food 10%. Partners: Germany 32.4%, Netherlands 6.0%, Italy 5.6%, Russia 5.5%

Imports: $15.6 billion. Commodities: fuels and power 17%, machinery 36%, chemicals 17%, food 8% (1992). Partners: Germany 23.9%, Russia 8.5%, Italy 6.9%, UK 6.7%

Industries: machine building, iron and steel, extractive industries, chemicals, shipbuilding, food processing, glass, beverages and textiles

Agriculture: accounts for 7% of GDP and a much larger share of labor force; 75% of output from private farms, 25% from state farms; productivity remains low by European standards; leading European producer of rye, rapeseed, and potatoes; wide variety of other crops and livestock; major exporter of pork products; normally self-sufficient in food

Business Organizations: Corporations exist in two forms; the joint stock company or the company with limited liability. Application must be made to the Polish government and requires an application for deed notarization and submission of all articles of incorporation, the company's registration certificate, power of attorney for a representative in Poland, and a board of director's resolution concerning the establishment of the company. Final application and registration for incorporation must be made to a Registration Court. In addition, companies must register with the Statistics and Tax Registry offices. Minimum capitalization for joint stock companies is *ZL* (*Zloty*) 1 billion; for limited liability companies, the minimum allocation is *ZL* 40 million.

POLAND

Taxes

Corporate Taxes: is levied at a flat rate of 40 percent of total taxable income. Branches of foreign corporations are liable to corporate income tax laws. Under some special conditions, joint venture companies may be exempted from corporate income tax liability. Currently a company must pay 20 percent in taxes on wages paid to Polish workers. Additionally, companies must pay 45 percent of gross wages of both U.S. and Polish employees to unemployment insurance and two percent to the Polish Social Security Fund. Personal Income Taxes: Residents of Poland are taxed on their worldwide income while non-residents are taxed only on Polish income. For non-residents, income derived from intellectual property rights, commission fees, salary remuneration, independent and consulting or production fees are taxed 20 percent unless a bilateral tax treaty on double taxation between Poland and the individual's country of residence exists (the United States and Poland have signed such an agreement.)

Other Taxes: Value-added taxes (VAT) was submitted to Parliament for a 22 percent VAT for most items. Select articles, *e.g.* food, would be taxed at seven percent.

Useful Contacts

Check for a Polish embassy, chamber of commerce or trade development agency in your country.

- **U.S. Trade Development Center**, Ulica Wiejska 20, Warsaw 00-490
  Tel: (48 22) 214 515 Fax: (48 22) 216 327

- **Ministry of Finance**, 00-916, ul. Wietokrzyska 12, Warsaw, Poland
  Tel: (48 22) 30-03-11

- **Foreign Investors Chamber of Industry and Commerce,**
  47/51 Krakowski Prezedmiescie Str., 00-071 Warsaw, Poland
  Tel: (48 22) 26-85-93

- **American Chamber of Commerce in Poland,**
  Plac Powstancow Warszawy 1, 00-950 Warsaw, Poland
  Tel: (48 22) 26-39-60 Fax: (48 22) 26-51-31

RUSSIA

Business Opportunities: The Russian Federation encourages foreign investment and is actively seeking foreign investors to participate in the privatization of state assets. In 1991, the Government of the Russian Federation embarked on a three-year privatization program, the goal of which is to liquidate 70 percent of state property over the next decade. This program began in early 1992 with the sale of smaller stores and restaurants. In January 1992, Russia announced that foreign investors would be permitted to buy shares in privatized Russian enterprises, and would be given the opportunity to acquire full ownership in certain "failing" Russian firms. New lease provisions allow foreign investors to obtain leases for up to 99 years.

Restrictions: There are some areas of privatization which are closed to foreign participation. These areas include: large companies and insurance and intermediary ventures, as well as companies dealing with securities.

Incentives: In the past, Russian enterprises in the business of producing goods (as opposed to extraction) with foreign participation in excess of 30 percent could receive a two-year tax holiday. However, the government eliminated this incentive when it reduced corporate income tax rates in early 1992. Qualifying enterprises are still permitted to carry forward losses for up to five years and deduct any spending for environmental protection.

Commercial Policies: Free-Trade Zones: A series of free-trade areas have been authorized throughout the country. These areas will permit duty-free imports for most goods.

Exchange Controls: The Central Bank of the Russian Federation (cooperating with the central bank of other former Soviet republics which are participating in the "Ruble Zone") controls the monetary policy of the Russian Federation in conjunction with the Ministry of Finance. In July 1992, the government abolished the policy of maintaining several different exchange rates for the ruble. Replacing the multi-tiered set of rates is one uniform, floating exchange rate for commercial transactions.

Profits are not freely repatriable. In order to increase hard currency reserves, the government has declared that Russian companies must surrender 50 percent of their hard currency revenues to the government. (Enterprises with 30 percent or more foreign ownership are exempt from these requirements.) The Russian government is expected to raise the hard currency surrender rate from 50 percent to 100 percent.

Exports: $43 billion Commodities: Petroleum and petroleum products, natural gas, wood and wood products, metals, chemicals, and a wide variety of civilian and military manufactures. Partners Europe, North America, Japan, Third World countries, Cuba.

Imports: $27 billion. Commodities: Machinery and equipment, chemicals, consumer goods, grain, meat, sugar, semi-finished metal products. Partners: Europe, North America, Japan, Third World countries, Cuba

Industries: Complete range of mining and extractive industries producing coal, oil, gas, chemicals and metals; all forms of machine building from rolling mills to high-performance aircraft and space vehicles; ship-building; road and rail transportation equipment; agricultural machinery, tractors, and construction equipment; electric power generating and transmitting equipment; medical and scientific instruments; consumer durables.

RUSSIA

Agriculture: Grain, sugar beet, sunflower seeds, meat, milk, vegetables, fruits; because of its northern location does not grow citrus, cotton, tea, and other warm climate products.

Business Organizations: Since the recent market reform package introduced by the Russian government legalized wholly-owned subsidiaries, they have gradually begun to replace joint ventures as the main form of direct foreign investment. All enterprises must register with the Russian Ministry of Finance. Foreign investment over *RR*100 million must receive approval from the Russian Council of Ministers before beginning operations.

Taxes

Corporate Taxes: The Government of the Russian Federation passed a new corporate income tax law in January 1992 which significantly altered the existing tax rate structure. The new law effectively cuts the standard income tax rate for most entities (including foreign-owned enterprises) from 32 percent to 18 percent. Income generated from consulting and auditing services is taxed at 25 percent. Income from exchange services, brokerage offices and other similar financial operations is taxed at 45 percent. The law does not provide for tax holidays. Only companies with 200 or fewer employees can continue to benefit from tax holidays granted before the new legislation was passed.

Personal Income Taxes: The Russian government passed legislation on personal income taxes in December 1991. This law obligates Russian and foreign citizens to pay tax on all income accrued throughout the calendar year. Non-residents are taxed only on income received from Russian sources.

Other Taxes: A Value-Added Tax (VAT) is applicable to any Russian or foreign legal entities operating in Russia that are engaged in commercial activities. All goods which are produced or sold in Russia, as well as services rendered, are subject to the VAT. Exports, however, are exempt. Since the VAT on the purchase of fixed assets is not creditable, the actual VAT rate is somewhat higher than the original rate of 28 percent. The VAT rate is scheduled to be reduced to 20 percent in 1993.

RUSSIA

Useful Contacts

• U.S. Embassy in Russia, Ulitsa Chaykovskogo 19/21/23, Moscow
  Telephone: (7095) 252-2450 Facsimile: 011 (7095) 255-9965

• Union of Chambers of Commerce and Industry of the Russian Federation, Ul Mezhdunarodnaya 10, Moscow
  Telephone: 206-7364 Facsimile: 278-7089

• Russian Chamber of Commerce and Industry, Kuibysheva St. 6, Moscow K-5 103684, Russia
  Telephone: (7095) 921-0811/2863

• Moscow Chamber of Commerce, Chekhova St. 13-17 , Moscow 103050
  Telephone: (7095) 299—7612

• St. Petersburg Chamber of Commerce, Krasny Flot Embankment 10, St. Petersburg 190000
  Telephone: 70812 314-9953

• Russian Trade Representative, 2101 Connecticut Avenue, NW, Washington, DC 20008
  Telephone: (202) 232 5988 Facsimile: (202) 232-2917

SPAIN

Business Opportunities: Royal Decree 671/1992 simplified foreign investment regulations. The number of cases requiring prior government approval was reduced by raising the value and control criteria for foreign investments.

Investment restrictions remain for investments by Non-EC Residents in "specified" sectors. These sectors are gambling, television, radio, air transport and defense-related investments (which includes strategic minerals and certain telecommunications services). Investments in these "specified" sectors are regulated by separate legislation; foreign investment in any of these sectors also requires prior authorization of the Council of Ministers.

Incentives: A combination of EC, national, regional and local level investment incentives are offered. Incentives range from grants, tax benefits, access to local financing, and duty-free imports, to facilitation of property purchases and necessary permits. National investment incentives are coordinated by the Ministry of Economic Incentives. The level of incentive is based on the type of project and the level of economic development in the geographic area in which the project will be based. Three types of regional development plans are as follows:

- Economic Promotion Zones (ZPE): These regions are areas with the lowest amount of economic activity and income.

- Zones of Industrial Decline (ZID): These regions are geographic areas affected by industrial decline.

- Special Zones (ZE): In these regions, specific national investment incentives are available for investments in steel, shipbuilding, electronics, chemicals, pharmaceuticals, and textiles. Approval is required from relevant Spanish Ministries.

Exports: $72.8 billion. Commodities: cars and trucks, semifinished manufactured goods, foodstuffs and machinery. Partners: EC 71.2%, U.S. 4.8%, other developed countries 7.9%

Imports: $92.5 billion. Commodities: machinery, transport equipment, fuels, semifinished goods, foodstuffs, consumer goods and chemicals. Partners: EC 60.7%, U.S. 7.4%, other developed countries 11.5%, Middle East 5.9%

Industries: textiles and apparel (including footwear), food and beverages, metals and metal manufactures, chemicals, shipbuilding, automobiles, machine tools and tourism

Agriculture: accounts for about 5% of GDP and 14% of the labor force; major products: grain, vegetables, olives, wine grapes, sugar beets, citrus fruit, beef, pork, poultry and dairy; largely self-sufficient in food; fish catch 1.4 million metric tons is among top 20 nations.

SPAIN

Business Organizations: Corporations (*Sociedad Anonima*—denoted SA) is the most common form of business organization in Spain. SAs need at least three investors to initially subscribe to the share capital; once established, the number of shareholders can be reduced to one. The board of directors must have at least three directors. Formation must be by public deed (*escritura publica*) before a notary. Banks, insurance companies and leasing companies must incorporate as an SA. A Limited Liability Company (*sociedad de responsabilidad limitada*—denoted SL is similar to a SA and is subject to the same general regulations. The SL is limited to no more than 50 shareholders, with the capital being divided among investors. Branch and Subsidiary are fully permitted for foreign companies to open a branch or subsidiary in Spain. Although a branch is not its own legal entity, it must register in the same manner as an SA. A subsidiary is similar to a branch, but is considered to be a "Spanish" legal entity. Subsidiaries are taxed on worldwide income, whereas a branch is taxed only on Spanish-source income. Licensing/Franchising is relatively new to the Spanish market. It follows EC franchising guidelines and the 1991 International Franchising Code of Ethics. Licensing agreements are reviewed by the General Directorate of Foreign Transactions (DGTE) in the Ministry of Economy and Commerce. Payments for licensing fees, technical assistance, consultants' fees, trademarks, patents, technology transfers, and other non-patented matters are freely transferable abroad. In most cases, such payments are subject to Spanish taxation and normally taxes will be withheld at time of payment.

Taxes

Corporate Taxes: basic corporate tax rate is 35 percent. Branch offices are subject to the same rate, but income remitted by the branch is subject to a withholding tax at a source rate of 25 percent. Taxable income is total income less deductible expenses. Non-Resident companies are liable for corporate income tax on income and capital gains sources derived in Spain at a rate of 35 percent. However, a 25 percent rate applies to dividends, interest, real estate, royalties and fees.

Personal Income Taxes: All residents, including resident aliens, are liable for Spanish income tax, which is levied on the total domestic and foreign net income and capital gains of residents. Taxable income includes salary and all types of remuneration. The general income tax rate falls between 20 and 53 percent. Very few deductions are permitted. With certain exceptions, non-residents are taxed only in Spanish-source income at the rate of 25 percent.

Other Taxes: The Spanish value-added tax (VAT) is 15 percent. A reduced rate of six percent is applied to sales and imports of human and animal foodstuffs, water, books, newspapers, magazines, pharmaceutical products, personal dwellings and school supplies. A 28 percent VAT tax is applied to sales and imports of luxury items.

SPAIN

Useful Contacts

Check for a Spanish embassy, chamber of commerce or trade development agency in your country.

- **U.S. Embassy in Spain**, Serrano 75, 28006 Madrid, Spain
  Tel: (34 1) 577-4000 Fax: (34 1) 575-8655

- **U.S. Consulate in Barcelona**, Paseo Reina Elisenda de Montcada 23, 08034 Barcelona, Spain
  Tel: (34 3) 280-2227 Fax: (34 3) 205-5206

- **The American Chamber of Commerce in Spain**, Avenida Diagonal 477, 08036 Barcelona, Spain
  Tel: (34 3) 405-1266 Fax: (34 3) 405-3124

- **American Chamber of Commerce in Spain, Madrid,**
  Hotel Euro Building, Padre Damian 23, 28036 Madrid, Spain
  Tel: (34 1) 359-6559 Fax: (34 1) 359-6520

SWEDEN

Business Opportunities: Foreign investment in Sweden is largely regulated by two pieces of legislation: *The Law on Foreign Acquisition of Swedish Firms* and *The Law on Foreign Acquisition of Real Property*. In general, Sweden is receptive to foreign direct investment, and with few exceptions, accords foreign investors the same treatment as Swedish nationals. Although the legal trend is toward the liberalization of foreign investment, Sweden does not offer special tax incentives to attract foreign capital.

The following guidelines govern foreign investment in Sweden:

- There are no restrictions on foreign ownership of Swedish corporations, and few restrictions on investing in the industrial sector.

- No prior approval is needed for investing in the share capital of a new company, for increasing the share capital, or for raising loan capital.

- The Swedish government must grant permission in order to establish a bank, an insurance company, or finance company using public funds.

Private investment is restricted in the following areas: the railroads, mail service, telecommunications, radio and television broadcasting, the production and sale of wine, beer and liquor, and the manufacture of tobacco products.

The government's policy usually does not permit foreign ownership of mineral rights, mines, farm land, and forest land. In addition, foreign ownership is not permitted or is severely restricted in air transportation, the merchant marine, manufacture of war materials, and forestry.

Incentives: Sweden offers no special tax concessions or tax holidays to attract foreign investors. However, the low level of corporate tax and a tax treaty with the United States (which allows for virtually tax-free repatriation of profits) serves to encourage U.S. investors. Liberal depreciation and deduction allowance on taxes also encourage foreign investment in Sweden.

As for non-tax incentives, despite a trend to cut government support to industry, Sweden actively appropriates resources for retraining labor, training immigrants, and for research into new products and processes. To a limited extent, incentives are also available for tourism ventures. Their general aim is to encourage innovation and structural adjustment in targeted depressed areas. There are no industry-specific incentives.

Export credits and guarantees are available from the National Industrial Board, and several regional development funds offer significant incentives to firms locating in targeted development areas. These incentives are in the form of grants and loans for financing new buildings and equipment, training, and personnel. In addition, payroll taxes are reduced from four to two percent for companies that invest in the development or support areas. Foreign-owned companies enjoy the same access as Swedish-owned enterprises to the country's credit sources and government-sponsored incentives to business.

Exports: $49.7 billion. Commodities: Machinery, motor vehicles, paper products, pulp and wood, iron and steel products, chemicals, petroleum and petroleum products. Partners: EC 55.8% (Germany 15%, UK 9.7%, Denmark 7.2%, France 5.8%), EFTA 17.4% (Norway 8.4%, Finland 5.1%), U.S. 8.2%, Central and Eastern Europe 2.5%

SWEDEN

Imports: $42.3 billion. Commodities: Machinery, petroleum and petroleum products, chemicals, motor vehicles, foodstuffs, iron and steel, clothing Partners: EC 53.6% (Germany 17.9%, UK 6.3%, Denmark 7/5%, France 4.9%) EFTA (Norway 6.6%, Finland 6.0%), U.S. 8.4%, Central and Eastern Europe 3%

Industries: Iron and Steel, precision equipment (bearings, radio and telephone parts, armaments), wood pulp and paper products, processed foods, motor vehicles

Agriculture: Animal husbandry predominates, with milk and dairy products accounting for 37% of farm income; main crops-grains, sugar beets, potatoes; Sweden is about 50% self-sufficient in most products; farming accounted for 1.2 of GDP and 1.9% of jobs in 1990.

Taxes

Corporate Taxes: Limited liability companies and branches of foreign corporations are taxed at the same 30 percent corporate tax rate. The Swedish corporate income tax presently includes liberal rules for depreciation of machinery and equipment. The taxpayer may select the 20 percent straight-line method or the 25 percent declining-balance method of computing depreciation. The cost of assets with a service life of less than three years may be written off immediately. Depreciation of factories and office buildings is on a straight-line basis, usually around three percent each year. No withholding taxes exist on the transfer of profits from a branch to its head office, interest payments, management fees, and service fees. However, dividends transferred from subsidiaries to parent corporations are subject to a withholding tax that may be lower if a tax treaty is in effect. Dividends paid to non-residents are subject to a 30 percent withholding tax, unless a treaty is in effect.

Other Taxes: The most important indirect tax is the Value-Added Tax (VAT). It is levied at a rate of 25 percent on most goods and services, and 18 percent on restaurant meals and tourism services. It applies to both domestic transactions and imported goods and services. Although exports from Sweden are not subject to the VAT, the VAT applies to almost all goods and services, with just a few exceptions. Of great importance to U.S. exporters of machinery and equipment is that all capital equipment enjoys virtual exemption from the VAT.

Useful Contacts

• American Chamber of Commerce in Sweden, Box 5512, 114 85 Stockholm, Sweden
   Tel: 46-08-783-5300 Facsimile: 46-08-662-88-84

• U.S. Embassy in Sweden, Strandvagen 101, S-115 27 Stockholm, Sweden
   Tel: (468) 783-5300

• U. S. Consul General in Goteborg, Sodra Hamngatan 2, S-411 04 Goteborg
   Tel: 46 31 100590 Telex: 21954 AQMCONS

SWITZERLAND

Business Opportunities: When dealing with Swiss authorities, foreign investors must be sure to differentiate between federal and canton law and must make allowances for both. Although the federal government allows foreign investment, it does maintain several laws and practices which hinder some forms of investment and foreign enterprise. For example, Swiss law restricts foreign ownership of real estate or trade/sale of Swiss real estate by non-residents. Furthermore, there are restrictions on work permits for foreign residents in Switzerland. To determine whether canton laws apply, investors should contact the individual canton or the Department of Economic Affairs.

Incentives: Investment incentives in Switzerland are based on a scheme of regional development policies. The federal government does not offer any incentives for investment, although it may support different regional development policies which increase employment or secure existing jobs. Tax relief for foreign investors can be granted only by the relevant canton.

Many cantons also encourage the formation of Swiss-based export businesses through relief or full exemption from taxation. This is done primarily for business which conduct most of their operations outside of Switzerland, or act as a holding company. In these cases, non-tax incentives may also be offered, including cash grants, loan guarantees, or salary supplements.

Exports: $63 billion. Commodities: machinery and equipment, chemicals, watches, metal products, precision instruments, textiles and clothing. Partners: Western Europe 63.1% (EC countries 56%, other 7.1%), U.S. 8.8%, Japan 3.4%

Imports: $60.7 billion. Commodities: machinery and transportation equipment, chemicals, textiles, vehicles, precision instruments, construction materials agricultural products. Partners: Western Europe 79.2% (EC countries 72.3%, other 6.9%), U.S. 6.4%

Industries: machinery, chemicals, watches, textiles, precision instruments

Agriculture: dairy farming predominates; less than 50% self-sufficient in food; must import fish, refined sugar, fats and oils (other than butter), grains, eggs, fruits, vegetables and meat.

Business Organizations: Stock Corporations (*societe ananyme* or a *Aktiengesellschaft*) must be formed by a minimum of three different shareholders, although post-formation procedures allow full stock control to be held by one individual. The corporation must be registered with the Registrar of Commerce in the canton (province) of residence, and the initial capital must be deposited in an accredited bank in the same canton. The minimum initial subscribed capital for a corporation is *SFr* 50,000. The majority of directors must be Swiss nationals residing in Switzerland as well as shareholders. Limited Liability Companies (SARL or *GmbH*) is similar to the stock corporation in structure and formation. However, a limited liability company can be formed with a minimum of two shareholders and maximum capital held by the firm is *SFr* 2 million. Because of this limitation, the limited liability company loses some of its appeal for foreign investors. Partnerships may be of limited, joint-venture and cooperative society format. Generally, the formal partnership must be registered in the Registrar of Commerce, but reporting and accounting are done for the individual partners and need not be reported to the state (except in the case of the cooperative society). In most partnerships, the full partners are liable for losses and debts owed by the corporation. Branches of foreign corporations must be registered in the individual canton in which they are located and are subject to corporate taxes. Branches must be able to act and make decisions independently of the foreign parent corporation.

SWITZERLAND

Taxes

Corporate Taxes: Federal income taxes on corporations are based on a ratio of net profit and worth and range from 3.63 percent to 9.8 percent. In addition, individual cantons levy communal and cantonal taxes, which are the major corporate taxes in Switzerland, so that income tax rates vary from 22 to 35 percent on pre-profit tax depending on the company's level of profit and canton of residence and operation. Taxable income from profits is determined by total worldwide income of the business, including royalties, dividends, rent, and interest received. Capital gains are considered income and are subject to federal income tax as well as tax in many cantons.

Personal Income Taxes: Tax must be filed annually (or every two years) and employed individuals must enclose official employer certification and statement of wages, salary, tips, and benefits (including living arrangements which are based on employment contract). Individuals who live in, or are employed or self-employed in, Switzerland for over six months are taxed as residents. Non-residents are taxed only on their Swiss income and assets, although procedures for deduction are independent on the tax treaty between Switzerland and foreign national's country of residence.

Other Taxes: In 1995 a value added tax (VAT) replaced the sales tax. Stamp Taxes are levied on the issue of stock in corporations or mutual funds as well as on the profit sharing declarations earned on Swiss corporations. The stamp tax is 2.9% for mutual funds and three percent for all other taxable categories. A nominal stamp tax is also assessed on the transfer of securities of foreign and Swiss corporations and is payable to the broker at the rate of 0.15 percent for Swiss securities and 0.3 percent for securities from foreign issuance or issuer.

Useful Contacts

Check for a Swiss embassy, chamber of commerce or trade development agency in your country.

• **U.S. Embassy in Switzerland**, Jubiläumstraße 93, 3005 Bern, Tel: (41 31) 43 7011

• **U.S. Consulate General**, Botanic Building, 1-3 Ave. De la Paix, 1202 Geneva
  Tel: (41 22) 738 7613

• **Swiss American Chamber of Commerce**, Talacker 41, 8001 Zurich, Switzerland
  Tel: 41-1-211-24-54 Fax: 41-1-211-95-72

UKRAINE

Business Opportunities: The Ukrainian government is relying on foreign investment to assist in the country's transformation into a market economy. Foreign capital is particularly important as the state-controlled industries are undergoing privatization. The parliament has passed a series of measures which are designed to encourage and protect foreign investment. For example:

- Foreign investors have the right to be compensated for losses, including lost opportunities resulting from actions or omissions on the part of governing bodies.

- Foreign investments in Ukraine are not subject to nationalization. Government bodies can not expropriate foreign investments except in emergency measures such as natural disasters and only the Cabinet of Ministers may authorize expropriations under these circumstances.

- In the event of suspension or termination of investment activity, foreign investors have the right to recoup their investment in the form of money or commodities within six months of the date of termination.

The foreign investment law provides liberal tax holidays, exemptions from import and export taxes, security clauses and many other investment incentives.

The provisions for compensation, guarantees, and repatriation will be limited until the Ukraine's currency become convertible. Another area of concern is Ukraine's underdeveloped judicial system which currently makes contracts, regulations and laws difficult to enforce. In any case, U.S. investors should consult with the growing number of U.S. law firms operating in Ukraine.

Incentives: In 1992 the parliament passed a package of tax incentives to encourage foreign investment. These incentives include the following:

- Entities establishing joint ventures with foreign participation of at least US$ 100,000 (or more than 20 percent of founding capital) are entitled to a five-year tax holiday, followed by an additional period of reduced tax rates. Such businesses are also exempt from paying the Value-Added Tax (VAT).

- 100 percent foreign-owned firms are allowed a tax deduction equal to the amount of their investment, and this deduction may be carried forward to offset future profits.

- Taxable profits for foreign investments are reduced by the amount of their profits reinvested in Ukrainian business.

- Exemption from customs duties and import taxes for periods (specified by the Law of the Ukraine on Business Associations) exists for property imported to Ukraine as part of the foreign investor's enterprise; property imported for investment on the basis of contractual agreements; and finished products, raw materials, semi-manufactured goods, components, spare parts and accessories.

In addition to these new incentives, the Ukrainian government is honoring all tax holidays granted by the former Soviet Union to entities established before January 1, 1992.

UKRAINE

Exports: $3 billion to countries outside of the FSU (1993). Commodities: coal, electric power, ferrous and nonferrous metals, chemicals, machinery and transport equipment, grain & meat. Partners: FSU countries, Germany, China, Austria

Imports: $2.2 billion from outside the FSU countries. Commodities: machinery and parts, transportation equipment, chemicals, textiles. Partners: FSU countries, Germany, China, Austria

Industries: coal, electric power, ferrous and nonferrous metals, machinery and transport equipment, chemicals, food-processing (especially sugar)

Agriculture: accounts for about 25% of GDP: grain, vegetables, meat, milk, sugar beets

Travel in Ukraine: Tourist Arrivals: N/A. Tourist Receipts: N/A Attractions: N/A

Business Organizations: Joint-Stock Associations has authorized capital divided into a specific number of shares (of equal value). Stockholders are liable only for the shares that they own. The total value of the issued stocks, which must not be less than RR100, constitutes the authorized capital oft the association. Joint-stock associations may be either "open" or "closed." Open joint-stock associations are distributed by means of open subscription and trading of shares on the stock exchange. Founders must hold a minimum of 25 percent of the shares for at least two years. Closed joint-stock association shares are distributed among the founders and cannot be openly traded. However, a closed joint-stock association can be changed to an open joint-stock association by amending the constituent documents. Limited Responsibility Associations is divided into parts whose size depends on the specifications set down by the constituent documents. Participants of limited responsibility associations take responsibility within the limits of their contributions. Authorized capital must be a minimum of RR50,000. Before registration of such a company, each participant must pay at least 30 percent of his or her contribution, which must be confirmed by a corresponding bank certificate. Additional Responsibility Associations' authorized capital is divided into parts whose size is determined by constituents documents. The participants are responsible for the association's debts and the limits of individual responsibility set forth in the constituent documents. Complete Associations are defined as those entities in which all investors who take up a common enterprise activity carry joint responsibility for the association's commitments, regardless of percentage of ownership.

UKRAINE

Taxes

Corporate Taxes: Rate of 18 percent includes foreign-owned businesses. A further rate of 15 percent applies to joint ventures with 30 percent or more foreign participation, as well to 100 percent foreign-owned Ukrainian companies which are involved in developing industry or agriculture. A withholding tax of 15 percent is levied on dividends, interest, royalties, and other Ukrainian-source income.

Personal Income Taxes: A progressive personal tax is levied which treats foreigners residing in the Ukraine on the same basis as Ukrainian citizens. Income must be declared and calculations include salaries as well as benefits such as compensation for children's tuition, room and .board, vacations of the taxpayer's family and other similar items.

Other Taxes: The standard value-added tax (VAT) rate is 28 percent. Goods with regulated prices are taxed at a reduced rate of 22 percent.

Useful Contacts

Check for a Ukrainian embassy, chamber of commerce or trade development agency in your country.

- **U.S. Embassy in the Ukraine**, 10 Vul, Yurity Kotsubinskoho, Kiev, Ukraine
  Tel: (001 7044) 244 7349

UNITED KINGDOM

Business Opportunities: The United Kingdom generally welcomes foreign investment. British business and investment law does not discriminate between nationals and foreigners or in any of the other regulations affecting the establishment or operation of a business in the United Kingdom.

Incentives: The United Kingdom encourages investment in "Development Area" and "Intermediate Areas." Known collectively as "Assisted Areas," they are concentrated in Scotland, Wales, Northern Ireland, and the north of England.

To attract investment into Development Areas where new industries and additional employment are needed, the government offers programs that provide special graduated benefits such as grants toward capital expenditures on new premises and on new equipment, tax allowances, training assistance, and special wage premiums. These are available both to British and foreign firms. In addition to U.K. incentives, there are substantial EC regional development funds devoted to these lagging regions and regions in decline.

Exports: $190.1 billion. Commodities: manufactured goods, machinery, fuels, chemicals, semi-finished goods and transport equipment. Partners: EC countries 56.7% (Germany 14.0%, France 11.1%, Netherlands 7.9%), U.S. 10.9%

Imports: $221.6 billion. Commodities: manufactured goods, machinery, semifinished goods, foodstuffs & consumer goods. Partners: EC countries 51.7% (Germany 14.9%, France 9.3%, Netherlands 8.4%), U.S. 11.6%

Industries: production machinery including machine tools, electric power equipment, equipment for automation of production, railroad equipment, shipbuilding, aircraft, motor vehicles and parts, electronics and communication equipment, metals, chemicals, coal, petroleum, paper and paper products, food processing, textiles, clothing and other consumer goods

Agriculture: accounts for only 1.5% of GDP and 1% of the labor force; highly mechanized and efficient farms; wide variety of crops and livestock products produced; about 60% self-sufficient in food and feed needs

Business Organizations: Limited Companies are public and private. The public limited company (PLC) may raise funds by issuing public shares or bonds. The private limited companies does not offer public issuance of shares. The private limited company can have a minimum of two members (shareholders) and a maximum of 50. Liability is limited to the value of subscribed shares of each individual member or shareholder. Branches are easily established, and can operate as a U.K. company. Government approval is not required but before opening a branch, the name under which a foreign company conducts business must be approved by the Secretary of State of Trade and Industry. The company need not maintain minimum capital or reserves for the branch. The foreign parent firm is liable for any debts or liabilities. Partnerships: In many cases, membership is limited to 20 partners. Liability is unlimited and extends to all private assets of the partners. Limited partnerships may be established but, business activities may only be conducted by partners with unlimited liability. Joint Ventures between foreign and British companies usually take the form of a limited company. Foreign firms may identify potential joint venture partners through several means, including through appropriate trade associations in the United Kingdom. Sole Proprietorship is operated by a sole beneficial owner of the business, but operating in this manner, all of the individual's assets are at risk. Unlimited Companies members are personally responsible for all debts of the business. Such companies are not common in the United Kingdom.

UNITED KINGDOM

Taxes

Corporate Taxes: resident companies are taxed on their worldwide income, and non-resident companies are taxed only on income derived in the United Kingdom. The standard rate (for companies with profits over £1,125,000) is 33 percent, but smaller companies, (*i.e.,* those with profits of less than £250,000) are subject to a rate of 25 percent. Income is determined by disclosed profits from operation, inventory valuation, exchange differences, capital gains, and foreign income. Deduction are given for depreciation and depletion, net operating losses, payments to foreign affiliates, and other items. Branches are taxed at the same rate as other business entities.

Personal Income Taxes: The UK taxes on its residents' domestic and foreign income and capital gains, and taxes *nonresidents* on their United Kingdom income. There are two tax brackets, with rates of 20% on the first £2,000 of taxable income, 25% on the next £23,700 and 40 percent on income over the £23,700. All individuals are taxed on their wage, tip and salaried income, and residents are also taxed on capital gains and investment income.

Other Taxes: The value-added tax (VAT) is levied on domestically produced products and services as well as imports. The Vat for imported items is assessed on the c.i.f. duty-paid value of goods and services. Certain items such as food, medicines, and books are not subject to VAT. The Vat rate, currently 17.5 percent is paid when goods enter the country or after the expiration of a deferral period. A social security contribution; a community charge payable to local authorities; an inheritance tax; municipal taxes of one percent on documents of transfer of assets, and a 0.5 percent stamp duty. A tax of 75 percent is levied on profits accrued from oil and gas extracted in the United Kingdom or in British territorial waters.

UNITED KINGDOM

Useful Contacts

Check for a British embassy, chamber of commerce or trade development agency in your country.

• **Invest in Britain Bureau,** Department of Trade and Industry,
Kingsgate House, 66-74 Victoria Street, London SW1E 6SW
Tel: (44 71) 215 2544 Fax: (44 71) 215 8451

• **American Chamber of Commerce,** 75 Brook Street, London W1Y 2EB, England
Tel: (44 71) 493-03-81 Fax: (44 71) 493-23-94

Appendix 3:
Asia and the Pacific Rim

AUSTRALIA

Business Opportunities: The Australian government supports long-term foreign investment that will assist Australia's economic development. For example, there are investment opportunities in railway network construction, and airport terminal projects. The government has liberalized its stance on foreign investment by increasing the value of projects which are exempt from review by the Foreign Investment Review Board (FIRB) to US$36 million, and by abolishing limitations on foreign equity in new mines and restrictions on acquisition of existing mines. However, certain categories of investment continue to require FIRB screening, including purchases of urban real estate and equity investment in restricted sectors.

Foreign firms wishing to invest in Australia should first consider whether they need the approval of the Australian Government under the FIRB process. FIRB approvals are usually granted within 30 days of notification. However, restrictions on foreign investment apply in specific areas where the government considers few benefits will accrue to the Australian economy from foreign investment. One example is the acquisition of developed non-residential commercial real estate.

Incentives: A number of incentives are offered to foreign companies wishing to invest in Australia. Most are offered by national and state governments and include tax and non-tax incentives. For example:

- Low interest loans to buy land, erect factories, or provide housing for key personnel.

- Subsidies for training employees or to lower freight costs.

- Bounties (incentive payments) for the manufacture of certain goods.

- Tax deductions for research and development projects.

- Incentives by Australian state governments for locating industries outside major cities.

Exports: $44.1 billion. Commodities: Coal, gold, meat, wool, alumina, wheat, machinery and transport equipment. Partners: Japan 25%, U.S. 11%, South Korea 6%, NZ 5.7%, UK, Taiwan, Singapore, Hong Kong

Imports: $43.6 billion. Commodities: Machinery and transport equipment, computers and office machines, crude oil and petroleum products. Partners: U.S. 23%, Japan 18%, UK 6%, Germany 5.7%, NZ 4%

Industries: Mining, industrial and transportation equipment, food processing, chemicals, steel

AUSTRALIA

Agriculture: Accounts for 5% of the GDP and over 30% of export revenues; world's largest exporter of beef and wool, second-largest for mutton, and among top wheat exporters; Major crops: Wheat, barley, sugarcane, fruit; Livestock: Cattle, sheep, poultry

Business Organizations: The most common forms of investment used in Australia by both resident and non-resident investors are: companies, including branch offices of foreign companies; joint ventures; partnerships; and trading trusts. Foreign firms may incorporate in Australia after completing all relevant documentation (i.e., Certificate of Incorporation, Articles of Association and Memorandum of Association). Foreign companies granted a Certificate of Incorporation are accorded the same rights, powers, and privileges as a domestic company enjoys.

Branches of foreign corporations must register with the state or territory Corporate Affairs Commission. Branches are accorded the same treatment as Australian companies.

Taxes

Income tax in Australia is levied at the federal level. Resident taxpayers, including foreign citizens living in Australia and foreign incorporated companies with management and control in Australia, are taxed on worldwide income. All Australian-source income is subject to Australian tax. Taxation of income by more than one country is avoided either through a foreign tax credit system or through exemption depending on the circumstances. Personal income taxes are payable on a progressive scale with a threshold of A$5,400 and a maximum of 47 percent payable on earnings over A$50,000.

Corporate Taxes: Corporations which are based and managed in Australia and branches of foreign corporations in Australia are taxed at a rate of 39 percent. In addition, a branch profits tax of five percent is applied to non-resident companies. A withholding tax is applied to dividends and interest paid in Australia by foreign subsidiaries.

Personal Income Taxes: Income taxes in Australia are levied on a progressive scale. The minimum tax rate is 20 percent, while the top marginal rate is 47 percent. Non-residents are taxed only on income arising from Australian sources.

Other Taxes: A sales tax of 20 percent is levied on the sale of goods. However, many goods are subject to special rates. Alcohol, tobacco and petroleum products are subject to an excise tax. State governments also levy payroll taxes, stamp taxes on business transactions, and land taxes.

Useful Contacts

•**American Chamber of Commerce in Australia—Sydney**
Suite 4, Gloucester Walk, 88 Cumberland St., Sydney, N.S.W. 2000
Telephone: 612-241-1907 Facsimile: 612-251-5220

•**Australian Tourism Industry Association**, Box E328, Canberra City, ACT 2600
Telephone: 06-273-1000 Facsimile: 06-273-4999

•**Australian Institute of Travel & Tourism**, 309 Pitt Street, 3rd Floor, Sydney, N.S.W. 2000
Telephone: 02-264-9616

PEOPLE'S REPUBLIC OF CHINA

Business Opportunities: Oil, coal, and hotel and property development projects account for large amounts of foreign investment. Recently, investment funds have shifted to manufacturing ventures. Ventures using advanced technology or focusing on exports are generally more encouraged than consumer products and service sector projects.

Potential investments go through a multi-tiered screening process often involving a number of government clearances at both the national and local levels. Implementation of national investment laws at the local level can vary widely. Generally, the five SEZs (Shenzhen, Zhuhai and Shekou in Guangdong Province, the Hainan SEZ, and the Xiamen SEZ in Fujian Province) provide good investment incentives and have established streamlines approval procedures. Many of the major cities on China's coast have economic and technical development zones offering incentives similar to those existing in the SEZs.

Exports: $92 billion. Commodities: textiles, garments, footwear, crude oil, toys. Partners: Hong Kong, U.S., Japan, Germany, South Korea, Russia

Imports: $104 billion. Commodities: rolled steel, motor vehicles, textile machinery, oil products. Partners: Japan, Taiwan, US, Hong Kong, Germany, South Korea

Industries: iron and steel, coal, machine building, armaments, textiles, petroleum, cement, chemical fertilizers, consumer durables, food processing

Agriculture: accounts for 26% of GDP; among the world's largest producers of rice, potatoes, sorghum, peanuts, tea, millet, barley and pork; commercial crops include cotton, other fibers, and oilseeds; produces variety of livestock products; basically self-sufficient in food; fish catch of 13.35 million metric tons (including fresh water and pond raised) (1991).

Business Organizations: Representative Offices for foreign companies is the most common way to establish a presence in China. Registration with the State Administration of Industry and Commerce (SAIC). Although representative office personnel cannot directly sign contracts or receive fees, they can perform market research, consulting, or liaison type of work. A foreign firm must find a sponsor organization that will approve its application to establish an office. Equity Joint Ventures are limited liability companies. Normally, the foreign partner must contribute at least 25 percent of the capital although there are no limitations on the number of partners. Profits are distributed according to each partner's investment. The foreign investor may not recover its investment until liquidation or sale of the venture.

Contractual Joint Ventures are often referred to as "cooperative joint ventures." The parties determine the form of operation through negotiation of a contract. Generally, the parties agree to operate jointly like partners or to form a new limited liability company. There are set government requirements on the duration of the venture, on the amount of capital the foreign investor must contribute, or on how profits are to be distributed. On successful completion of the pre-approval procedures MOFERT or a corresponding local authority will make a decision on approval within 45 days.

Wholly foreign–owned ventures will depend on whether the enterprise is deemed to benefit the development of China's national economy. The Chinese government prefers enterprises which employ advanced technology and equipment to manufacture products important to the national economy and is not produced in China.

Other types of business establishments include consignment sales and service centers established to market foreign company products and to service those products, and foreign bank branches.

Taxes

Corporate Taxes: Wholly owned foreign–owned ventures, equity joint ventures, and contractual joint ventures pay a combined national and provincial tax of 33 percent of pre-tax income. Depending on the location, purpose, length and profit investment plans of a foreign-invested venture, there are opportunities to lessen, defer or exempt income from taxation. Consignment sales and service centers established by a Chinese entity to market a foreign company's products, or to maintain or sell spare parts for the foreigner's products, are subject to a 33 percent tax. Foreign company representative offices which engage solely in liaison activities on behalf of head offices normally have no Chinese source of income and do not pay income tax but must file an income tax return. Offices of foreign service companies such as consultants, accountants, banks and trading companies that derive income form services may be taxed on their income. Commercial Industrial and Commercial Tax (CICT) applies to the production of industrial and agricultural goods, commercial retailing, and service, transportation and communications applies to activities conducted in China. The tax is levied on the gross amount of proceeds received by the sale and services at each stage of production when transferred from one entity to another. The typical CICT rate is five to 10 percent, although they may range from 1.5 to 69 percent. Taxpayers importing goods pay CICT on the amount of their purchases.

Personal Income Taxes: Individuals residing in China are subject to income tax pay progressive rates ranging from five to 45 percent of their wages and salaries earned in China. Compensation for personal services, royalties, interest, dividends and other income are taxed 20 percent.

Per diem or periodic allowances paid to employees of foreign companies in China are normally considered taxable income but company expenditures such as lodging, business entertainment and transportation costs are not personal income for the employee.

PRC

Useful Contacts

Check for a Chinese embassy, chamber of commerce or trade development agency in your country.

• **U.S. Embassy in the People's Republic of China Beijing**, Xiu Shui Bei Jie 3, 100600, Beijing,
People's Republic of China
Tel: (861) 532-3831

• **American Chamber of Commerce for China—Beijing**, G/F Great Wall Sheraton Hotel,
N. Donghuan Road, Beijing, China
Tel: (861) 500-5566 Fax: (861) 508-8494

• **American Chamber of Commerce in Shanghai,**
Shanghai Centre, 4th Floor, Suite 435, 1376 Nanjing Xi Lu, Shanghai 200040, People's Republic of China
Tel: 86-21-279-7119 Fax: 86-21-279-8802

HONG KONG

Business Opportunities: Hong Kong welcomes foreign investment to diversify its industrial base and to develop high-technology industries. This includes areas such as radio, televisions, and selected telephone services, which the Hong Kong government has privatized. There are no export performance requirements, and no distinction is made based on the source of the investment.

Hong Kong does not require local participation in ownership or management or otherwise restrict foreign ownership. The government permits 100 percent foreign ownership, and there is generally no approval or screening procedure for foreign investment. However, foreign companies must register with the Registrar of Companies within one month of establishing a business within Hong Kong. In registering a branch, the parent company must submit its articles of incorporation.

Incentives: There are no special incentives to attract foreign investment to Hong Kong because the low rate of corporate taxes and minimal government regulation serve this purpose. The industrial Investment Unit within the Industry Department does provide assistance to overseas companies interested in investing in the territory. Foreign businesses are also advised to obtain a copy of the Companies Ordinance since they will have to comply with many of its provisions.

Exports: $145.1 billion (including re-exports of $104.2 billion) Commodities: Clothing, textiles, yarn and fabric, footwear, electrical appliances, watches, clocks, and toys. Partners: China 32%, U.S. 23%, Germany 5%, Japan 5%, UK 3%

Imports: $149.6 billion Commodities: Foodstuffs, transport equipment, raw materials, semi-manufacturers, petroleum. Partners: China 36%, Japan 19%, Taiwan 9%, U.S. 7%

Industries: Textiles, clothing, tourism, Electronics, plastics, toys, watches, clocks

Agriculture: Minor role in the economy, local farmers produce 26% fresh vegetables, 27% live poultry, 8% land area suitable for farming.

Business Organizations: The primary forms of business organizations in Hong Kong are: sole proprietorship, partnership, corporation and branch. All businesses must register with the Inland Revenue Department and obtain a Business Registration Certificate from the Registrar of Companies.

Corporations must have a minimum of two subscribers and may be either private or public companies. Private companies may not have more than 50 shareholders nor offer its shares or debentures to the public, and the right to transfer shares in a private company may require board approval or be subject to a right of pre-emption by the other shareholders. Public companies, on the other hand, are subject to minimum capitalization requirements and to regulation in the issuance of prospectuses and stock offerings, and must file annual statements with the Registrar of Companies.

Hong Kong companies, whether public or private, can have limited or unlimited liability. In a "limited" company, the shareholders are liable only for the amount unpaid on their shares or alternatively, for the amount that they have pledged to contribute. Companies in which the shareholders have unlimited liability are rare. Most foreign investors choose to establish private limited companies or branch operations.

HONG KONG

Taxes

Corporate Taxes: Personal Income Taxes: Other Taxes

Useful Contacts

• **American Chamber of Commerce in Hong Kong**, 1030 Swire House, Central G.P.O. Box 355, Hong Kong
  Telephone: 852-22526-0165 Facsimile: 852-2810-1289

• **Hong Kong Government Trade Department**, 700 Nathan Road, Kowloon, Hong Kong
  Telephone: 852-789-7555 Facsimile: 852-789-2491

• **Hong Kong Government Industry Department, Ocean Centre**, Canton Road, Kowloon, Hong Kong
  Telephone: 852-737-2473 Facsimile: 852-730-4633

• **Hong Kong Trade Development Council, Convention Plaza, 1 Harbour Road, Hong Kong**
  Telephone: 852-584-4333 Facsimile: 852-824-0249

• **Hong Kong Customs an Excise Department, Harbour Building, 38 Pier Road, Central Hong Kong**
  Telephone: 852-852-1411 Facsimile: 852-398-0145

• **Hong Kong Trade Development Council**, 38/f Office Tower, Convention Plaza, 1 Harbor Road, Wanchai, Hong Kong
  Telephone: (852) 833-4333 Facsimile: (852) 824-0249

INDIA

Business Opportunities: The government has liberalized the number of industries open to foreign investment, loosened approval requirements and allowed majority foreign equity ownership. There are frequent changes in the regulations governing equity percentage permitted and the industries open to foreign participation. Companies wishing to enter the Indian market should make efforts to obtain the most-up-to-date information.

Foreign investment is encouraged in large-scale projects, projects that will have a favorable impact on the Indian balance of payments position, and investment that will bring new technology to India. The government has designated a list of 34 high-priority industries open to foreign investors.

Rules and regulations governing foreign investment in India stipulate:

- All foreign investment projects, not considered a priority industry eligible for automatic clearance by the Reserve Bank of India, require approval by the Foreign Investment Promotion Board or a newly created committee for review of smaller investment projects.

- The government permits foreign firms to hold up to 51 percent equity in Indian venture on a case-by-case basis.

- Automatic approval is granted to foreign investments of up to 51 percent equity in 34 high-priority industrial sectors.

- For businesses that solely focus on export-oriented manufacturing, 100 percent ownership is available.

- Foreign companies are permitted to acquire land and own buildings as long as permission is obtained from the Reserve Bank of India.

The following restrictions are placed on foreign investment: foreign investment in non-priority sectors is generally restricted to 40 percent of common stock; and restrictions on 100 percent foreign ownership may apply, depending on the nature of the business.

Incentives: No specific tax incentives exist to attract foreign investment. However, there are incentives available to Indian companies with some share of foreign ownership. Tax and non-tax incentives may be granted to businesses that will increase Indian exports. For example:

- Tax depreciation allowances and investment allowances for various businesses and tax holidays for projects undertaken in specified underdeveloped areas.

- Tax deductions during the first 10 years of operation for new industrial undertakings established anywhere in India. These deductions apply to the hotel and shipping industries.

- Under certain conditions, 100 percent export-oriented projects are exempt from taxation.

- Soft loans and concessional credits are available to specified industries.

- Five-year tax holiday for industrial undertakings in free trade and export processing zones. Exemption from licensing regulations, excise taxes, customs duties, and sales tax are also available to businesses operating in these areas.

INDIA

- Businesses that manufacture and process goods for export are eligible for customs and excise duty drawbacks. These drawback schemes also apply to raw materials.

Some non-tax incentives are offered by the state governments. Examples of these include the availability of land on concessional terms, facilities for business use, and water and power at reduced rates.

Exports: $21.4 billion Commodities: Gems and jewelry, clothing, engineering goods, chemicals, leather manufactures, cotton yarn and fabric. Partners: U.S. 18.9%, Germany 7.8%, Italy 7.8%

Imports: $22 billion Commodities: Crude oil and petroleum products, gems fertilizer, chemicals, machinery. Partners: U.S. 9.8%, Belgium 8.4%, Germany 7.6%

Industries: Textiles, chemicals, food processing, steel, transportation equipment, cement, mining, petroleum, machinery

Agriculture: Accounts for 40% of the GDP and employs 65% of labor force; Principal crops: rice, wheat, oil seeds, cotton, jute, tea, sugarcane, potatoes; Livestock: cattle, buffaloes, sheep, goats, poultry; Fish: catch about 3 million metric tons ranks India among the world's top fishing nations.

Business Organizations: The most common business entity used by foreign investors in India is the locally incorporated company. Branches, sole proprietorships and partnerships are essentially closed to foreign companies. Foreign investors may participate in either public or private companies. Private companies must restrict the transfer of their shares, limited the number of shareholders to 50 and prohibit any invitation to the public to subscribe for shares.

Taxes

Corporate Taxes: Indian corporate tax rates are high and the pertinent laws complex. The standard corporate income tax rates are 45 percent for public companies, 65 percent for branches of foreign compnies and 50 percent for all other companies. If companies utilize tax incentives available to them, the typical rates vary between 30 and 50 percent. The tax rates are lowest for widely held companies incorporated in India. Companies are strongly encouraged to employ a tax specialist familiar with the Indian tax structure.

A 25 percent tax is levied on dividends paid to non-resident corporate bodies, with a minimum 30 percent tax being applied if the non-resident is not a corporation. Interest is taxed at a rate of 25 percent, with a -3.125 percent surcharge. Royalties are taxed at a rate of 30 percent.

Other Taxes: There is a five percent sales tax applicable to most goods along with excise taxes on alcohol, drugs, automobiles, cosmetics, cigarettes and air conditioners. States also levy sales tax ranging from four to 10 percent. A number of luxury, real estate and other taxes may also apply.

INDIA

Useful Contacts

• **U.S. Embassy in India,** New Delhi, Shanti Path, Chanakyapuri 110021
  Telephone: (9 11) 600651 Telex: 82065 USEM IN

• **Indian Chamber of Commerce,** 445 Park Avenue, 18th Floor, New York, NY 10022
  Telephone: 212) 755-7181

• **Government of India Tourist Office,** 88 Janpath, Delhi, India 110001
  Telephone: 11-3811

• **U. S. Consulate General, Lincoln House,** 78 Bhulabhai Desai Road 400026, Bombay
  Telephone: 91 022 822-3611

INDONESIA

Busniess Opportunities: The government views foreign investment as a way of attracting high technology and business to Indonesia. Investment is coordinated by the BKPM, which works with various government ministries to formulate investment policy. Indonesia has made strides to improve the foreign investment climate by opening up more industries and allowing a wider variety of manufacturing inputs to be imported. The BKPM publishes a "negative list" which identifies the sixteen areas completely closed to foreign investment, and the forty-four areas where foreign investment is conditionally permitted.

In Indonesia, foreigners are not permitted to own land; all foreign investors must have an Indonesian joint venture partners to invest in an Indonesian venture. In April, 1992, the Government of Indonesia loosened restrictions transferring majority ownership to nationals. Under these rules, foreign investors are limited to 80 percent equity in a limited liability company, which must be reduced to 49 percent within 20 years of commencement of commercial production.

Incentives: Various fiscal measures are available to both foreign and domestic investors. Investors may import duty free (or at reduced rates) capital goods, tools, and spare parts which are to be used in the start-up of a venture. Additional incentives include indefinite postponement of the Value-Added Tax (VAT) on inputs imported for use in items manufactured for re-export, unrestricted foreign exchange transfers, and exemption from the capital stamp tax on initial foreign capital.

Exports: $38.2 billion. Commodities: Petroleum and gas 28%, clothing and fabrics 15%, plywood 11%, footwear 4%. Partners: Japan 32%, U.S. 13%, Singapore 9%, South Korea 6%

Imports: $28.2 billion. Commodities: Machinery 37%, semi-finished goods 16%, chemicals 14%, raw materials 10%, transport equipment 7%, foodstuffs 6%, petroleum products 4%, consumer goods 3%. Partners: Japan 22%, U.S. 14%, Germany 8%, South Korea 7%, Singapore 6%, Australia 5%, Taiwan 5%

Industries: Petroleum and natural gas, textiles, mining, cement, chemical fertilizers, plywood, food, rubber

Agriculture: Accounts for 21% of GDP; subsistence food production; small-holder and plantation production for export; main products are rice, cassava, peanuts, rubber, cocoa, coffee, palm oil, copra, other tropical products, poultry, beef, pork, eggs

Business Organizations: A Limited Liability Company (*Perseoan Terbatas*—denoted PT) is available under foreign joint ventures based on the Penanman Modal Asing (PMA). PMA companies may be either private or publicly listed on the stock exchange. For most foreign investors, this type of incorporation is the most relevant. Branch of a Foreign Corporation: The foreign investment law provides that enterprises may operate as a branch in limited circumstances. In practice, this applies to some banks, and to certain mining operations. Representative Office: A foreign company may establish a representative office in Indonesia. The representative office must be licensed by either the *Department of Trade* or the *Ministry of Public Works*. A representative office registered under the Department of Trade may not engage in business activities, but may conduct promotional or quality control activities. A representative office registered under the Ministry of Public Works may engage in specific business activities. Regional Representative Office: A foreign company may establish a Regional Representative Office (RRO) if domiciled in one of Indonesia's main cities. Approval is by the Investment Coordinating Board (BKPM) and the license is valid indefinitely. An RRO's function is to oversee operations of foreign organizations in more than one Asian country. Full Partnership (Firma): In principle, foreign participation in Indonesian partnerships is permitted. However, as a matter of long-standing government policy, no such participation is permitted in practice. Partners are personally liable for all obligations of the enterprise.

Taxes

Income Taxes: There is a three-tiered income tax system:
- Income up to Rp 10 million is taxed at 15 percent.
- Income from Rp 10 million to Rp 50 million is taxed at 25 percent.
- Income above Rp 50 million is taxed at 35 percent.

Dividends from resident corporations, interest, rents, royalties and other income derived from property, management compensation, and after-tax profits paid to non-residents are subject to an additional withholding tax of 20 percent. When paid to a resident, they are subject to a withholding tax of 15 percent. There are depreciation deductions for most assets (excluding buildings). Deductions vary from five to 50 percent depending on the life of the product.

Indirect Taxes: Indonesia has implemented a Value-Added Tax (VAT) system to replace the previous sales tax system. The VAT rate is 10 percent on imported goods, except for goods and basic materials used to produce export commodities and machinery and equipment used in developing industries. In addition to the VAT, there is a sales tax of between 10 and 30 percent levied on luxury goods.

Tax Treaties: The United States and Indonesia have a bilateral tax treaty, which specifies that U.S. corporations in Indonesia cannot be taxed more than resident corporations and that American individuals and businesses will not be double-taxed on the same income.

Useful Contacts

- **American Chamber of Commerce**, Landmark Centre, 22nd Floor, Suite 2204, J1. Jendral Sudirman
  Telephone: 722-1-571-0800 Fax: 622-1-571-0656

- **National Development Information Office**, Jalan Medan Medeka Selatan 17, Jakarta 10110, Indonesia
  Telephone 62-21-384-7412 Fax: 62-21-350-442

- **Indonesian Chambers of Commerce and Industry**, Jalan M. H. Thamrin 20, Jakarta, Indonesia
  Telephone: 62-21-310-5683 Fax: 62-21-350-442

- **Importers' Association of Indonesia**, P. O. Box 2244/JKT, Jala E pintu Timur Arena PRJ, Jakarta, Indonesia
  Telephone: 62-21-377-008 Fax: 62-21-324-422

JAPAN

Business Opportunities: In recent years, the Japanese government has made efforts to open the Japanese market to foreign companies and official regulations on foreign investment are minimal. The following rules pertain to foreign investment:

- There are no requirements on local equity, export performance, or local content.

- The Foreign Exchange and Foreign Trade Control Law and the Implementing Cabinet Order state that prior approval of certain foreign investment is no longer necessary.

- Capital may be freely repatriated.

- Foreign companies may be listed on the Nikkei (the Tokyo Stock exchange).

Investment in some select areas is restricted. These areas include weapons, atomic energy, aircraft. space development, narcotics and vaccine manufacturing, security guard devices, agriculture, forestry and fisheries, public utilities, petroleum refining and marketing, air and rail transportation, and ship building. Foreign investment in the banking and the securities industries reflects a reciprocity requirement.

Incentives: There is a variety of financial support programs designed to help international business executives participate in the Japanese marketplace. The majority of these programs are provided by the Japan Export-Import Bank, MITI and the Japan Development Bank (JDB) and in many cases are a collaborative effort with U.S. government agencies. Support comes in the form of trade/import financing, R&D grants and project financing. Many other incentive programs are provided through local government on a project specific basis.

Additionally, some tax concessions are available to branches of foreign corporations. These include carry-back and carry-forward tax losses, and tax credits for qualifying expenditures.

Exports: $360.9 billion. Commodities: manufactures 97% (including machinery 46%, motor vehicles 20%, consumer electronics 10%). Partners: Southeast Asia 33%, U.S. 29%, Western Europe 18%, China 5%

Imports: $240.7 billion. Commodities: manufactures 52%, fossil fuels 20%, foodstuffs and raw materials 28%. Partners: Southeast Asia 25%, U.S. 23%, Western Europe 15%, China 9%

Industries: steel and non-ferrous metallurgy, heavy electrical equipment, construction and mining equipment, motor vehicles and parts, electronic and telecommunication equipment and components, machine tools and automated production systems, locomotives and railroad rolling stock, shipbuilding, chemicals, textiles, food processing

Agriculture: accounts for only 2% of GDP; highly subsidized and protected sector, with crop yields among highest in the world; principal crops-rice, sugar beets, vegetables, fruit; animal products include pork, poultry, dairy and eggs; about 50% self-sufficient in food production; shortages of wheat, corn, soybeans; world's largest fish catch of 10 million metric tons in 1991

Travel in Japan: Tourist Arrivals: 2,104,000. Tourist Receipts: $3,435,000,000 Tourist Attractions: Tokyo (*Emperor's Palace, museums and art galleries, Iris garden*); Honshu (*Nikko National Park and Fuji area, Nikko-temples and shrines*); Mt. Fujiyama;

JAPAN

Osaka (*castle, shrines, theaters, music festival*); Kyoto (*architecture, cultural artifacts, Kurashiki folk art museum*); Nagasaki (*Peace Park*); Hokkaido (*winter sports*).

Business Organizations: Corporations must be reported to the *Legal Affairs Bureau of the Ministry of Justice* two weeks after the first constituent general meeting. In some cases, because of tax and market changes, the advantages of forming a corporation in Japan are diminishing. Branch operations are expected to become a more common method for foreigners to enter the marketplace. Branches are established by appointing a qualified representative and must register with the Legal Affairs Bureau of the Ministry of Justice within three weeks of opening the Japanese office. However, under the *Structural Impediments Initiative* (SII), the government has committed itself to repealing the prior notification requirement and replaced it with *ex post facto* notification to the Bank of Japan. Engaging in subsidiary operations, joint ventures, or acquiring stock in Japanese companies is generally more complicated and expensive than opening a branch in Japan. This is partially due to the cross-shareholding relationships that exist in the Japanese marketplace. A company may choose to establish a representative office which may provide guidance and support to agents, manage marketing activities and collect market data and provide information for potential clients. No prior approval is necessary to establish an office in Japan, however representative offices cannot generate taxable income. Licensing and franchising are both feasible methods to operate in Japan. If technology transfers are involved, a company is required to report to the Ministry of Finance and any other ministry involved in regulation of the given industry. Under the SII, the Government has committed to eliminate the need for U.S. corporations to serve prior notification. Foreign companies may also become involved in the Japanese business community by participating in the government procurement system. However, in most cases, a prequalified agent should be employed in order to sell to the government.

Taxes

Corporate Taxes: In general, the corporate tax rate is 37.5 percent. Capitalized at or under ¥100 million the first ¥8 million is taxed at 27.5 percent and income above is taxed 37.5 percent. A 20 percent withholding tax is applied to dividends, interest, and royalties that are distributed by a Japanese firm. Under a U.S.-Japanese tax treaty, the rate is reduced to 15 percent for U.S. shareholders on interest and royalties and to 15 percent for dividends. The withholding tax does not apply to profit repatriation by branches.

Personal Income Taxes: An individual who enters Japan intending to stay for more than one year becomes a resident upon entry. However, an individual is consequently classified in permanent or non-permanent status with taxable income being dependent on the type of classification. Japanese rates are steeply graduated. Non-residents are subject to tax only on income from Japanese sources, which is usually a flat rate. Non-resident tax status may also be affected by a tax treaty with the relevant country.

Other Taxes: There is a three percent value-added tax (VAQT), also called consumption tax, applied to all goods (4.5% on autos) and most retail sales. In addition there is a stamp tax, registration and license tax, and taxes on liquor and alcohol.

JAPAN

Useful Contacts

Check for a Japanese embassy, chamber of commerce or trade development agency in your country.

- **Keidanren (Federation of Economic Organizations)**, 1-9-4 Otemachi, Chiyoda-ku, Tokyo 100 Japan
Tel: (813) 3279-1441

- **The American Chamber of Commerce in Japan—Tokyo**, Bridgeston Toranomon Bldg,
5F, 3-25-2, Toranomon, Minato-ku, Tokyo 105, Japan Tel: 813 3433-5381 Fax: 813 3436-1446

- **American Chamber of Commerce in Okinawa**, P.O. Box 235, Okinawa City 904, Okinawa, Japan
Tel: 81-98933-5146 Fax: 81-98933-7695

KOREA

Business Opportunities: Most foreign firms continue to face difficulties in establishing and operating foreign investments in Korea, however, the United States and Korea have resumed discussions on investment issues. Following a 1989 U.S.-Korea investment agreement, the Korean government has made efforts to improve the investment climate and remove various restrictions. Remaining obstacles include: high domestic interest rates and a prohibition on offshore borrowing; a ban on the purchase of land for investments on services industries; and long delays on the governmental approval process.

All foreign investment in Korea is governed by the *Foreign Capital Inducement Law* and its subordinate regulations. The *Ministry of Finance* (MOF) administers regulations on the foreign investment laws. The following regulations are applicable to almost all businesses investing in Korea: the minimum amount of foreign investment is *W* (*Won*) 50 million; remittance of both dividends and capital is guaranteed by law.

Restrictions on foreign investment in Korea are governed by a variety of regulations. A negative list system classifies sectors of the economy where investment is prohibited or restricted. Investment in sectors on the negative list is possible with approval from the *Ministry of Finance*. Approval or disapproval occurs within 60 days.

Sectors in which foreign investment is prohibited include the production of tobacco products, the press, generation of electric power, the operation of drinking establishments, the postal, telephone and telegraph services, television broadcasting services and gambling.

Restrictions usually take the form of an equity limitation clause for the foreign investor or of specific conditions being attached to a given product.

Foreign ownership and representation on boards are restricted to minority shares in aviation, mining, fisheries and fish processing, and marine transportation. As of the end of 1991, 62% of current foreign investment projects involved foreign equity of 50% or less, with wholly foreign–owned businesses amounting to 24 percent of the total projects.

Incentives: Most enterprises with foreign investment are treated as domestic businesses under Korean law. Consequently, foreign investors are entitled to tax and non-tax investment incentives.

Commercial Policies

Free-Trade Zones: There are two free export zones for the bonded processing of imported materials into finished goods for export. Foreign invested firms can manufacture, assemble, or process export products using freely-imported, duty-free raw materials or semifinished goods. The majority of wholly foreign-owned projects operate in these zones.

Exchange Controls: Korea's Foreign Exchange Control Law subjects all foreign exchange transactions to control. Foreign investors who wish to remit dividends, interest, royalties, and capital an application must be filed with the president of a Class A foreign exchange bank for approval. The government guarantees unlimited remittance of profits at the prevailing exchange rate at the time of transfer.

Labor Force: 20 million. By occupation: services and other 52%, mining & manufacturing 27%, agriculture, fishing &

KOREA

forestry 21%. Unemployment rate: 2.6%

Population: 45,082,880. Ethnic divisions: homogeneous (except for about 20,000 Chinese)

Exports: $81 billion. Commodities: electronic and electrical equipment, machinery, steel, automobiles, ships, textiles, clothing, footwear, fish. Partners: U.S. 26%, Japan 17%, EC 14%

Imports: $78.9 billion. Commodities: machinery, electronics, electronic equipment, oil, steel, transport equipment, textiles, organic chemicals, grains. Partners: Japan 26%, U.S. 24%, EC 15%

Industries: electronics, automobile production, chemicals, shipbuilding, steel, textiles, clothing, footwear, food processing

Agriculture: accounts for 8% of GNP and employs 21% of work force (including fishing and forestry). Principal crops—rice, root crops, barley, vegetables, fruit; livestock and livestock products—cattle, hogs, chickens, milk, eggs; self-sufficient in food, except for wheat; fish catch of 2.9 million metric tons, seventh largest in the world.

Travel in South Korea: Tourist arrivals: 3,196,000. Tourist receipts: $3,426,000,000. Tourist attractions: The Yi dynasty palaces in Seoul—*Kyongbok, Changdok and Toksu*—are recommended, since they constitute the National Museum of Korea and the Korean Folk Museum. The folk village of Suwon, located less than an hour's drive from Seoul, is a fine example of a "living museum." Sorok Mountain and Cheju Island are popular scenic attractions; Pusan and Masan are examples of a modern port and industrial site. The southwestern city of Kyongju has many fine antiquities. English is widely spoken at major tourist sites and facilities in the principal cities; in other areas, English speakers may be readily found.

Business Organizations: In principle, foreigners are permitted to establish and operate a joint stock corporation, a limited partnership, a limited company and a branch. However, there are certain limitations on a foreigner's lattitude to invest both in regards to industry and business form A joint stock company is the form of business most popular with foreign investors. Seven or more promoters are required for the incorporation of a joint stock company. After incorporation the number of shareholders may be reduced to one. A registration fee must be paid and a company must apply to a district tax office for a business license within 30 days of commencing business.

Branches of foreign corporations must register with the Bank of Korea and obtain a license if the branch plans to make remittances overseas. Foreign branches that plan no remittances are simply required to file reports on establishment with the Bank of Korea. Branches cannot own shares on Korean companies, engage in manufacturing or participate in the financial sector of the Korean economy.

KOREA

Taxes

Corporate Taxes: The corporate tax rates in Korea are 20 percent for taxable income up to W100 million and 34 percent for taxable income in excess to W100 million. Additional defense and resident surtaxes apply at the rates of 20 and 7.5 percent respectively. There are withholding taxes on dividends, interest and royalties. Dividends and interest are taxed at the rate to 25 percent for non-residents. Royalties are also taxed at 25 percent. In January 1991, the Korean government began to asses a tax of 27 percent on excess retained earnings of large, unlisted corporations.

Personal Income Taxes: The Korean income tax system aggregates gross income from all sources and taxes it at progressive rates ranging from five to 50 percent. A resident surtax applies at the rate of 7.5 percent. Foreigners in the Republic of Korea are classified as residents or non-residents for tax purposes in the following manner: residents, and individuals who stay in Korea for more than one year are taxed in most respects as Korean nationals; non-residents are taxed only on income derived from sources within the Republic of Korea.

Other Taxes: The 10 percent VAT applies to all goods and services. There are also special excise taxes on liquor, gasoline, education, tobacco and various luxury items. Numerous other taxes exist ranging from real property to automobiles.

Tax Treaties: The Republic of Korea and the United States established a tax treaty to avoid double taxation. This treaty reduces U.S. withholding tax rates to 12 percent on interest payments, and 10 to 15 percent on dividends and royalties.

Useful Contacts

- **U.S. Embassy in Korea**, 82 Sejong-Ro; Chongro-ku, Seoul, Korea 110-050
  Telephone: (822) 397-4114 Fax: (822) 738-8845

- To mail from within the United States:
  U.S. Embassy in Seoul, Korea, APO San Francisco 96301

- **Embassy of Korea in the United States**, 2320 Massachusetts Ave. NW, Washington, DC 20008
  Telephone: (202) 939-5600

- **The American Chamber of Commerce in Korea**, Room 307, Chosun Hotel, Seoul, Korea
  Telephone: (882) 753-6471 Fax: (882) 755-6577

MALAYSIA

Business Opportunities: The Malaysian Industrial Development Authority (MIDA) serves as a one-stop shop clearinghouse for regulatory information and investment project approval.

Very few industries are protected from foreign investment. However, the major restrictions are as follows:

- No equity conditions are imposed on projects that export 80 percent or more of their production.

- For projects that export between 50 and 80 percent of their production, foreign equity ownership can be up to 100 percent provided that the investment is at least M$ 50 million in non-land fixed assets or else provides 50 percent value-added and the product does not compete with domestic products. If the first condition is not met, foreign equity ownership cannot exceed 79 percent. The level of equity permitted depends on: technology level, spin-off effects, investment size and location, value-added and utilization of local parts and materials.

- Projects that export between 20 and 50 percent of their production allow a maximum of 51 percent foreign ownership. Projects that export less than 20 percent of their production are not permitted in excess 30 percent foreign ownership.

Incentives: The government has made investment in the economy a priority, and as such has provided foreign companies with a wide array of incentives designed to make it easier to conduct business and operate in the Malaysian marketplace. Incentives are awarded on a case-by-case basis according to guidelines established by MIDA and the Malaysian government's Foreign Investment Committee (FIC).

Incentives include:

- Pioneer industry status: This status can be granted to any company in the manufacturing, agricultural, or other industrial or commercial sectors. Companies in targeted industries pay only 30 percent of their income for a period of five years.

- Investment tax allowance: Companies can receive an allowance of 60 percent of qualifying capital expenditures incurred during the first five years to offset the first 70 percent of income. Any unused balance can be carried forward.

- Reinvestment allowance: Companies can receive an allowance of 40 percent of capital expansion or diversification expenditures to offset income.

- Export allowance and export income abatement: Although these will be phased out by 1994, export-oriented companies can qualify for tax breaks based on the proportion of production that is exported.

- Other allowances: These are granted for a range of promotional activities, ranging from research and development to staff training.

Exports: $46.8 billion. Commodities: electronic equipment, petroleum and petroleum products, palm oil, wood and wood products, rubber, textiles. Partners: Singapore 23%, U.S. 15%, Japan 13%, UK 4%, Thailand 4%, Germany 4%

Imports: $40.4 billion). Commodities: machinery and equipment, chemicals, food, petroleum products. Partners: Japan 26%,

MALAYSIA

Singapore 21%, U.S. 16%, Taiwan 6%, Germany 4%, UK 3%, Australia 3%

Industries: Peninsular Malaysia: rubber and palm oil processing and manufacturing, light manufacturing industry, electronics, tin mining and smelting, logging and processing timber. Sabah: logging, petroleum production. Sarawak: agriculture processing, petroleum production and refining, logging

Agriculture: accounts for 17% of GDP Peninsular Malaysia: natural rubber, palm oil, rice. Sabah: mainly subsistence, but also rubber, timber, coconut, rice. Sarawak: rubber, timber, pepper, deficit of rice in all areas.

Business Organizations: Four types of businesses may be set up in Malaysia: private companies, public companies, branches of foreign companies, and sole proprietorship/partnerships. Three types of companies may be incorporated: a company with limited shares, a company limited by guarantee, and an unlimited company with or without share capital. In companies limited by shares, the liability of a member is limited to a specific amount of money. In companies limited by guarantee, the liability of a member is limited to a specific amount undertaken to be contributed to assets after a company's termination. Private companies (*Sendirian Berhad*... abbreviated *Sdn. Bhd.*) may be limited or unlimited. Private limited companies restrict the right to transfer shares, limits its membership to no more than 50, and prohibits public sale of shares or invitation to the public to deposit money with the company. Public limited companies (*Berhad* or *Bhd.*) are companies whose shares may be offered to the public. Foreign companies, partnerships, and sole proprietorships must register with the Registrar of Companies (ROC) before they can be established. Companies must pay registration fees on the amount of authorized capital, as well as stamping and filing fees.

Taxes

Corporate Taxes: Non-resident individuals and corporations are taxed at a flat rate of 35% on all sources of Malaysia income, excluding interest payments, royalties, management service fees and rental of business equipment or moveable properties.

Personal Income Taxes: Generally, non-residents are not subject to income tax from employment if the period of employment is less than 60 days.

Other Taxes: There is a development tax of 4% on net income from business or property rental sources. However, the government has suggested that this be abolished. There is a sales tax of 5% on certain goods, though it was lifted in 1990 for certain foodstuffs, sporting goods, and household equipment.

MALAYSIA

Useful Contacts

Check for a Malaysian embassy, chamber of commerce or trade development agency in your country.

• **U.S. Embassy in Malaysia,** 376 Jalan Tun Razak, P.O. Box 10035, 504 Kuala Lumpur, Malaysia
  Tel: (60 3) 248-9011 Fax: (60 3) 242-2207

• **American-Malaysian Chamber of Commerce,** 11.03 Lev 11, Amoda/22 Jalan Imbi,
  55100 Kuala Lumpur, Malaysia
  Tel: (60 3) 248-2407 or 2540 Fax: (60 3) 242-8540

PHILIPPINES

Business Opportunities: The government is making efforts to open up its economy to foreign investment and increase commercial links with its major trading partners, the United States, Japan, the European Community, and the states belonging to the Association of Southeast Asian Nations (ASEAN).

The government passed the Foreign Investment Act which replaced requirements for investments and in effect opened the Philippine market to the world. The major provisions of the law provide that:

- Foreigners may own up to 100 percent of domestic market enterprises that are not on the so-called "negative list". One hundred percent foreign ownership is allowed in any enterprise that exports 60 percent of its output or more, even if the enterprise is included on this negative list. (Previously the government stressed its preference for joint ventures with 60 percent Filipino ownership.)

- Foreigners may invest in partnerships, associations, and corporations registered with the Securities and Exchange Commission (SEC) or sole proprietorships registered with the Bureau of Trade Regulations and Consumer Protection.

- The Board of Investment (BOI) must approve and register investments of firms that wish to utilize available investment incentives. (An America Desk has been established in the BOI to facilitate U.S. business activities in the Philippines.)

Incentives: There are many investment incentives that the government has instituted to attract investors to the Philippines. Many of these are tax packages, but there are also no-tax incentives and export processing zones (EPZs). Enterprises registered with the BOI are entitled to the following incentives:

- Income tax holidays are awarded for a period of six years for commercial operations for pioneer firms and four years for non-pioneer firms, with the possibility of extension for an additional year if the project meets certain conditions specified by the BOI. Firms that are engaged in expansion are entitled to income tax exception proportionate to the expansion for three years.

- Newly established firms may receive deductions of 50 percent of the wages, corresponding to the number of skilled and unskilled workers employed, for a period of five years after registration with the BOI.

- Firms may be granted low import duties and taxes on capital equipment. In addition, they may receive exemptions or reductions on taxes and duties associated with the import of supplies and spare parts for consigned equipment.

- Companies may also receive relief from taxes and duties on raw materials used in the manufacture, processing or production of exports.

- Customs procedures can be simplified for equipment, spare parts, raw materials, and supplies.

- Companies may employ foreign nationals in supervisory, technical, or advisory positions for up to five years, with limited extensions in some cases.

Exports: $11.1 billion. Commodities: electronics, textiles, coconut products, cooper, fish. Partners: U.S. 39%, Japan 18%, Germany 5%, UK 5%, Hong Kong 5%

222

PHILIPPINES

Imports: $17.1 billion. Commodities: raw materials 40%, capital goods 25%, petroleum products 10%. Partners: Japan 21%, US 18%, Taiwan 7%, Saudi Arabia 6%, Hong Kong 5%, South Korea 5%

Industries: textiles, pharmaceutical, chemicals, wood products, food processing, electronics assembly, petroleum refining, fishing

Agriculture: accounts for about 20% of GDP and about 45% of the labor force. Major crops: rice, coconuts, corn, sugarcane, bananas, pineapples, mangoes; animal products—pork, eggs, beef; net exporter of farm products; fish catch of 2 million metric tons annually

Business Organizations: The main forms of business organizations are sole proprietorships, partnerships, and corporations. Other less-common forms include joint stock companies, joint accounts, business trusts, and cooperatives. The Philippines' *Securities and Exchange Commission* (SEC) monitors registration of partnerships and corporations. Representative Offices undertake non-income–generating activities as information dissemination and promotion of foreign company's products. Offices must be registered with the SEC. Branches which are considered to be simple extensions of the parent company must register with the SEC. After obtaining a license, a branch must deposit cash or government securities equivalent of P100,000, and two percent of gross income in excess of P5 million each fiscal year thereafter. Branch offices are allowed to conduct all types of business operations that are approved by the Board of Investment (BOI), including marketing, rendering of services, processing or assembling of semi-finished products, manufacturing, and licensing. Licensing/Franchise Agreements allow U.S. companies to provide patents, trademarks, services, technology, and other assets to Philippine companies in exchange for royalties. In order for royalties to be remitted in full, net of taxes, contracts for royalties or technical service contracts must be registered with the Central Bank. It must be for a fixed term of no more than five years; cannot prohibit the licensee from exporting or limit exportation; and royalty payments may not exceed rates established by the government's *Technology Transfer Board* (TTB) for specific technology or industrial rights. *Joint Venture Agreements* are a common way for U.S. firms to do business in the Philippines. The local company can contribute hands-on market information and financial resources.

Taxes

Corporate Taxes: are subject to manufacturer's or producer's sales taxes and income taxes. Non-resident foreign corporations (corporations that are not engaged in trade or business in the Philippines) are taxed only on their Philippine income on a flat rate of 35 percent of gross income, with no allowable deductions. Interest income on foreign loans earned by non-resident foreign corporations is subject to a 20 percent tax. Resident foreign corporations with operations in the Philippines are taxed in the same manner as non-resident corporations. Branches are taxed only on income derived from Philippine sources. Subsidiary remittances to the parent office are taxed at 35 percent. A branch is required to deposit to the *Securities and Exchange Commission* P100,000 after license issuance.

PHILIPPINES

Personal Income Taxes: Are on worldwide income. A non-resident individual is taxed only on Philippine source income. Taxable income is 29 percent on up to P500,000 and 35 percent over.

Other Taxes: There is a value-added tax (VAT) of 10 percent, imposed on sales and transactions of taxable goods, as well as selected services. It is also imposed on imports, whether for business or private consumption. There are several exemptions, including business deemed to be "small enterprises"; the sale of non-food agricultural, marine, or forest products in their original state; and books and regular periodicals.

Useful Contacts

Check for a Filipino embassy, chamber of commerce or trade development agency in your country.

- **United States Embassy in the Philippines**, 1201 Roxas Blvd., Manila, Philippines
  Tel: (63 2) 521-7116 Fax: (63 2) 522-4361

- **U.S. and Foreign Commercial Service**, 2nd Floor, Thomas Jefferson Cultural Center,
  395 Sen. Gil J. Puyat Ave., Makati, 1200 Metro Manila
  Tel: (63 2) 818-6674 Fax: (63 2) 818-2684

- **American Chamber of Commerce in the Philippines**, Corinthian Plaza, 2nd Floor,
  P.O. Box 1578 Paseo de Roxas, Makati, Metro Manila, Philippines
  Tel: (63 2) 818-7911 Fax: (63 2) 816-6359

SINGAPORE

Business Opportunities: Singapore's government promotes and facilitates foreign investment, and investors face few restrictions. The only major restrictions on foreign investment in Singapore involve sectors that the government has deemed vital to national interest. These include telecommunications, weapons and munitions manufacture, and (in special instances mandated by the parliament) the print media.

Incentives: Singapore offers many incentives designed to increase foreign investment in the country. These include tax concessions and holidays, research and development incentives, export incentives, and loan/grant programs. Industry incentive programs are administered by the Economic Development Board (EDB). Specific incentives include:

- Approved Foreign Loan Scheme—Corporations borrowing a minimum of S$200,000 from a foreign lender for the purchase of capital goods may be exempt from withholding tax on interest in Singapore.

- Expansion - Businesses that spend more than S$10 million on new productive equipment and machinery for expanding facilities are eligible for tax relief for up to five years after the new facilities begin operations in the form of an exemption from the 31 percent tax on profits in excess of pre-expansion levels.

- Investment Allowance - Companies may receive exemption of taxable income of up to 50 percent of a new fixed investment for up to a five-year period.

- International Direct Investment Incentive—Companies which are majority Singapore-owned may set off against other taxable income losses incurred from the sale of shares in a foreign enterprise up to 100 percent against equity invested.

The Monetary Authority of Singapore (MAS) provides incentives for financial operations. These include incentives for:

- Operation Headquarters: Companies that provide management, technical, or other support services to affiliates outside of Singapore are subject to a reduced tax rate on income arising from provision in Singapore of approved services and may be eligible for tax relief on income received from foreign affiliates.

- Finance and Treasury Centers (FTC): Qualifying income of FTCs can receive a reduced tax rate of 10 percent for a period of five to 10 years, subject to review at the end of the period.

- Fund Management Scheme: Income arising from portfolio management activities is taxed at a reduced rate of 10 percent.

- Asian Currency Unit (ACU): Income from offshore loans and credit facilities is taxed at a reduced rate of 10 percent.

- Withholding Tax: Nonresidents and companies who place deposits with ACU are not subject to withholding tax.

Exports: $147 billion (1994). Commodities: electronics, fabricated metal products, petroleum products, telecommunication products. Partners: U.S. 21%, Malaysia 12%, Hong Kong 8%, Japan 8%, Thailand 6% (1992)

Imports: $156 billion (1994). Commodities: aircraft, petroleum, chemicals, foodstuffs. Partners: Japan 21%, U.S. 16%, Malaysia 15%, Saudi Arabia 5%, Taiwan 4%

SINGAPORE

Industries: petroleum refining petrochemicals, electronics, oil drilling equipment, processed food and beverages, ship repair, *entrepot* trade, financial services, biotechnology

Agriculture: occupies a position of minor importance in the economy; self-sufficient in poultry and eggs, must import much of other food; major crops-rubber, copra, fruit, vegetables

Business Organizations: The primary forms of business enterprises are companies (public and private), branches and subsidiaries of foreign corporations, sole proprietorships, and joint ventures or partnerships. Incorporated companies and foreign enterprises are registered and regulated under the Companies Act, while partnerships (including joint ventures) and sole proprietorships are registered under the Business Registration Act. Joint ventures are usually temporary enterprises, formed by two or more parties for the purpose of completing a specific project. They may be registered either as an incorporated company or partnership (which is generally a more permanent, profit-motivated form of joint venture). They may be formed by individuals or corporations. All foreign businesses are required to hire a resident manager to oversee operations, and branches of foreign corporations must employ at least two resident agents to be liable for the company's actions and liabilities.

Taxes

Corporate Taxes: The tax system is administered by the *Inland Revenue Department of the Comptroller of Income Taxes*. The following basic points regarding the tax system should be noted:

- Singapore falls into the medium-tax jurisdiction; The corporate tax rate is 27%, and personal tax rates are a maximum of 30%.

- There are no capital gains taxes.

- Individuals who reside in Singapore for 183 days or more in any one year are considered non-residents and are subject to income taxes on the same basis as citizens. Individuals who reside in Singapore for more than 60 but fewer than 183 days in any year are subject to a special tax of 15 percent or the normal resident tax, whichever is higher. Singapore income generated by non-residents for 60 or fewer days is tax exempt.

- All employees are required to contribute to the Central Provident Fund, Singapore's social security scheme.

SINGAPORE

Useful Contacts

Check for a Singapore embassy, chamber of commerce or trade development agency in your country.

- **U.S. Embassy in Singapore**, 30 Hill Street, Singapore 0617 Tel: (65) 338-0251 Fax: (65) 338-4550

- **The American Chamber of Commerce in Singapore**, Scotts Road, #16-07 Shaw Center, Singapore 0922
  Tel: (65) 235-0077 Fax: (65) 732-5917

- **Singapore Economic Development & Board**, 55 East 59th Street, New York, NY 10022
  Tel: (212) 421-2203 Fax: (212) 421-2206

TAIWAN

Business Opportunities: Taiwan encourages foreign investment, especially in technology-oriented and capital-intensive projects. The Taiwan authorities have established two departments that handle the foreign investment process in Taiwan. The *Industrial Development and Investment Center* deals with matters relating to repatriation, registration and investment incentives and the *Investment Commission* handles approval of rejection of the foreign investor's application.

Foreign business entities wishing to locate in one of Taiwan's export processing zones should note that the appropriate zone administration handles investment applications and procedures for a particular zone. Nationalization of companies has never occurred and guarantees of 20 years are available to companies in which foreign investors hold equity of 45 percent or more.

Foreign investment is restricted in the following sectors:

- Strategic sectors, *i.e.*, military goods, petroleum refining, sugar and sal

- Public utilities, *i.e.*, water supply, telephone, and power industries

- The oil sector is reserved for the state and foreign enterprises may only enter this field through joint ventures with the Chinese Petroleum Company

- The *Taiwan Tobacco and Wine Monopoly* forbids private investment

- Foreign business entities are not permitted to purchase or lease land without government approval. Foreign enterprises should be aware that approval may entail a long process.

Incentives: The following investment incentives are available to qualifying firms:

- Accelerated depreciation on capital goods is available for newly established companies.

- Four-year tax holiday and/or accelerated depreciation of fixed assets for enterprises that plan undertake expansion.

- Tax credits of five to 20 percent of the costs of various new equipment, research and development investments, personal training, and international marketing.

- Industrial estates with prepared sites and industrial harbors are available with government financing.

- The state-run Bank of Communications provides a NT (New Taiwan) $20 billion credit facility for 1 investment in the information, machinery, electronics and textiles industries; purchases of automated machinery; and government supported investment projects.

- A tax credit of 20 percent is available for enterprises locating in a district that is short of resources or with slow development.

- Special loans from the Central Bank are available at low interest rates for purchases or imports of machinery and equipment necessary for key industries.

- There are numerous research and development incentives available.

TAIWAN

Free-Trade Zones: Taiwan currently has three export processing zones (EPZs) and is planning additional zones. Two of the zones are located in Kaoshiung; the third is at Taichung. Industries established in these zones are expected to export production although special permission to sell to the local marketplace may be obtained. Each zone caters to a specific industry and all operations in these zones are free of import duties and commodity taxes on imports. Enterprises planning to set up in the zones are expected to invest in new or underdeveloped industries, make a minimum capital expenditure and make full use of the land. Enterprises planning to operate outside these zones are permitted to set up bonded warehouse facilities.

Exchange Controls: Foreigners may freely remit profits, royalties, and dividends as long as the investment is approved by the *Ministry of Economic Affairs*. In addition, there is a ceiling placed on remittances abroad. An enterprise or an individual may not remit more than $5 million within one year without obtaining approval from the Central Bank of China. Inward remittances over $5 million are not permitted unless the business obtains permission from the Central Bank of China or the foreign exchange is accrued through the export of goods or services.

Labor Force: 7.9 million. By occupation: industry and commerce 53%, services 22%, agriculture, fishing & forestry 15.6%. Unemployment rate: 1.5%

Population: 21, 298, 930. Ethnic divisions: Taiwanese 84%, mainland Chinese 14%, aborigine 2%

Exports: $85 billion. Commodities: electrical machinery 19.7%, electronic products 19.6%, textiles 10.9%, footwear 3.3%, foodstuffs 1.0%, plywood and wood products 0.9%. Partners: U.S. 27.6%, Hong Kong 21.7%, EC 15.2%, Japan 10.5%

Imports: $77.1 billion. Commodities: machinery & equipment 15.7%, electronic products 15.6%, chemicals 9.8%, iron & steel 8.5%, crude oil 3.9%, foodstuffs 2.1%. Partners: Japan 30.1%, U.S. 21.7%, EC 17.6%

Industries: electronics, textiles, chemicals, clothing, food processing, plywood, sugar milling, cement, shipbuilding, petroleum refining

Agriculture: accounts for 4% of GNP and employs 16% of labor force (includes part-time farmers); heavily-subsidized sector; principal crops—rice, fruit, tea; livestock and livestock products—hogs, poultry, beef, milk; not self-sufficient in wheat, soybeans, corn; fish catch 1.4 million metric tons

TAIWAN

Business Organizations: The *Company Law of Taiwan* permits four classes of business organizations:

- The unlimited company may be organized by two or more shareholders with unlimited joint liability among them.

- The unlimited company with liability shareholders can be organized by one or more shareholders of unlimited liability and one or more shareholders of limited liability.

- The limited company, organized by not fewer than five or more than 21 shareholders with each shareholder liable for only his or her capital contribution.

- The company limited by shares, which must have at least seven shareholders whose liability is restricted to the division of the total capital allotted to each shareholder.

The most common business organization for a foreign investor is the company limited by shares. All firms in Taiwan must be incorporated and certified by the *Ministry of Economic Affairs*. There are no limitations placed on foreign equity but local participation is encouraged.

Foreign companies may also organize branch offices in Taiwan. Branches must apply for recognition from the *Ministry of Economic Affairs* (MOEA) and also register with the MOEA. These two processes include the supplying the MOEA with facts about the parent company and the parent company's articles of incorporation. There is a minimal capital requirement of *NT*$1 million although if the branch will be involved in importing and exporting, the minimum capital requirement increases to *NT*$5 million. The parent must appoint a branch manager and an individual legally authorized to receive documents.

Foreign companies are also permitted to set up representative offices; representative offices are now allowed to do business and generate income.

Partnerships and joint ventures are also permissible. Only general partnerships may be organized and partners bear unlimited liability for the obligations of the partnership. Also, partners generally have unlimited liability. The joint venture is not recognized as a legal taxable entity and is usually organized as a jointly-owned company.

Taxes

Corporate Taxes: Taiwan imposes the following corporate tax rates on both locally-owned and foreign-owned firms:

- Income up to *NT*$50,000 is exempted from income tax.

- Taxes of 15 to 50 percent are levied on income ranging from *NT*$50,000 and *NT*$100,000.

- Income between *NT*$100,000 and *NT*$500,000 is taxed at 25 percent.

- The tax rate for income in excess of *NT*$500,000 is 30 percent.

TAIWAN

Foreign branches are taxed only on income derived from sources within Taiwan. A 25 percent withholding tax is usually levied on dividends paid to non-residents. A 20 percent withholding tax is applied on interest payments to non-residents, which may be waived under certain conditions. Interest payments to residents are taxed at 10 percent, which is credited to personal income tax.

Royalties paid to non-residents are taxed at 20 percent, while royalties paid to residents are taxed at 15 percent. Exemptions from the withholding taxes on royalties may be granted from the *Ministry of Economic Affair's Investment Commission* and the *National Bureau of Standards*.

Personal Income Taxes: Nonresidents and individuals residing in Taiwan for fewer than 183 days are taxed at a flat rate of 20 on income derived in Taiwan. Individuals resident in Taiwan are subject to tax rates ranging from six to 40 percent.

Other Taxes: The following is a list of the other taxes applicable in Taiwan:

- There is a 5% value-added tax (VAT).

- A commodity tax of two to 60 percent is levied *ad valorem* on the production of certain local goods or imported goods.

- A 5% business receipts tax may be applied to banking, insurance, and securities brokerage.

- Bars, clubs, restaurants and entertainment establishments are taxed from 15 to 20 percent.

- A tax of between 0.6 to 1.25 percent is levied on domestic gross receipts.

Tax Treaties: The United States and Taiwan have concluded tax treaties covering air and sea transport.

Useful Contacts

- **American Institute on Taiwan (AIT)**, # 7 Lane 134, Hsin Yi Rd., Section 3, Taipei, Taiwan
  Tel: (8862) 709-2000 Fax: (8862) 702-7675

- **China External Trade Development Council**, 41 Madison Ave., 14th Floor, New York, NY 10010
  Tel: (212) 532-7055 Fax: (212) 213-4189

- **American Chamber of Commerce in Taiwan**, Room 1012, #96, Chung Shan N. Rd. Sec. 2,
  P.O. Box 11-1095, Taipei, Taiwan Tel: (8862) 581-7089 Fax: (8862) 542-3376

- **Tourism Burear, Ministry of Communications**, 280 Chunghsiao E. Rd., Section 4, Box 1490, Taipei, Taiwan
  Tel: (8862) 721-8541

Appendix 4:
Middle East & Sub-Saharan Africa

ISRAEL

Business Opportunities: Israel's government encourages foreign investment, In 1951, the U.S. and Israel entered into a Friendship, Commerce, and Navigation Treaty (FCN), which to a large extent acts as a bilateral investment treaty. It ensures equal treatment under the law for foreign and domestic businesses, and protects against expropriation (except in the case of the public interest and then only with appropriate compensation). There are no significant investment barriers, and the Israeli government allows for 200 percent foreign ownership of businesses in the country.

The Ministry of Industry and Trade promotes and approves investment into the country, and authorizes all incentives provided to foreign companies. Foreigners wishing to purchase real estate in Israel must have their request approved by the Director of Land Registry or the Controller of Foreign Exchange.

Incentives: The Israel Investment Authority and the Ministry of Industry and Trade authorize all investment incentives, which come generally in the form of investment grants and tax relief for "approved enterprises". Approved enterprises are those which increase Israeli exports, or generate new jobs in less developed areas of the country. The Ministry, through its various industry-specific departments, decides which companies should receive this status. To be considered for such status, a company must submit an investment plan, and meet certain capital, ownership, and employment criteria. The Industrial Development Bank then assesses the economic viability of the proposed project.

Cash grants of up to 38 percent of costs are awarded to approved enterprises, based on their geographic location. Costs covered by such programs include site development, plant construction, and equipment acquisition. Firms which locate their operations around Tel Aviv receive the lowest amount of grants, and those farthest away from such developed metropolitan centers receive the most benefits. Approved enterprises also receive a lower tax rate. There are two- to 10-year tax exemptions and 10 to 25 percent company tax rates available to such firms.

Imports: $20.3 billion. Commodities: military equipment, investment goods, rough diamonds, oil, other productive inputs, consumer goods. Partners: U.S., EC

Industries: food processing, diamond cutting and polishing, textiles and apparel, chemicals, metal products, military eqpt, transport eqpt, electrical eqpt, miscellaneous machinery, potash mining, high technology electronics, tourism

Agriculture: accounts for 7% of GDP; largely self-sufficient in food production except for grains; principal products are citrus and other fruits, vegetables, cotton; livestock products include beef, dairy, poultry

ISRAEL

Business Organizations: Limited corporations and branches of foreign corporations are the most common entities utilized by foreign investors in Israel. *The Companies Ordinance of 1959*, as amended, regulates the formation and conduct of corporations. This legislation provides for the formulation of unlimited companies, companies limited by guaranty, limited share companies, and companies with share capital. Israeli partnership legislation states that a registered partnership is a legal entity and can sue or be sued. Any foreign partnership can register with the *Registrar of Partnerships* and operate in Israel. Israeli companies do not need government approval to enter into licensing agreements with foreign firms, and once a company has produced certified statements, royalties may be transferred freely through authorized banks. The normal duration for licensing agreements is five years, with automatic renewal for an additional five years. The normal royalty payment is four to five percent of turnover, although higher rates for luxury products are common. Royalties are deductible from income taxes.

Taxes

Corporate Taxes: Pay a company tax equivalent to 40 percent of taxable income. The balance is subject to a further income tax of 8.33 percent.

Personal Income Taxes: Are levied on gross income derived form employment, trade, business, dividends, interest, pensions, rents and royalties. Limited deductions are available. The rates range from 20 to 48 percent, with the highest rate being for income over US$25,000 annually.

Other Taxes: Israel has a value-added tax (VAT) of 18 percent which is levied on most transactions of goods and services. The VAT applies to imports, based on their landed-cost plus customs duties. There is also a capital gains tax of 10 percent on the sale of tangible and intangible property excluding inventory and securities.

Useful Contacts

Check for a Isreali embassy, chamber of commerce or trade development agency in your country.

• **U.S. Embassy in Israel**, 71 Hyarkon Street, Tel Aviv, Israel
  Tel: (972 3) 517-4338 Fax: (972 3) 658-0330

• **Israel-American Chamber of Commerce and Industry**
  35 Shaul Hamelech Blvd., P.O. Box 33174, Tel Aviv, Israel 61333
  Tel: (972 3) 695-2341; 696-7628 Fax: (972 3) 695-1272

KUWAIT

Business Opportunities: Foreign business activity in Kuwait has increased since liberation. However, this activity has been largely trade-related and there has been little foreign direct investment.

The Government of Kuwait has directed and financed most of the reconstruction and redevelopment efforts. The Central Tenders Committee (CTC) is responsible for issuing government tenders and contract awards. Since the completion of the emergency phase of reconstruction, all bids must be entered by Kuwaiti firms, either in a joint venture, or by a Kuwaiti agent or representative.

Financing of bid bonds is generally done in the form of a bank guarantee. Performance bonds indicate that the bank guarantee is payable to a Kuwaiti bank from an American bank. Contractors generally receive an advance payment to cover start-up expenses. Investors who wish to partake in government tenders should register with the government for pre-qualification procedures.

Incentives: The government of Kuwait offers tax incentives and non-tax assistance on inward investment for new and/or existing companies and joint ventures. Incentives for investment include:

- Tax holidays of up to 10 years for companies introducing new technology to Kuwait.

- No restrictions on repatriation of profits, fees, capital or personal salaries.

- Tariff protection for a maximum of 10 years.

- Free use of industrial sites.

- Government assistance for financing research and feasibility studies.

- Pre-qualification for government tendering and purchases.

Taxes

Corporate Taxes: Corporate taxes are based on a progressive scale ranging from five to 55 percent of the firm's total Kuwait-source profit. Foreign firms which participate in joint ventures are taxed only on their share of the joint venture income. There are no withholding taxes in Kuwait and capital gains are taxed as normal income within the corporate tax structure. Personal Income Taxes: Personal income taxes are not levied on Kuwaiti citizens or foreign residents. Other Fees: There are a variety of government fees for social services, including residence fees for all expatriates. Tax Treaties: Kuwait is a signatory to the Arab Tax Treaty with other GCC members. Kuwait is interested in establishing a treaty on double taxation with the United States and has requested further consultation.

Exports: $10.5 billion. Commodities: Food, construction materials, vehicles and parts, clothing. Partners: U.S. 35%, Japan 12%, UK 9%, Canada 9%

Industries: Petroleum, petrochemicals, desalination, food processing, building materials, salt, construction

KUWAIT

Agriculture: Practically none; dependent on imports for food; about 75% of potable water must be distilled or imported.

Business Organizations: Foreign firms are prohibited by law from establishing independent business entities in Kuwait. All foreign firms wishing to establish a business in Kuwait must do so through approved joint ventures with Kuwaiti firms or through a registered agreement with a Kuwaiti government agency.

Joint Ventures: Foreign investors are offered a number of incentives to participate in joint ventures with Kuwaiti firms, such as limited liability exposure, relief from Kuwaiti corporate taxes, and management options. All government procurement bids must be conducted through Kuwaiti citizens or Kuwaiti firms (joint ventures between foreign investors and Kuwaiti nationals fulfill this requirement). (Exceptions exist for bids to the Ministry of Defense and the Ministry of the Interior.) Kuwait discourages joint ventures in the oil, insurance, banking and finance sectors.

Useful Contacts

• **Ministry of Information, State of Kuwait**, Box 193 , SAFAT, Kuwait
   Telephone: 241-5301 or 242-7141

• **U.S. Embassy in Kuwait**, P. O. Box 77, SAFAT 13001 Kuwait
   Telephone: 965 242-4151 Facsimile: 965 240-7368

• **Embassy of Kuwait in the United States**, 2940 Tilden Street, NW, Washington, DC 20008
   Telephone: (202) 966-0702 Facsimile: (202) 966-0517

• **Central Tenders Committee**, P. O. Box 1070, SAFAT, 13011 Kuwait
   Telephone: (965) 240-1200 Facsimile: (965) 241-6574

• **Kuwait Chamber of Commerce and Industry**, Cambers Building, Ali Salem Street, Kuwait
   Telephone: (965) 243-3864 Facsimile: (965) 243-3858

• **U.S. Arab Chamber of Commerce**, 1825 K Street, NW, Suite 1107, Washington, DC 20006
   Telephone: (202) 331-8010

SAUDI ARABIA

Business Opportunities: Saudi Arabia actively encourages foreign investment, especially if the projects have a lasting developmental effect on the country's economy and promote industrialization and technology transfer. Saudi law requires that any project involving foreign capital result in "economic development" and transfer needed technology. Moreover, foreign investors must find Saudi partners in order to benefit from Saudi investment incentives and practically speaking, to obtain authorization from the relevant Saudi authorities. The petroleum and mineral extraction industries are owned and controlled by the government, and are generally closed to foreign investment. The following should be kept in mind when planning an investment in Saudi Arabia:

- All foreign investment must be licensed by the Ministry of Industry and Electricity (MIE) and registered with the Ministry of Commerce.

- Obtaining the requisite governmental approvals entails the involvement of many Saudi agencies at different stages of the investment planning and implementation process. An investment proposal may be implemented only after the MIE issues an investment license to the applicants. Once granted, the investment license will stipulate the permitted corporate objectives of the entity subject to the license.

- Most foreign investment is carried out through limited liability companies organized for this purpose by the foreign investors and their Saudi partners. These "investment companies" must be formed in accordance with Saudi company law and registered with the MOC.

- At the present time, only foreign capital invested in a foreign-owned branch office or in the share capital of either a joint stock or limited liability company will qualify for an investment license.

Incentives: As part of its program to develop non-oil industries, the government provides various tax and other incentives for foreign investors. For government-approved projects with at least 25 percent Saudi participation, foreign investors in agricultural and industrial ventures are eligible for a 10-year exemption from income tax. Investors in non-individual projects which meet the 'local participation' requirement may be eligible for a five-year income tax exemption.

The government also provides loans of up to 80 percent of fixed assets for agricultural products under *SR*3 million and 40 percent for projects over *SR*3 million. The Saudi Industrial Development Fund grants loans to Saudi companies amounting to 50 percent of the total cost of the project. Customs duty exemptions (on importation of products used for the project) and protection (i.e., imposition of protective duties on importation of goods produced by the project) are also available.

Exports: $42.3 billion. Commodities: petroleum and petroleum products 92%. Partners: U.S. 21%, Japan 18%, Singapore 6%, France 6%, Korea 5%

Imports: $26 billion commodities: machinery and equipment, chemicals, foodstuffs, motor vehicles, textiles. Partners: U.S. 18%, UK 12%, Japan 10%, Germany 5%, France 5%

Industries: crude oil production, petroleum refining, basic petrochemicals, cement, two small steel-rolling mills, construction, fertilizer, plastics

SAUDI ARABIA

Agriculture: accounts for 10% of GDP, 16% of labor force; subsidized by government; products-wheat, barley, tomatoes, melons, dates, citrus fruit, mutton, chickens, eggs, milk; approaching self-sufficiency in food.

Business Organizations: Limited Liability Companies (LLCs) are the most common form of business organization utilized by foreign investors. LLCs must have at least two but not more than 50 shareholders. Such companies may not deal in insurance or financial operations, and must be capitalized with at least *SR*500,000. LLCs are required to set aside 10 percent of net annual profits as reserve capital. Joint Stock Companies are privately or publicly-held limited liability companies resembling U.S. corporations. Joint Ventures are unincorporated associations which resemble general partnerships. Each party to the venture holds title to his agreed contribution. The joint venture agreement must be submitted to the *Ministry of Commerce* and must include objectives, rights and liabilities of the venturers, and the manner of the division of profits. Branches may only be established and registered in the *Commercial Register at the Ministry of Commerce* if approval is granted from the *Foreign Investment Capital Committee (FCIC)* at the *Ministry of Industry and Electricity*. Approval of the FCIC depends on whether the branch is conducive to the economic development of the country. Local legal representation is necessary to register a branch. A Representative Office may supervise and coordinate the entity's administrative activities in the country, but would be prohibited from directly or indirectly engaging in commercial activities. *Technical and Scientific Services Office* may obtain a license from the *Ministry of Commerce* to provide technical and scientific support to the parent company's Saudi distributor (s), conduct market surveys, and undertake product research. They may not engage in commercial activities.

Taxes

Corporate Taxes: range from 25 percent (on annual taxable income of up to *SR*100,000) to 45 percent (on annual taxable income of over *SR*1,000,000).

Personal Income Taxes: Salary and benefits of non-Saudi employees are not subject to income tax at present. However, non-Saudis who derive income from investments in Saudi businesses or from professional activities, and those who are nonresidents, are taxed at rates ranging from five percent (for taxable income up to *SR*16,000) to 30 percent (for taxable income over *SR*66,000). The *Zakat* is a wealth tax levied on Saudi and GCC nationals*, who wholly Saudi and GCC shareholders in limited liability companies. The rate is approximately 2.5 percent of an individual's net worth or of an entity's assets (less deductions).

Other Taxes: Currently, no local, regional, property or other sales taxes are imposed.

GCC (Gulf Cooperation Council): consists of the United Arab Emirates of Bahrain, Qatar and Abu Dhabi, plus Kuwait, Oman and Saudi Arabia.

SAUDI ARABIA

Useful Contacts

Check for a Saudi embassy, chamber of commerce or trade development agency in your country.

- **U.S. Embassy,** Collector Road M, Riyadh Diplomatic Quarter, Saudi Arabia
  Tel: (966) 1 488-3800 Fax: (966) 1 488-3278

- **U.S. Consulate General in Dhahran,** P.O. Box 81 Dhahran, Dhahran Airport, Saudi Arabia
  Tel: (966) 3 891-3200 Fax: (966) 3 891-3296

- **U.S. Consulate General in Jeddah,** Palestine Road, Ruwais, P.O. Box 149, Jeddah, Saudi Arabia
  Tel: (966) 2 667-0080 Fax: (966) 2 669-3074

- **American Business Association,** Eastern Province, P.O. Box 88, Dhahran Airport, Dhahran 31932, Saudi Arabia
  Tel: (966) 3 857-0595 Fax: (966) 3 857-8139

- **American Businessmen's Group of Riyadh,** P.O. Box 34992, Riyadh 11478, Saudi Arabia
  Tel: (966) 1 477-7341 Fax: (966) 1 411-2729

UNITED ARAB EMIRATES

Business Opportunities: Foreign investment is actively encouraged by the UAE government. Particularly favored are those investments which aid in the development and diversification of the economy. Most U.S. investment has been in the petroleum industry, but the UAE is presently trying to encourage other projects.

Generally, UAE firms enter into joint ventures with foreign firms. The local firm may be responsible for the land, capital, expertise, labor permits, and other necessary in-country preparation. Incentives are available in the form of tax preferences, and financial support for ventures which are USE majority-controlled.

Exports: $22.6 billion. Commodities: crude oil 66%, natural gas, re-exports, dried fish, dates. Partners: Japan 39%, Singapore 5%, Korea 4%, Iran 4%, India 4%

Imports: $18 billion commodities: manufactured goods, machinery and transport equipment, food. Partners: Japan 14%, UK 9%, U.S. 8%, Germany 6%

Industries: petroleum, fishing, petrochemicals, construction materials, some boat building, handicrafts, pearling

Agriculture: accounts for 2% of GDP and 5% of the labor force; cash crops (including dates); food products—vegetables, watermelons, poultry, eggs, dairy products, fish; only 25% self-sufficient in food.

Business Organizations: Companies must be registered with the Chamber of Commerce and the local Emirate government. UAE law stipulates that Emirate nationals must own at least 51 percent of a company's share capital in the country. Public shareholding companies require a minimum of 55 percent public participation, and shareholder liability is limited to the nominal value of their shares in the company's capital. The minimum capital for a public shareholding companies is *Dh*10 million. Private shareholding companies must have at least three shareholders, and a minimum capital os *Dh*2 million. Limited liability companies may have up to five UAE citizens as managers. Branches can be established with local sponsorship and must be registered with the *Ministry of Economy and Commerce* and local Emirate officials. They are by nature 100 percent foreign-owned, and are not hampered by any regulations against specific commercial activities.

UAE

Taxes

Corporate Taxes: Corporate taxes exist, though only oil-producing companies and branches of foreign banks are responsible for these taxes.

Personal Income Taxes: There are no personal income taxes.

Other Taxes: There are no indirect taxes, excluding certain custom duties and taxes imposed on hotel services and property rental.

Useful Contacts

Check for a UAE embassy, chamber of commerce or trade development agency in your country.

- **U.S. Embassy in the UAE**, Al-Sudan Street, P.O. Box 4009, Abu Dhabi, United Arab Emirates
  Tel: (971 2) 336691

- **U.S. Consulate General**, Dubai International Trade Center, P.O. Box 9343, Dubai, United Arab Emirates
  Tel: (971 4) 313115 Fax: (971 4) 375121

- **American Business Council of Dubai/Northern Emirates**, World Trade Center, Suite 1610, P.O. Box 9281, Dubai, UAE
  Tel: (971 4) 314735 Fax: (971 4) 314227

UNION OF SOUTH AFRICA

Business Opportunities: South Africa promotes and encourages foreign investment. Official assistance is available from the Department of Trade and Industry, which will examine and advise on proposals for the establishment of new industries or the expansion of existing operations.

Incentives: Incentives are offered to both domestic and foreign investors. For more than 50 years the government-owned Industrial Development Corporation of South Africa (IDC) has provided development capital for new projects in urban and rural areas, (excluding self-governing homelands) in the form of medium-and long-term loans to finance fixed assets, as well as direct equity participation.

The factors listed below are considered to be among the incentives which make South Africa an attractive climate for foreign investors:

- The Financial Rand enables foreigners to invest in South Africa at a discounted rate, guaranteeing a minimum of 16 percent (as of April 1992) rate of return;

- Guaranteed transfer of profits;

- Special incentive programs for exporters;

- Operations can be wholly owned;

- Minimum of regulations, those in place are wholly transparent;

- Well-developed physical, financial, and commercial infrastructure;

- Entry point to markets of the southern African region;

- Growing domestic consumer market; and

- No nationality requirements on managerial staff.

Initiated in 1991, the *Regional Industrial Development Program* is a new package of incentives to promote industrial development. The program includes a scheme to reimburse the relocation costs of approved foreign undertakings up to a maximum of R 1 million per project. The incentives apply in full (100 percent) to most of the country, 60 percent to the metropolitan Cape Town area, and excludes the PWV (Pretoria-Witwatersrand-Vereeniging) region and the city of Durban.

Exports: $24.3 billion. Commodities: gold 27%, other minerals and metals 20–25%, food 5%, chemicals 3%. Partners: Italy, Japan, U.S., Germany, UK, other EC countries, Hong Kong

Imports: $18.1 billion. Commodities: machinery 32%, transport equipment 15%, chemicals 11%, oil, textiles, scientific instruments partners: Germany, U.S., Japan, UK, Italy

Industries: mining (world's largest producer of platinum, gold, chromium), automobile assembly, metalworking, machinery, textile, iron and steel, chemical, fertilizer, foodstuffs

SOUTH AFRICA

Agriculture: accounts for about 5% of GDP and 30% of the labor force; diversified agriculture, with emphasis on livestock; product-cattle, poultry, sheep, wool, milk, beef, corn, wheat, sugarcane, fruits, vegetables; self-sufficient in food

Business Organizations: The most common business organization is the limited liability company. Firms can be limited by guarantee (primarily not-for-profit) or shares. Companies having share capital may be either public or private companies. Public companies have the "Ltd." after their names, whereas private companies are identified with "*Pty. Limited.*" A South African resident must be appointed as a public officer of the company to handle income tax matters. Foreign firms may operate through a branch rather than a subsidiary in South Africa. Foreign companies wishing to establish a branch must file copies of the memorandum and articles (authenticated by a South African council) with the *Registrar of Companies.* The *Close Corporation* (CC) has become popular, particularly for small businesses. A *Close Corporation* may be formed by at least one but not more than 10 individual members (including non-residents). Each member stands in fiduciary relationship to the corporation and may be liable to the corporation for losses suffered as a result of a breach of faith.

Taxes

Corporate Taxes: The standard tax rate of 48 percent applies to foreign branch operations which are taxed only on income from sources located within South Africa. Dividends are exempt from general or "normal" South African income tax. There is a withholding tax of 15 percent on royalties and dividends paid to non-resident investors.

Personal Income Taxes: The rates of income tax for non-resident and residents are the same:

Married women: All earned income on a graduated scale reaching 40 percent at taxable income of R 50,000.

Married man: All earned income on a graduated scale reaching 43 percent at taxable income of R80,000.

•**Unmarried person:** All income is taxed on a graduated scale reaching 43 percent at a taxable income of R56,000

Property owners pay local assessment rates based on the certain appraised value of their properties. In addition, certain *Regional Services Councils* levy nominal services and establishment taxes. (These may be treated as deductible business expenses for income tax purposes). Capital gains and dividends on shares are not taxed.

Other Taxes: The added-value tax (VAT) is 10 percent to replace the previous sales tax. Financial services are exempt and exports zero rated. Other taxes include bank transactions duties, a stamp tax levied on legal documents, a securities transfer tax, excise duties and ad valorem taxes on items such as gasoline and alcohol.

Useful Contacts

Check for a South African embassy, chamber of commerce or trade development agency in your country.

- **U.S. Embassy in South Africa**, 887 Pretorius St. Arcadia 0083, Pretoria, Republic of South Africa
  Tel: (27) 12 342-1801 Fax: (27) 12 342-2629

- **Department of Trade and Industry**, P. Bag X753, Pretoria 0001, Republic of South Africa
  Tel: (27) 12 310-9791 Fax: (27) 12 322-0298

- **American Chamber of Commerce in South Africa**, P.O. Box 1132, Houghron 2041 South Africa
  Tel: (27) 11 788-0265; 0266 Fax: (27) 11 880-1632

- **World Trade Centre Johannesburg**, Jurgens Park, Jones Road, Jet Park, P. O. Box 500, Kempton Park 1620, South Africa
  Telephone: (011-27-11) 975-8011 Fax: (011-27-11) 975-9415 ATTN.: C. P. Swart, Executive Chairman

- **Foundation for African Business and Consumer Services** (FABCOS), P. O. Box 8785, Johannesburg 2000, South Africa
  Telephone: (011-27-11) 832-1911 Facsimile: (011-27-11) 836-5920 ATTN.: Ashley Mabogoane

Index

Country Index

About this book

The International Business Plan is published by a family-owned publisher. We try to provide our readers with the very finest small-business books. We solicit and welcome all your comments, including your criticism as well as your praise. Please direct your correspondence to the address on the facing page.

The printing was done by our good friends at *Thomson-Shore* in Ypsilanti, Michigan, U.S.A. They're a pleasure to do business with.

This book is printed on 50-lb. acid-free paper, so it won't turn yellow for 200 years. *Move over, Dead Sea scrolls.*

We film-laminate our covers so that they won't curl when the humidity rises, and notch-bind them so that they last longer for you.

Free!

Would you like to tap the resources of the Internet? Puma Publishing now maintains a list of **Internet resources** that can direct you to sources of international business assistance. This will help you to get your international business enterprise off to a running start. If you'll photocopy the form below and mail or fax it to

Puma Publishing, 1670 Coral Drive, Santa Maria, California, U.S.A. 93454
fax: 805-925-2656

We'll send you a current copy promptly.

- -

Yes! Please send me a copy of your list of Internet resources.

Your name: _____

Your company's name: _____

Address:_____

City:_____State or Province:_____Country: _____

Fax number: _____e-mail address:_____

Where did you hear about this book? _____

How would you like to see this book improved?_____

_____

(optional) My business is:_____

Dear Puma Publishing: Here is an Internet resource that we have found to be useful, and should be included on Puma's Internet Resource list. The e-mail address or URL (Universal Resource Locator) of this resource is: _____

Brief description of this Internet resource: _____

_____

_____

_____

The Business Bookshelf

These books have been carefully selected as the best on these subjects.
Your satisfaction is guaranteed or your money back.

Money Sources for Small Business

How You Can Find Private, State, Federal, and Corporate Financing

By William Alarid. Many potential successful business owners simply don't have enough cash to get started. *Money Sources* shows how to get money from Federal, State, Venture Capital Clubs, Corporations, Computerized Matching Services, Small Business Investment Companies plus many other sources. Includes samples of loan applications.

ISBN 0-940673-51-7   224 pages   8½ x 11   paperbound $19.95

Small Time Operator

How to Start Your Own Business, Keep Your Books, Pay Your Taxes, and Stay Out of Trouble

By Bernard Kamaroff, C.P.A. The most popular small business book in the U.S., it's used by over 250,000 businesses. Easy to read and use, *Small Time Operator* is particularly good for those without bookkeeping experience. Comes complete with a year's supply of ledgers and worksheets designed especially for small businesses, and contains invaluable information on permits, licenses, financing, loans, insurance, bank accounts, etc.

ISBN 0-917510-10-2   190 pages   8½ x 11   paperbound $14.95

The Instant Business Plan

Twelve Quick and Easy Steps to a Successful Business

By Gustav Berle, Ph.D., and Paul Kirschner. Learn the secrets of simplifying the business planning process, raising needed cash for your business quickly, and saving money on business plan preparation. Includes sections on dealing with banks, government loans, and how to get OPM (Other People's Money).

ISBN 0-940673-71-1   200 pages   8½ x 11   paperbound $14.95

The Business Planning Guide

Creating a Plan for Success in Your Own Business

By Andy Bangs. The perfect companion to the *Instant Business Plan, The Business Planning Guide* has been used by hundreds of banks, colleges, and accounting firms to guide business owners through the process of putting together a complete and effective business plan and financing proposal. The *Guide* comes complete with examples, forms and worksheets that make the planning process painless. With over 150,000 copies in print, the *Guide* has become a small business classic.

ISBN 0-936894-96-2   208 pages   8½ x 11   paperbound $22.95

Free Help from Uncle Sam to Start Your Own Business

(Or Expand the One You Have)
3rd Edition, Completely Revised

By William Alarid and Gustav Berle. *Free Help* describes over 100 government programs that help small business and gives dozens of examples of how others have used this aid. Included are appendices with helpful books, organizations and phone numbers.

ISBN 0-940673-54-1   304 pages   5½ x 8½   paperbound $13.95

The Instant Marketing Plan

Your Simple Enjoyable Easy-to-Follow Road Map to Skyrocket Your Business

By Mark Nolan. No business can survive without marketing. Here for the first time in print marketing genius Mark Nolan reveals the secrets he usually charges $400 per hour to reveal. Mark's writing style is fun and informal. You'll enjoy his experiences and you formulate a knock-out plan to bring customers to your door and have them come back again and again.

ISBN 0-940673-74-6   200 pages   8½ x 11   paperbound $15.95

To order by credit card from within the USA, call toll free (800) 255-5730 extension 110.

Please have Visa, MasterCard, American Express or Discover card ready.

To order by credit card from outside the USA,
please fax your credit card number, date of expiration and name on card to **(805) 925-2656.**

To order by check please mail it to:
Puma Publishing, 1670 Coral Drive, Department IIBP, Santa Maria, California 93454 USA.
Sales tax: Please add 7¾% for shipping to California addresses.

Shipping airmail to addresses in USA $4.00 for first book + $2.00 per additional book. Overseas airmail shipping $16.00 for first book + $4.00 per additional book.

E-MAIL: Pumapub871@aol.com • Visit our home page http://www.worldprofit.com/money/mapuma.htm